WRITING MASCULINITY IN THE LATER MIDDLE AGES

Medieval discourses of masculinity and male sexuality were closely linked to the idea and representation of work as a male responsibility. Isabel Davis identifies a discourse of masculine selfhood which is preoccupied with the ethics of labour and domestic living. She analyses how five major London writers of the late fourteenth and early fifteenth centuries constructed the male self: William Langland, Thomas Usk, John Gower, Geoffrey Chaucer and Thomas Hoccleve. These literary texts, while they have often been considered for what they say about the feminine role and identity, have rarely been thought of as evidence for masculinity; this study seeks to redress that imbalance. Looking again at the texts themselves, and their cultural contexts, Davis presents a genuinely fresh perspective on ideas about gender, labour and domestic life in medieval Britain.

ISABEL DAVIS is Lecturer in Medieval and Early Renaissance Literature at Birkbeck College, University of London.

T0371431

CAMBRIDGE STUDIES IN MEDIEVAL LITERATURE

GENERAL EDITOR
Alastair Minnis, *Ohio State University*

EDITORIAL BOARD
Zygmunt G. Barański, *University of Cambridge*
Christopher C. Baswell, *University of California, Los Angeles*
John Burrow, *University of Bristol*
Mary Carruthers, *New York University*
Rita Copeland, *University of Pennsylvania*
Simon Gaunt, *King's College London*
Steven Kruger, *City University of New York*
Nigel Palmer, *University of Oxford*
Winthrop Wetherbee, *Cornell University*
Jocelyn Wogan-Browne, *University of York*

This series of critical books seeks to cover the whole area of literature written in the major medieval languages – the main European vernaculars, and medieval Latin and Greek – during the period *c.* 1100–1500. Its chief aim is to publish and stimulate fresh scholarship and criticism on medieval literature, special emphasis being placed on understanding major works of poetry, prose, and drama in relation to the contemporary culture and learning which fostered them.

Recent titles in the series

A complete list of titles in the series can be found at the end of the volume.

Frontispiece. Misericord from St Nicholas's church, King's Lynn, c. 1419.
© V&A Images/Victoria and Albert Museum.

WRITING MASCULINITY IN THE LATER MIDDLE AGES

ISABEL DAVIS

CAMBRIDGE
UNIVERSITY PRESS

CAMBRIDGE UNIVERSITY PRESS
Cambridge, New York, Melbourne, Madrid, Cape Town, Singapore,
São Paulo, Delhi, Dubai, Tokyo

Cambridge University Press
The Edinburgh Building, Cambridge CB2 8RU, UK

Published in the United States of America by Cambridge University Press, New York

www.cambridge.org
Information on this title: www.cambridge.org/9780521142175

© Isabel Davis 2007

This publication is in copyright. Subject to statutory exception
and to the provisions of relevant collective licensing agreements,
no reproduction of any part may take place without the written
permission of Cambridge University Press.

First published 2007
This digitally printed version 2010

A catalogue record for this publication is available from the British Library

ISBN 978-0-521-86637-8 Hardback
ISBN 978-0-521-14217-5 Paperback

Cambridge University Press has no responsibility for the persistence or
accuracy of URLs for external or third-party internet websites referred to in
this publication, and does not guarantee that any content on such websites is,
or will remain, accurate or appropriate.

For my supervisors:
Felicity Riddy and Jeremy Goldberg

Contents

Acknowledgements

This book has been a very collaborative effort: its arguments have been variously tried out before my teachers, colleagues, friends, job-interview panels and conference audiences everywhere, and this brief statement of thanks cannot hope to acknowledge every debt I owe. However, my special thanks go to my PhD supervisors: Felicity Riddy and Jeremy Goldberg; this book is dedicated to them in recognition of their inspiring and scholarly lead. I am grateful too to the AHRB who funded my postgraduate work, during which time a lot of the ideas for this book were seeded. My work is much indebted to the academic community connected with the Centre for Medieval Studies at York (past and present) and, in particular, Anthony Bale, Cordelia Beattie, Pamela Hartshorne, Matthew Holford, Lara McClure, Nicola McDonald, Mark Ormrod, Sarah Rees Jones, Craig Taylor, Marion Turner and Sarah Williams. I am grateful to the two anonymous readers, and general editor, Alastair Minnis, at Cambridge University Press for their careful reading and constructive comments. Thanks are also due to Linda Bree, Maartje Schetens, and Debby Banham for their expertise. Many thanks, too, to Rachel Wevill for her patient and exacting reading of the text. Other thanks go to all my friends and family who have supported me in ways too wonderful and various to list here. As ever, I want to thank my parents on whose unstinting faith and support I have always been able to rely. Finally, though, this project would neither be finished nor quite the same without the loving and patient help of Richard Rowland, whose generosity I can never hope to repay.

Abbreviations

ANQ	*American Notes and Queries*
EETS, ES	*Early English Text Society*, extra series
EETS, OS	*Early English Text Society*, original series
EETS, SS	*Early English Text Society*, special series
ELH	*English Literary History*
ELN	*English Language Notes*
LCC	'The Long Charter of Christ'
MED	*Middle English Dictionary*, H. Kurath *et al.* (ed.) (Ann Arbour, 1956–)
N&Q	*Notes and Queries*
OED	*Oxford English Dictionary*, J. A. Simpson *et al.* (ed.), 2nd edn, 20 vols. (Oxford, 1989)
PL	*Patrologia Latina*, J.-P. Migne (ed.)
PMLA	*Proceedings of the Modern Language Association of America*
Chaucer: *T&C*	*Troilus and Criseyde*
CkP	*The Cook's Prologue*
CkT	*The Cook's Tale*
CYP	*The Canon's Yeoman's Prologue*
CYT	*The Canon's Yeoman's Tale*
FranP	*The Franklin's Prologue*
GP	*General Prologue*
MerT	*The Merchant's Tale*
MilP	*The Miller's Prologue*
MilT	*The Miller's Tale*
PardP	*The Pardoner's Prologue*
PardT	*The Pardoner's Tale*
PThop	*The Prologue to the Tale of Thopas*
ParsT	*The Parson's Tale*
ShipT	*The Shipman's Tale*

WBP	*The Wife of Bath's Prologue*

Unless otherwise stated, all quotations from the works of Chaucer will be from the *Riverside Chaucer*, L. Benson *et al.* (eds.), 3rd edn (Oxford, 1989).

Gower:
CA	*Confessio Amantis*
MO	*Mirror de l'omme*
PP	'In Praise of Peace'

Hoccleve:
J'sW	'The Tale of Jereslaus's Wife'
LaMR	'La male regle'
RP	*The Regiment of Princes*

All quotations from the Bible are from Jerome's vulgate (http://www.drbo.org/lvb/); English translations are taken from the Douay–Rheims version (http://www.drbo.org).

Short references have been used in the notes to the text; for the full bibliographic information please refer to the bibliography.

Introduction: Writing masculinity in the later Middle Ages

Ego certe, domine, laboro hic et laboro in me ipso. Factus sum mihi terra difficultatis et sudoris nimii.

(Augustine, *Confessions*, X, xvi, 25)[1]

A man in the house is worth two in the street.

(Mae West, *Belle of the Nineties*, 1934)

The frontispiece of this book shows a misericord depicting a master-craftsman, a wood-carver, working in his workshop with his three apprentices. The fact that he is represented with his apprentices identifies the subject as a householder at a time when apprentices would have lived in the house attached to the workshop where they were trained. The coincidence of medium and subject matter here – this is a wood-carving of a wood-carver carving – invests this with a subjectivity not found in those other misericords that depict, say, the labours of the agricultural year; it is, I shall argue, a piece of life writing or, rather, life carving. The initials of the maker – a 'W' and a 'V' – on either side of the central 'portrait' and arranged around the tools of his trade – the saw and gouge – are an embedded signature in what are more usually anonymous pieces. The very stuff of this carving, its material, writes it into the life of its maker. That is not to say, of course, that this carving is a window onto actual and everyday life, as earlier misericord scholars sometimes thought. It is evidently implicated in prevailing cultural ideologies about the authority of the male householder and master craftsman, a masculine model that is also prominent in the records of the urban guilds and the municipal authorities, which wished for a transparent, male-governed and

I

household-based manufacturing sector.[2] Its representation of self should
be treated as sceptically as any other first-person narrator from any other
life-written text. While this piece, however, may say very little about the
King's Lynn carver with the initials W. V., or even the daily grind of
making misericords in the early fifteenth century, it does tell us about
contemporary ideals of masculinity and how they operated.[3] Furthermore, there is a palpable and playful interaction between these ideals and
a preoccupation with the self, wherein is found a representation of the
subject. This volume will seek to explore similar intersections between
medieval masculine subjectivity and the ethics of labour and living,
within a group of texts that are geographically proximate and that span
the two generations between *c.* 1360 and *c.* 1430: William Langland's *Piers
Plowman*, Thomas Usk's *The Testament of Love*, John Gower's *Confessio
Amantis* (principally Book IV), Geoffrey Chaucer's *Canon's Yeoman's
Prologue* and *Tale*, and the poetry of Thomas Hoccleve.

Where the carver depicted on this misericord dominates and fills the
workshop space, his apprentices are much smaller, in a neat illustration of
the differential in their ages and their statuses within the workshop.
Whilst two apprentices work together at a bench behind the master, the
single figure on the right of the piece hesitates on the threshold of
the room. It is significant that there are three apprentices rather than just
one, signalling this master's moral fitness as an educator of the young and
the manager of a business concern that was larger and more financially
successful than was the average.[4] The size and centrality of the master-
carver articulates his authority and proprietorial rights over the space, its
personnel and the products of their labour. The positioning of the
apprentice on the margins of the carving suggests his liminal status as a
trainee, an adolescent, a temporary resident and also possibly an immigrant. The dog under the table signals that this is a domestic workshop
attached to a household and provides an iconographic sign that this
business and, by extension, the associated home are governed through
unbreachable bonds of fidelity.

This is a bold and self-assertive piece of work; carving himself into his
local church – St Nicholas's, King's Lynn – with a mark more memorable, although usually less permanent than the mason's, this maker
proudly advertises and autographs his craft with a statement about his
status as a householder, a 'good' man and a respected member of the
community.[5] This carver has a confidence in his work that encourages
him to inscribe his initials quite indelibly on the church furniture, riv-
alling the way that wealthy benefactors were writing theirs, alongside the

saints', in stained glass lights. Glass, however, was an expensive medium – most was imported from the continent through entry points like King's Lynn, and was then painted with costly pigment and fired in workshops like those which proliferated in East Anglia; in contrast wood was cheap and the price of the labour was the only real cost of a misericord.[6] Here we might see a connection with the literature of the same period that was exploiting English (another vernacular medium, like home-grown wood) and using it to create works which presumed to rival those in Latin and French, languages which, like Rhenish or French glass, had more cultural cachet. Even in these acts of self-assertion, however, in their overly earnest insistence on industry and competence, can be detected a vulnerability, an anxiety about the possible insufficiency of the masculine self being represented.

In just the same way that countless Middle English texts opened with an acknowledgement of the unexceptional nature, the deficiency of the language in which they were composed, wooden misericords have also been seen as a lowly medium. M. D. Anderson prefaces the most authoritative catalogue of English misericords like this:

Misericords are a very humble form of medieval art and it is unlikely that the most distinguished carvers of any period were employed in making them, except perhaps, during their apprentice years.[7]

There are all sorts of assumptions here about both misericords and apprentices; in a similar vein, Anderson suggests elsewhere that the creator of the pulpit in Ely Cathedral, being a man of evident taste, cannot also have been responsible for the misericords found in the same building, which he attributes, instead, to day-waged journeymen.[8] But of course misericords were – unlike pulpits and stained glass – out of sight, underneath seats, usually in the choir, and this position, coupled with their inexpensive medium, makes them 'humble'. However, it was precisely the cheapness of misericords and their location in the church that gave misericord-makers their licence; their decorative schemes were clearly less controlled from the top than those of the windows, or even of the more noticeable woodwork, in church buildings. If there ever were, for example, a window that showed a medieval glass painter, it has been destroyed – which is of course possible given the frustratingly breakable nature of the medium and people's propensity, especially in the middle of the seventeenth century, to throw stones. However, it is unlikely that such a reflexive figure would have been suggested or sanctioned by those that paid for the glass. The subject matter of misericords was less consistently the insignia of important families, or religious iconography; often they showed carnivalesque, scurrilous and fantastic scenes or scenes of 'ordinary life' – indeed themes that were suitable to be sat on. The quirky repertoire of the misericord-maker includes representations of the non-aristocratic self, the self, unsuitable for stained glass, in his work-a-day, domestic setting. Misericords, then, are a kind of joke or graffiti. Missing the grandiloquence of stained glass they articulate a comic version of the self, which is even a parodic comment upon the vanity of the patrons depicted in church windows. Not just aspirational but also self-fashioning, the literature considered in this book also finds, in the mundane materials of vernacular English, scope to discuss a new kind of masculine selfhood that was constructed out of the quotidian language of labour and the bourgeois household.

Of course, it may be that Anderson is right and that misericords *were* apprentice pieces and part of a training process. Then, of course, the joke is even more pronounced since the trainee, however affectionately, depicts his master as a domestic tyrant – a caricature which may or may not have squared with his reputation within the community that used the church – and then the apprentice carver covers his transgressive impudence by showing himself small, insignificant, indistinguishable from his peers and, anyway, on the way out. The most central of the pair of apprentices on the left of the King's Lynn carving has had his head chipped off, but the one whose head is still intact has it turned to his friend, mouth open mid-sentence. Their gossip takes place behind their master's back and beyond his supervision. The apprentice carver thus represents himself in modest relation to and in awe of his master – his social and gender role model – but his humility is bafflingly close to impudence. The protagonists and narrators in the literary texts studied here are also consistently measured against intelligible models of appropriate masculine labour, whether feudal icons, like the arable agriculturalist (as in *Piers Plowman*) and the knight-errant (in Book IV of the *Confessio Amantis*), or more up-to-the-minute, urban identities, like the good apprentice (in *The Canon's Yeoman's Prologue* and *Tale*) or the professional writer (in the writings of Usk and Hoccleve). Like the King's Lynn misericord these poetic works use labour to connect what they portray and how they are made. These texts hover between a corroboration of and a satire on models of masculine labour and they interpose the reflexive subject at the confluence of these two divergent dynamics. It is in this equivocal and metamorphic tone that the autobiographical subject is written.

These texts constitute a new kind of London life writing that is concerned to place the subjective self in relation to the contemporary ethics of masculine labour and living. This brings me onto the question of terminology that exercises the introduction of so many books about life writing in the past. In this book I use the terms 'life writing' mostly and 'autobiography' occasionally; I do so advisedly and in full knowledge of the discomfort that accompanies their deployment or rejection elsewhere.[9] I do this not in an effort to redefine the genre but because they are the best terms that we have to refer to the reflexive writing practices of the kind reviewed in this book. 'Life writing' is designed to be a broad term, broader than 'autobiography' and I use it here without apology. 'Autobiography' is more difficult but I use it in preference to the alternatives that have been suggested. I reject the phrase 'ego document' on the grounds of inelegance; James Olney's 'perigraphy' (writing around or about [the self]) is nicer than 'ego document' but not really better, being less current and familiar than 'life writing', which has been defined similarly.[10] Lawrence de Looze's 'pseudo-autobiography' is heedful of the particular textures of medieval life writing but assumes three things that are not part of the approach of this volume: first it suggests that the textual personae are definitely *not* avatars of their authors (which, while it may be true of the texts he investigates, is not quite the case with those I look at here); secondly it assumes that there is a 'true' kind of autobiography which produces an authentic representation of the authorial self; and thirdly it implies that within that 'true' autobiography the text's subjectivity is exclusively sited within the protagonist-narrator.[11]

The word autobiography, of course, comes from the Greek: *autos* (self), *bios* (life), *graphein* (to write). The problem comes in relation to the second of these. Although the life writing investigated here does discuss past events (*The Testament of Love* being a good example), I do not think that their authors are ever principally engaged in representing a historical life. These writings are less acts of memorialization or recollection than expressions of confession and conscience; I am concerned, then, more with the *autos* than the *bios*, which is where, I think, medieval life writing practices are more likely to direct us.[12] Further, a gendered study such as this one is also, inevitably perhaps, guided to consider the motifs and mechanics of confession, a narrative form that foregrounds the sexual life. Given the superfluity of the *bios*, then, the term 'autography' – which has been coined by H. Porter Abbot to discuss the reflexive fiction of Samuel Beckett – seems potentially useful.[13] There is a possible ambiguity, though, with using that term in a discussion of a manuscript culture where (as in the case of Thomas Hoccleve, for example) the text may literally be in the author's own hand and so I have plumped for 'auto-biography' to avoid such a confusion. 'Autobiography' as a genre has been strictly policed and has typically excluded life-written narratives that are chronologically idiosyncratic, often those from marginal or minority groups or from people in the past. The texts I look at here are evidently not 'autobiography' in the narrowest definition of that term, they are not written on a normative *Bildung* template, but they are certainly auto-biographical in content and I intend the word in that limited sense. My principle interest, though, is not really to stretch a category but to find a practicable terminology to investigate the less pedantic question, similar to that raised by James S. Amelang's study of artisan autobiography in early modern Europe, of how people in the past wrote about themselves.[14]

Many medievalists, like de Looze, have been circumspect about using the word 'autobiography' because of the legacy of Jakob Burkhardt's *Civilization of the Renaissance in Italy*.[15] Others though, like Jeremy Tambling, have made short work of rejecting Burkhardt's thesis about the 'discovery of the individual' in the Renaissance period:

there is no ahistorical 'individualism' or 'humanity' to be discovered; for each age and dominant ideology will seek to produce the concept of the individual it wants – in relation to power structures, patriarchy and modes of control.[16]

There is, however, still some more work to be done: the modern studies of masculinity, which have recently been written to compliment women's studies and complete the picture of gender in the past, are very much entangled in this old debate about selfhood and modernity. 'Anxiety' has been the watchword in men's studies, and attempts to historicize the Freudian notion of anxiety have revisited Burkhardt and also Max Weber, whose *Protestant Ethic and the Spirit of Capitalism* has also played its part in constructing the alterity of the Middle Ages.[17] Studies of masculinity, in fact, often recycle previous, implicitly phallocentric theses – like those of Burkhardt and Weber – and, by making them overtly about men, have produced new accounts of *modern* masculinity as desiring, anxious and subjective.[18] This strategy has the unfortunate effect of describing the Middle Ages as one which antedates the developments that 'seem parti-cularly important for the making of those configurations of social practice that we now call "masculinity"', consigning medieval men to a kind of Kleinian infancy in which they are unable to delimit themselves from object others.[19] I am not, in contrast, arguing for any kind of sameness between the medieval and modern periods; masculinity isn't timeless. Rather, in a move somewhat like Tambling's cited above, I argue that pre-Reformation masculine anxiety should be acknowledged and analysed, and its many differences from the cultural angst in other periods should be discovered through a close reading of its particular textures and manifestations. Whilst this volume does not attempt a comparison of the periods either side of the Reformation crisis, such a study would be a valuable area for further research and would find, I should imagine – perhaps a little like Christine Peters's recent work on women's lay piety – the difference in the detail, in the local variations that are typically written out of the neo-Weberian metanarrative.[20] This volume instead focuses on the textual community of late fourteenth- and early fifteenth-century London, describing and contextualizing a particular fashion for positioning the medieval, but nonetheless *anxious* masculine self at the interstices between his labour and his domestic life.

Elizabeth Heale's recent consideration of the self in Renaissance verse has laudably attempted to outline in its introduction, in a more sensitive and less simplistic way, exactly what are the differences and indeed continuities between the medieval and Renaissance representations of selfhood.[21] Finally, though, I don't think that Heale's conclusion, that medieval life writing finds 'closure and identity in the authorizing discourses of God conveyed through the authoritative words of Reason', which is predicated on the study of Hoccleve as the sole representative of his age, is a convincing reading either of Hoccleve's neurotic verse forms or of medieval religious and life writing practices more broadly. It is all too often fallaciously assumed that medieval religiosity contrasts with Renaissance secularism and, further, that faith precludes cerebral inwardness.[22] Faith purports to be, but is really not at all, an emptying of the self. The same is true of social and political conformity. Exterior bodies (God, political and social communities) turn out, after all, to be subjectively imagined, a part of, rather than either a foil to, or a substitute for the interiorized subject. The 'self-fashioning' subject in these texts is to be found in the homosocial and internal negotiations between the self and the world.[23] I do not seek necessarily to identify the authors of these texts unequivocally and exclusively with the narrators inside their writings, even where those narrators share their names and, perhaps, their occupations.[24] It is not clear, when we look at the King's Lynn misericord, whether the maker is a master or an apprentice; the carving is clearly concerned to show not the self in an isolated portrait but as part of a masculine community; its subjectivity is dialectic, confected in the

spaces between one individual and another, or between the individual as
is and what he imagines he *ought* to be.

Although scholars often look for selfhood and individuality in subversion and iconoclasm, I am at least as interested in the way in which the
texts or narrators discussed in this book conspire with and invest in
dominant ideologies. Chaucer's Canon's Yeoman, for example, has been
described as a symbol of insurrection, but I argue in chapter four that his
account of himself is just as telling about the dangers of trade complicity
and male confederacy, about misplaced allegiance and inappropriate
labour cohesion.[25] Will, in *Piers Plowman*, has also been seen as a
maverick narrator and yet the poem's subjectivity, I suggest in chapter
one, is not solely and exclusively located in the narrator but rather in the
relationship between the narrator and those masculine models – labour
models primarily – that he is exhorted to emulate by his conservative but,
crucially, interior interlocutors.[26] Obedience and faith are often glamorized in these texts as active strengths and iconic masculinity is
deployed to that end. Karl Weintraub has argued, specifically about pre-
modern identity, that:

The more the mind's eye is fascinated by the ideal model before it, the more a
man will strive to attain *it*, the less he will ask about the fit between the model
and his own specific reality. He is unlikely to suffer from a sense of 'falsifying
himself' by fitting into the norms demanded by his model, to feel 'hemmed in' if
the ideal expresses the values of the society, or to lament the lost opportunities of
his precious individuality.[27]

I could not disagree more strongly. It is precisely in the absence of a 'fit'
between iconic masculine models and the self that the subjective anxieties
I describe in this book are to be found. It is exactly what happens in this
gap that is dramatized in the texts here. I consider the autobiographical
motive, the subjectivity of the text, as it is constructed on the fraught
interface between the narrator-protagonist and his various interlocutors
over appropriate forms of masculine conduct.[28] These dialogues, I suggest, exteriorize the formation of the social conscience, staging the uneasy
concessions and accommodations necessary for the individual to find a
place in his world. In thinking about conscience I do not describe an
innate rational consciousness *per se*, rather I use it as a conceptual tool
with which to historicize an anxiety produced between the twin fears of
being, on the one hand, overly appetitive and ostracized and, on the
other, unassertive and exploited.[29] Because every community differs from
every other and places uneven expectations upon its members, I do not

present evidence for an ontological and historically transcendent set of human anxieties. Rather I describe singular and culturally specific patterns in the connections between these texts and their contexts, between their narrators and their authors' *milieux*, between their protagonists and the ethical expectations against which they are measured.

That these texts share an interest in, indeed a fixation on, work – which is not always thought to be a very poetical subject – is no coincidence. Indeed, they are evidence of a larger cultural perturbation about a contemporary labour crisis – which was itself a corollary of the demographic crises of the previous decades – a crisis that is exhibited in the labour legislation repeatedly reissued throughout the latter half of the fourteenth century. This legislation was part of a discourse that, although it purported to be retrospective, fabricated a new labour ethic that combined antiquated feudal values and their concomitant, reliable gender-paradigms with a regulatory framework for the burgeoning wage economy. Further, the national labour legislation was modelled upon *a priori* London law, a fact that indicates the precociousness and particularity of the metropolis during this period of economic and social transformation.[30] In particular, London was singular in terms of its reception of a significant number of economic migrants, especially from those places where the land was of indifferent fertility.[31] Many of those migrants were young people who came in search of household service jobs in the town. These migrations placed in tension notions of belonging and enterprise, social investedness and economic opportunism.

The London literature considered in this book is thought to originate from a circle that was curiously positioned in relation to the discursive preoccupation with labour and the ideals of industry that it generated.[32] First, these authors are often thought to have been close to, indeed implicated in, the administrative culture within which the labour legislation was made and disseminated; it is thought that Chaucer in particular had a hand in its enforcement.[33] Whatever the truth about their authors, the narrators of these texts embody a dilemma about the relationship between work and male desire, between working and domestic identities, that were in antagonized conflict in the lives of the late-medieval bureaucrats. As secular men in clerical roles, and frequently *clerici uxorati*, the bureaucrats occupied an unstable cusp identity untested in social practice.[34] The late fourteenth-century labour crisis precipitated a revival of and a restless insistence upon various conservative models of holistic social corporation – such as the ubiquitous three estates schema – within which the bureaucrat found it hard to classify himself.

Whilst his labour identity seemed to position him within the first estate, his marital or sexual status aligned him with the second or third. The late-medieval process of generating ethical codes for these relatively untried male lifestyles, which I have elsewhere described as a cultural rite of passage, is represented in the interior negotiations of a new kind of vernacular male life writing.[35]

The alienation produced by this disjunction between working and sexual status was exacerbated by fashionable moral discourses that continually related men's sexual and labouring roles, making industry and the social cohesion it would necessarily produce an attractive masculine commission by linking it to sexual success and patriarchal authority. The conceptual and lexical conflation of work and sex, of production and reproduction, was not new in this period: the Middle Ages inherited it from both classical and Judeo-Christian traditions. Aristotelian medicine, for example, used metaphors of arable husbandry to describe the processes of human fertility (men were figured as agriculturalists, women as passive fields and children as harvested fruit).[36] Production and reproduction were also the activities of the fallen human, labouring for food and in childbirth. Gregory Sadlek has traced other traditions, from Ovid's *Ars amatoria*, for example, showing how labour imagery supplied polite euphemisms for Alan of Lille's rejection of sodomy and the recommendation of reproductive sex in his influential *De planctu naturae*.[37] These were indeed old tropes but they were revised and given new meanings in the particular social and economic climate of post-Black Death England. For example, whilst the legislative energies of this generation were fixated on the production and enforcement of labour law, private households increasingly became the site where social and sexual behaviours were policed and managed.[38] The task of instilling discipline in the youthful and often transient population of the urban household was being delegated to male householders and the instruments that were supplied for the task were often regulations surrounding trade, employment and training. This tendency to regulate labour and social/sexual behaviours together was matched by the physical proximity of working and living in the ideal dual urban household, with its annexed workshop or shop. Indeed, the urban guilds and municipal authorities, in a systematic process of 'cognitive purification', encouraged householding men to demonstrate their authority through the regulation of their dependent wives, children, servants and apprentices – to conflate their working and their domestic identities.[39] Like the carver portrayed on the King's Lynn misericord, though, this was an ideal that was rarely realized in practice, and this discrepancy undoubtedly generated misgivings about masculine authority and sufficiency.

These literary texts all invest in the moral orthodoxies of their age, valorizing both conformity and industry, and yet they produce narrators that are, by comparison, compromised – sometimes tragically, sometimes comically and sometimes both. At the same time as engaging with cultural ideals of masculinity, the narrators of these literary texts identify themselves not as good, industrious men but variously as idle, avaricious or insufficient workers, inappropriate or unrewarded lovers or husbands, as adolescents or children. In so doing, they interiorize wider, cultural anxieties about male irresponsibility and appetite. In this way, these texts continually but variously represent the dialectic between the community and the self, dramatizing the construction of the social conscience and inflecting it with the lexicon of employment and service. Whilst on the one hand they pay sincere homage to literary and social conventions, creating humble and diffident personae, on the other this apparent respect can be read as an insinuation of the fragmented and disruptive subject into the symbolic heart of the community.

The singular commixture of comedy and anxiety in the portraits of these narrators is a representation of a new masculine modality: a kind of *urbanitas*, a pragmatic, non-heroic identity that is an unsteady accommodation between the 'common good' and the interior, appetitive self. At once socially interpolated and original, individually determined constructions, these narrators are homeless within their own texts. The concept of 'home', though, of finding resolution and settlement, is crucial to these works, which develop the affectivity, fidelity and piety of the bourgeois household ethos into a tragically unattainable, Boethian *summum bonum*. This quest for stability is presented as an interior process and often demonstrated by spilling and inordinate narrative forms. Langland's copious and compulsive revisions, Usk's vacillations between genres, Gower's theme of masculine errancy, the Canon's Yeoman's structural blurring of his *Prologue* and *Tale*, and Hoccleve's engulfing social invective dramatize their narrators' homeless searches for accommodation within the moral universe, within the social order, within the sinful self, within their own 'skyn[s]' (Hoccleve's 'Complaint', 303) and ultimately, in these reflexive texts.

CHAPTER I

The masculine ethics of Langland's
Piers Plowman

INTRODUCTION

The imagery and lexicon of labour and agriculture is omnipresent in *Piers Plowman*, inflecting the poem's other concerns and displacing their perhaps more expected figures and vocabularies.[1] In particular and most relevantly for this chapter, the language of work is often euphemistically used to discuss sexuality in a way that might seem casual if it were not so consistent. This, for example, is the description of the kingdom of Lechery in the Charter of Guile:

> And al the lordshipe of Leccherie in lengthe and in brede –
> As in werkes and in wordes and in waitynges with eighes,
> And in wedes and in wisshynges and with ydel thoughtes
> Ther as wil wolde and werkmanshipe fayleth.
>
> (B, II, 89–92)[2]

The description stands out with its extended alliteration of the 'w' over three lines. The rhythm created by the parataxis of lines 90–1 is reminiscent of the staccato breaths of the sexual fantasist. The crescendo of these conjunctive clauses builds an expectation, amplified by the word 'waitynges', which is ultimately flattened by the anti-climax of the last two words: 'werkmanshipe fayleth'. Tellingly, impotence is described as a labour failure caused by a superfluity of 'ydel thoughtes'. This, of course, was not a new association but one that was inherited from Classical and Judeo-Christian traditions. Medieval readings of the first three chapters of Genesis, for example, wrestled with the way that work and sexuality were intertwined in Christian origin myth.[3] However, this kind of language took on a new pertinence in a community transformed by the collapse of intensive arable agriculture, struggling with the economic consequences of the labour shortages left by the demographic problems of the early and mid-fourteenth century.

12

Langland set out in his poem a reflexive discourse about masculine ethics which combined ideas about work, sexuality and domesticity during a period in which the nature and value of both labour and the household were being redefined, a process of redefinition that often treated them both together. The poem's interest in the processes of production – its moral and political discussion of work – has been frequently noticed and contextualized against the labour crisis of the post-Black Death period. The labour legislation, which was anxiously redrafted throughout the period in which this poem was also being fretfully revised and reissued, shares both a physical locale and a moral register with Langland's work.[4]

Langland's poetry, I shall show, always considers the project of restoring social order as an especially masculine commission, relating it particularly to male domestic roles. Clearly there is a close relationship between the socio-economic registers of *Piers Plowman* and *Wynnere and Wastoure* but Langland made the household setting that he found in the (probably) earlier poem a much more evidently masculine space.[5] Although there is an extensive historiography on the centrality of female work during the labour shortage in the decades immediately following the Black Death of 1348–9, Langland is far more interested in men's than in women's economic contributions.[6] Piers allocates work, on the basis of estate, in Passus VI of the B-text and, in that allocation, women's responsibility for small-scale textile production is dealt with cursorily in just nine lines. In Passus XIX of the B-text, women are passed over completely when Grace comes to distribute professional and craft skills, which are weapons in the fight against the Antichrist and his henchmen: Ydelnesse, Envye and Pride. The narrator, in his defence of his labour in the *Apologia pro vita sua* (C, V), restricted by his subjective concerns, gives a list only of male vocations. Estates theory in this period was similarly erratic in the way that it classified women and their social contribution.[7] Whilst they were sometimes categorized as a fourth estate adjunct to the masculine community, women were as often given a whole estates system of their own, which was separate from but parallel to that of the male community, and which differentiated them from each other according to marital or social status; more usually they were entirely overlooked and thought to be represented by their husbands or fathers. Women were rarely found a reliable place within this ubiquitous schema, and Langland is not unusual in carving up societal responsibility along male occupational and status lines. The theme of marriage and sexuality is also treated with a similarly reflexive masculinism. The masculine subjectivity of the 'marriage of Meed' Passus has been well documented by feminist critics: Lady Meed is a woman trafficked in a male economy, the object of the male gaze, an amoral, blank slate given meaning through her marriage.[8] I shall not focus on the marriage of Lady Meed; instead I shall treat some of Langland's other discussions of marriage and its place within the Christian corporation. I shall, however, argue for a masculinist perspective in those discussions that testifies to their specular significances. Because in this poem the male gaze is, of course, reflexive; the female characters that have been most considered in gendered analyses are avatars of the dreamer-narrator's subjective consciousness.

Sociologists and historians considering men's lives and masculine ethics in later periods have emphasized the intersections between work and home: the way in which men's identities as fathers and husbands influence their identities as workers, and vice versa.[9] Whilst this poem has been a boon to historians of labour, and considered in terms of its interest in marriage, these themes have never been discussed in relation to the poem's masculine subjectivity.[10] The husband and worker is produced as a compelling ideal in this poem; he is invested with much of the responsibility for restoring social order just in the way that householders and working people were charged with the same in the records associated with labour in the period.[11] The problems associated with a population and labour shortage initiate a process of 'cognitive purification' whereby gender models are reformulated in response to a perceived social need.[12] The poem provides numerous positive accounts of marriage that are newly confected out of, by turns, resistant and corroborative readings of scriptural and exegetical accounts of Christian sexuality. Langland makes transformative use of inherited texts and debates and, in this chapter, I am interested in the way that he marginalizes the standard medieval preference for virginity, negotiating a more privileged place for marriage and fatherhood within his theological poetics. I shall also describe, however, the hesitation with which this new set of ethics is proposed in *Piers Plowman*. Will – whose authority is dubious, who resembles the objects of the poem's most stinging invective – is compromised by the masculine ethics that are supported by the poem's earnest hopes for the future of the community.[13] In particular, as a married clerk, he stands in curious relation to the estates taxonomy in which the poem is so invested, standing on a cusp between traditional identities.[14] Will's prosecution by his own Reason and Conscience and his account of himself in the C-text *Apologia pro vita sua* are, I shall suggest, as instructive on the question of his problematic marital status as his contravention of contemporary labour law.

As the debate between the interior faculties of Will, Reason and Conscience shows, the poem, even in its waking episodes like the C-text *Apologia*, is also a dramatization of the narrator's own cerebral intro-spection. Like John Burrow, I think that it doesn't much matter whether the dreamer-protagonist's 'autobiography', in Passus V of the C-text, is literally 'true'; the critic can maintain an agnosticism about the 'real' William Langland.[15] The poem is a spectacular and tragic representation of the fractured male *autos*, a representation produced in the relations between characters and in the discrepancies between their world views.[16] The name Will may also be a personified projection of an interior faculty: the sexual drive and/or the Augustinian notion of *voluntas*.[17] Will the dreamer and Will the protagonist in the dream are in enigmatic and mostly indistinguishable relation. The dreamer-narrator stands in com-petition with splinters of himself, developing protean connections with the various personae with whom he shares poetic space, and which are variously invested in the multifarious contemporary discourses of authority. In its many incarnations, *Piers Plowman* has been described as a mad text, the product of a fitful imagination.[18] The poem's many para-noid revisions – attempts to tidy and sanitize – actually complicate, proliferate and expand; it is a spilling and plural narrative form that mimics the narrator's unsated, impatient quest to find ethical accom-modation within the self.

LABOUR OR MARRIAGE?

Will authorizes his defence of his labour with a near-quotation from 1 Corinthians 7.20. In his rendition – '*In eadem vocacione in qua vocati estis*' – Will evokes St Paul's '*unusquisque in qua vocatione vocatus est in ea permaneat*', which is part of a larger argument in Corinthians about the subordination of marriage to virginity, and which deploys different notions of 'vocation' as metaphors to explain that hierarchy.[19] In the Corinthians passage, the distinction between marriage and virginity is being compared with two others. The first is that between the cir-cumcised and the uncircumcised (that is, between Jew and Gentile): by likening marriage to circumcision, St Paul describes it as irreversible: just as the foreskin cannot be reformed, virginity cannot be reclaimed and, further, marriages made in the eyes of God cannot be dissolved.[20] Sec-ondly, the relationship between marriage and virginity is compared to that between bondman and freeman. These analogies make the states of virginity and marriage akin to religious, racial or status categories. It is telling that Langland chooses to use a passage which is about marriage in order to discuss his narrator's labour; indeed, marriage and labour are connected by assumptions that are left wholly tacit. I suggest that the connection is this: St Paul begrudgingly accepts existing Corinthian marriages as a necessary evil to avoid social disintegration, whilst social disintegration, as it was perceived by Langland's generation, was inextricably bound up with the shortage of labour. The comparison between the married person and the bondman in 1 Corinthians makes for an association between divorce and social revolution – the married should stay married in order not to disrupt the social status quo. Thus St Paul expresses his preference for virginity without jeopardizing the future social order of Corinth and he obviates the potentially revolutionary implications of virginity and so of Christian conversion.

Medieval ideas about social corporation were indebted and often referred to Paul's first letter to the Corinthians, wherein he most clearly espoused his wish that disparate and divided parts might come together to form the body of Christ (1 Corinthians 12). Robert F. Yeager has given a clear exposition of the evolution of that idea into medieval thought and the political theory of, for example, John of Salisbury, producing a parallel figure for secular forms of authority in which disparate members were unified by the monarchical head.[21] These organic images disguised the innovations that they may have introduced and became ubiquitous in descriptions of ideal communities. After all, Paul sought to create a new rather than describe a pre-existing cohesive Christian Church.

The discourses of social unity of the late fourteenth century similarly formulated new cohesive structures in the language of indubitable and natural principle. The Statute and Ordinance of Labourers (1349–51), for example, produce a fantasy of a society ordered by labour practice and price regulations; this is a vision of social corporation – 'common weal' – invented around work and wages as unifying principles.[22] These attempts at social engineering reproduced feudal estates theory in a singular way. The clergy are mentioned only as a communication conduit: the Ordinance was to be disseminated via the pulpit.[23] These pieces of legislation were designed, the preamble to the Statute unashamedly acknowledges, to protect the interests of the 'great Men' as a group (although the Ordinance also legislates against individual employers' poaching labour from each other), interests that are understood to be identical to those of the common weal.[24] The articles of both the Ordinance and the Statute divided up the rest of society – both men and women – in terms of secular occupation, and made the restitution of a notional pre-Black

Death social order incumbent upon their proper observation of right practice. They list first arable agricultural workers (and especially harvest hands), then the urban liveried servants, next 'workmen of houses' (that is, the workshop artisans), and finally the victualling trade. Their final precepts attempt to guard against bribery and corruption amongst the officials – the bailiffs and so on – charged with enforcement. This is a new version of the perfect community produced from the collocation of disparate trades and statuses, each engaged by their respective duties. The Statute thus purports to be comprehensive and its omission of economic practices that were not so readily categorized – the piece-work, day-work and credit networks – reveals both its fictive naïvety and its proximity to other wishful visions of corporate, holistic communities.[25]

Anne Middleton in an encyclopaedic essay makes a suggestive case about the relationship between the C-text *Apologia pro vita sua* and the 1388 Statute on vagrancy. She has argued that the narrator acquits himself of the charges brought against him, which are framed in the terms of the said Cambridge Statute by Reason and Conscience, effectively defending himself and his labour in a way which deploys both the teachings of St Paul on the stability of estate identification and the terms of the Statute itself: 'in such a way as both to exploit and to dismantle its monologic facade'.[26] While I admire much of Middleton's case, my argument takes a different tack precisely over Langland's use of St Paul. The social and ethical vision of the late fourteenth-century labour legislation may have a 'monologic facade' but it is nevertheless still not wholly identical to the apostle's teaching in 1 Corinthians 7. Indeed, Statute law constructs a very different masculine ideal to that recommended and indeed embodied by the apostle – 'dico autem non nuptis et viduis bonum est illis si sic maneant sicut et ego' (1 Corinthians 7.8).[27] In particular it mostly excises the celibate clergy which, in other renditions of medieval estates theory, and in the reckoning of St Paul, were considered superordinate to the married laity. Will exploits a vulnerability within Pauline thinking, turning his pessimistic evaluation of marriage against his predilection for Christian corporation. Middleton has accurately described the way in which St Paul is used by the narrator to justify his estates philosophy.[28] Will takes the Corinthians verse out of context and uses it ostensibly to authenticate his pursuing the clerical career to which his schooling has suited him. The narrator goes on to extrapolate from that that just as *he* should remain in the clerical *milieu* to which his education has accus- tomed him, everyone should remain in the estate in which they were born and socialized. In doing so he also imitates – as Middleton notes – the statutory injunctions that enforced people to stay in the positions and especially agricultural positions with which they had previously been identified. In his list of estates, the narrator mimics the style and substance of the labour legislation that anatomized society on the bases of place and duty. Will deploys Paul's conservatism – a conservatism which chimes with contemporary discourses about labour and social order – to exempt himself from the most socially necessary forms of work, and especially agricultural labour during harvest time. The dreamer exploits a terror of social upheaval – of the kind displayed in the epistle to the Corinthians and contemporary labour legislation – to recommend himself to his own disapproving Reason and Conscience.

However, the Corinthians passage itself uses the idea of the bondman/freeman status descriptions only as a metaphor in a comparison of virginity and matrimony. The rest of the passage is concerned to establish the hierarchy of sexual states which was to dominate the teachings of the medieval Church on human sexuality, and which valued continence more than marriage. Whilst there were other more positive accounts about marriage in this period, which did not recommend virginity as a universal good, Langland chooses a text that unequivocally *does*. The question of sexual perfection and propriety thus haunts Will's discussion of his work. In particular, his identification as *clericus uxoratus* makes his use of Paul's hierarchy of sexual states even more pertinent and problematic. The estate taxonomies of the Middle Ages did not usually find a place for the anomalies, like Will, who were both married and clerical; indeed, the narrator doesn't, as he comes to admit in accord with his own Conscience (C, V, 89–98), fit into his own lists.[29] Incidentally, and by using Paul's words on marriage in his own service, Will incorporates his problematic marriage to Kytte, which he mentioned in the first lines of his confession, into the discussion of his work. He does so in a way that latently acknowledges that the 'parfit man' (as Will erroneously refers to himself at line 84) would not be both married and clerical.

And this is principally where my argument departs from Middleton: the narrator is uncomfortable and shifty, at odds with his own interior systems of surveillance, and unwittingly uses authorities and texts which compromise his case. St Paul's depiction of marriage as a permissible alternative only to unregulated sexuality or social flux becomes Will's compromise, which is in subtextual competition with the possibility of sexual continence. The narrator's marriage and his work are both, then, about damage limitation. His marital status, though, further weakens his other decidedly and self-confessedly 'wayke' arguments about his unsuitability for physical labour, the sort of labour that would seem to fit best with his domestic identity. Hanna has noted Will's punning on his healthy but inadequate limbs/lomes (tools), their innuendo re-enacting, Hanna argues, Will's emasculation in the disciplinarian medieval schoolroom. These puns express the same conflation of sexuality and labour, of (re)production that, as I shall show, is crucial to the portrait of the ideal husband-worker in Wit's marriage sermon; Will stands in problematic contrast to the 'wedded men' (C, X, 203) that his Kynde Inwit teaches him to admire. Hanna expresses surprise that the text should adopt this tone of sexual inadequacy in the *Apologia* when the narrator finds himself at the prime of his life and at the height of his sexual potency during his married years.[30] I suggest that it is precisely his marital status that confuses the masculine propriety of his clerical labour and his clerical labour that throws his marriage into an area of moral doubt that lies beyond traditional gender paradigms.

The exact nature of Will's vocation is a matter of some discussion; its indeterminacy is evidently a central feature of its construction. E. Talbot Donaldson suggested, and his finding, though qualified, is still upheld, that Will was intended to represent an acolyte whose anomalous marriage would have placed limitations on his career in the Church. He also noted that the medieval Church, out of a prejudice produced by scriptural authorities like Paul, was less inclined to recompense married clerks, and that this would have considerably complicated the married clerk's working patterns, obliging him to take on casual work either as a scribe or as a bedesman, moving between various private households.[31] Anne Middleton and Wendy Scase have both discussed Will in relation to gyrovague satire and fingered his itinerancy as one of the most troubling aspects of his portrait.[32] Will's admission that he lives both in London and 'opeland' makes him a peripatetic figure in a world in which travel and travellers were regarded with suspicion and their movements made the subject of regulatory laws. Indeed, 'uppelande' figures as a suspicious place of origin for men who illegally set up as barber surgeons in the 1376 London ordinance of that trade.[33] Fear of itinerancy was, of course, alarm at a labour force which, after the Black Death, was increasingly economically and socially as well as geographically mobile; there is also evidence, however, that the sexual behaviour of migrants was also reason for their being distrustfully regarded or, alternatively, that fears about mobile labour were thus hysterically displaced. Larry Poos has found evidence that migrant couples found the nature of their marriage unions scrutinized by those communities in which they settled; an intolerance of the sexual misbehaviour of migrant youth, and especially male apprentices, is a commonplace in the contemporary record.[34] Certainly Langland's poem regularly makes unexplained connections between mobility and sexual aberrance.[35] The migrant populations of late medieval England were at once economic and sexual unknowns and thus embody St Paul's double fears, against which marriage is a protection.

An epiphenomenon of the legal preoccupation with the enforcement of the labour legislation was the increasing privatization of social and sexual discipline, especially of young people who were less likely to be prosecuted in public courts and more likely to be reigned in by their masters or fathers. The householder-husband came to be glamorized as a masculine ideal in the medieval civic and urban guild records, as he is in the King's Lynn misericord.[36] Male householders had an important role in brokering the marriages of young people in their charge and marriage was often encouraged as a way of regulating perceived promiscuity within the youthful populations of the later medieval urban household.[37] On the other hand, fears of labour crisis also generated the rural ideal of the married labourer, made iconic by Langland, of course, in his most authoritative creation: Piers the Plowman himself.[38] Wit's sermon on marriage, which I shall go on to discuss in more detail below, recommends a masculine model of the industrious and married man – a man like Piers Plowman – as a remedy for both population and labour shortage. Piers's marriage is not the lesser of two evils in the Pauline way – it is made sound and affirming by his secular agricultural labour. Will's, on the other hand, is not morally buttressed by work in this way and is still vulnerable to the aspersions cast by Paul. In this way, Will stands in compromised relation on two fronts that are wholly dissimilar, separately answerable to the terms of the contemporary labour legislation and an older, Pauline partiality to sexual purity. The narrator's compromise is between old and new masculine ideals.

Wit's sermon on marriage and the ploughing of the half-acre are scenes that stand at the moral heart of all three versions of *Piers Plowman*. If we read Will's confession – as Middleton does – as a successful poke in the eye for the forces of late medieval surveillance, then we would also have to question those two crucial statements about the social ethics of labour and marriage, against which Will stands measured and is found to be woefully inadequate. Reason and Conscience, who oppose Will in the C-text scene, are surely, too, aspects of the poem's subjectivity, and vocalize its sincere investment in the discourses of social control of the kind that are manifest in the labour law. Will's prosecution by his *own* reason and conscience is, as Middleton says, a comic episode, but it is also tragic and affecting.[39] I do not see Will's inability to repent fully as a tacit legitimation of his vernacular errancy; the poem has heterogeneous reactions to competing sources of authority, representing and managing them at their confluence: the fractured self.

THE LIFE OF DO WELL

The full complexity of the Do Well, Do Bet, Do Best conceit is not one that there is space to tackle in this chapter. As many have noted, this is a hard triad to clarify definitively, and it combines ideas about ways of living, learning and assuring salvation.[40] The meanings of the three states are fluid and never made truly explicit, no two characters in the poem offering the same account of them. Although a bishop is the simile which is used to define the state of Do Best (e.g. B, VIII, 96), the exact relationship between Do Bet/Do Best and the orders of the clergy (which would inevitably carry distinctions of sexual status) is not definitively stated. Whilst some have seen the idea of the Do Well, Do Bet, Do Best triumvirate as an articulation of the difference between the laity, the clergy and the episcopy, the poem suggests it as a ladder of improvement that one individual might climb.[41] Self-evidently it isn't possible to ascend to virginity from marriage, in the way that Paul notes by likening husbands/wives and virgins to the uncircumcised and the circumcised.

Notwithstanding the possibility that the Do Well to Do Best spectrum is intended to correspond to social identities, it evidently also signifies a hermeneutic progress; the whole poem and the dreamer's journey purport to advance organically through these stages (although, anti-climactically, Will never reaches any kind of superlative condition).[42] The figure of Thought is clear that Do Bet, at least, is an extension of, rather than an alternative to Do Well. Part of the significance of the search for Do Well, though, as Wit's sermon makes axiomatic, is as a negotiation of the medieval ethics of marriage. Several critics have noted the poem's 'friendliness' towards marriage, the positive place it is given in the poem's social theory.[43] Tavormina has argued that the themes of marriage and family function as Langland's main repertoire of images: 'such an intrinsic part of his world-view that he could hardly avoid expressing himself in those terms'.[44] She does not consider, though, that they are as ideologically critical to the poem as, say, the themes of salvation, justice, mercy and truth. I think, however, that Langland's writing about sexuality is thoroughly bound up with those other questions. Furthermore,

I shall argue that the differences between the A, B and C versions reveal the strident case that is made for marriage in the B-text; that stridency, though, is hedged about and qualified in C in a way that indicates not only the political and theological importance of these supposedly private and domestic subjects, but also the edginess with which they are broached. The Langlandian confusions, the poem's apparent imprecision about the life of Do Well and its exact implications for the institution of marriage are, I suggest, testament to its originality, its contribution to a new and as yet not wholly authorized system of medieval ethics within which marriage, rather than virginity, held a central place. *Piers Plowman*'s discussion of matrimony vacillates between the ordinary and the extraordinary, protecting its orthodoxy through the use of the discrepant opinions of its various personae.

Whilst the meanings of Do Well and Do Bet are intricate and multivalent, the actual phrases are surely reminiscent of Paul's contrasting of virginity and matrimony in 1 Corinthians 7:

nam qui statuit in corde suo firmus non habens necessitatem potestatem autem habet suae voluntatis et hoc iudicavit in corde suo servare virginem suam bene facit igitur et qui matrimonio iungit virginem suam bene facit et qui non iungit melius facit.

[For he that hath determined being steadfast in his heart, having no necessity, but having power of his own will; and hath judged this in his heart, to keep his virgin, doth well. Therefore, both he that giveth his virgin in marriage, doth well; and he that giveth her not, doth better.]

(1 Corinthians 7.37–8)

Here the ideas of doing well or better are written into an account of how to master the will (*voluntatis*); this already suggests a personification of interior faculties of the kind found in Langland's drama of the self. If the phrases 'bene facit' and 'melius facit' – although admittedly not 'optime facit' – look unstudied here, they harden into established categories in the exegetical commentaries on this passage – from, for example, Ambrose, Jerome and Augustine – which are often also tracts on the relative merits of virginity as opposed to marriage. Jerome in his marriage tract *Adversus Jovinianum*, like other patristic writers, does not read this as an address to the fathers of Corinth on the relative merits of marrying off their daughters as later commentators do.[45] Instead he sees the phrase 'virginem suam' as a metaphor for 'carnem' [flesh]. This resolves the otherwise problematic first verse cited here; in this reading, the passage claims that the man who does well, who keeps his virgin from marriage, masters his *inner* desires. However, the Corinthians passage states that he does well, 'bene facit', if he keeps his virginity, but then in the next verse, says that he also does well if he marries. This is not the contradiction that it might appear to be, and Jerome, amongst others, makes short work of the apparent knot, expatiating thus: '[t]antum est igitur inter nuptias et virginitatem, quantum inter non peccare, et bene facere; immo ut levius dicam, quantum inter bonum et melius'.[46] In the Pauline account, to marry and to remain a virgin are similar in that they are both good when compared with sexual incontinence, but virginity is that and more; it is in fact better than marriage.

Of course, Langland's understanding of doing well or, indeed, doing better is never so narrowly and exclusively focused on the propriety of marriage. However, his expansive and protean reformulations are always insistent on including marriage in his discussion of what it is to do well. This is most prominently so in Wit's marriage sermon. In the A-text, Wit cites the same bit of St Paul that the narrator will use later in the C-text *Apologia* – '*In eadem vocacione qua vocati estis state*' (A, X, 112) – and recommends Do Well as the stable root that supports the flower Do Best. Here, Do Well, Do Bet and Do Best are complex concepts, partly about enduring a God-given lot or estate but also about the virtue of marriage as opposed to the other grades of chastity. Wit grounds social order and the generation of perfection on the lives of the working married: 'þoruȝ wedlak þe world stant' (A, X, 133).

The B-text improves this already positive account of marriage by writing out Do Bet and Do Best as comparisons. In the B-text, Do Well is more explicitly associated with matrimony with the bold assertion: 'In this world is Dowel trewe wedded libbynge folk' (B, IX, 108). This is not the exegetes' *id est* construction, which David Aers has argued resists a definitive association; Do Well here is not just like but actually *is* matrimony.[47] In the B-text, Langland appropriates St Paul's 'bene facit' only in the second way it is used (1 Corinthians 7.38): to validate the institution of marriage. And yet the poem is scrupulous to ignore the preceding verse and thus to avoid mapping St Paul's hierarchy of sexual states – marriage, widowhood and virginity – neatly onto the categories Do Well, Do Bet and Do Best respectively. There is no interest in finding an explicit place for virginity or widowhood in the schema.

The further adjustments made to Wit's marriage sermon in the C-text of *Piers Plowman* seem to recognize the perversity of the B-text's claim that Do Well is exclusively associated with the state of matrimony. In C,

however, the corresponding statement is phrased differently: 'Ho-so
lyueth in lawe and in loue doth wel, / As this wedded men þat this world
susteyneth' (C, X, 202–3). Now the life of Do Well might also be realized
in other ways other than through marriage. However, Do Bet and Do
Best are not reincorporated into Wit's speech in the later text; the C-text,
like the B-text, still resists a simple relation between Paul's hierarchy of
the grades of chastity and the three Dos. We will see again, in the
discussion below about the Tree of Charity section, how the C-text
changes seem to make B's strident claims for the place of marriage more
judicious, and yet, tellingly, they also fail to erase them. Langland's poetry
of marriage always looks for loopholes in the Catholic case for the pri-
macy of virginity.

MEN DOING WELL

Thought and Wit together systematically write a conflation of marriage
and work as a positive masculine model a little like that exemplified by
Piers Plowman in Passus V–VI of the B-text. The first definitions the
dreamer is given of Do Well are from Thought and Wit. The narrator
says he is over familiar with Thought and, conversely, unacquainted with
Wit, prefiguring the way that Hoccleve would personify his troubling
thoughts as unwelcome guests and his Wit as alien and truant; Thought
and Wit, who are both tall like the dreamer, are nevertheless projections
of Will's interiority. The dreamer's immediate and interior understanding
of Do Well, derived from Thought and Wit, is at once about labour and
marriage:

> Whoso is trewe of his tunge and of his two handes,
> And thorugh his labour or thorugh his land his liflode wynneth,
> And is trusty of his tailende, taketh but his owene,
> And is noght dronkelewe ne dedeynous – Dowel hym folweth.
>
> (B, VIII, 82–4)

Labourers and landowners are given a kind of parity of dignity within Do
Well that originates from their having the same physical self-sufficiency
and moral fortitude to fulfil their respective social duties. Wit's interpretation is not dissimilar, although he puts his concerns about labour
into the service of arguments about sexuality and the proper practice of
marriage. Indeed, he everywhere uses the vocabularies of, and ideas about
labour familiar from the *Visio*. Several critics have noted the way in which
money and sex are compressed into the single character of Lady Meed;

Wit's sermon extends that conflation into (re)production, offering an alternative to Meed's worldly delights in a good labour-team marriage.[48] Wit's subjective and unacknowledged masculinist inclination renders his defence of marriage into an ideal of manhood, glamorizing the authority and achievements of the industrious workman and husband. Whilst Augustine's writing on marriage, for example, was applicable to both men and women, Wit sees men as prime movers in the domestic sphere with women only as auxiliaries and dependents; for Wit the male decision to marry is more significant.

According to Wit in the B-text, the life of Do-well is exemplified by industrious married people: 'In this world is Dowel trewe wedded libbynge folk' (B, IX, 109a). Do Well is the virtuous lifestyle of the married lay-person, and offers him or her access to salvation. Together, married couples 'mote werche and wynne and the world sustene' (B, IX, 109b): both populate and feed the world. In Wit's reckoning, though, women are relegated, in a passage which implicitly refers to Genesis 2.18, to the role of assistant – 'The wif was maad the wye for to helpe werche' (B, IX, 113).[49] Men, according to medieval interpreters of Genesis, are both the primary producers and maintainers of their environment; it is socially and economically more important that men move into the context of household and family life.[50] Wit's sermon cites Paul's begrudging tolerance of marriage as a precaution against sexual anarchy but excises women; so that while Paul writes: 'propter fornicationes autem unusquisque suam uxorem habeat et unaquaeque suum virum habeat' [But for fear of fornication, let every man have his own wife, and let every woman have her own husband] (1 Corinthians 7.2), Langland adapts it to make: 'Bonum est ut unusquisque uxorem suam habeat propter fornicacionem' [It is good that for fear of fornication every man have his own wife] (B, IX, 191a). Whilst for St Paul sexual desire is unruly for both sexes, for Wit the young male's desire is a constant pressure towards sexual intercourse and it is only by marrying that a man can convert a potentially destructive drive into a creative force:

> Whiles thow art yong, and thi wepene kene,
> Wreke thee with wyvyng, if thow wolt ben excused:
> *Dum sis vir fortis, ne des tua robora scortis.*
>   (B, IX, 182–3)

This extract, with its use of phallic weapon imagery, encourages men to 'vent' – 'Wreke' – themselves, a verb which casts 'wyvyng' as a safety valve, releasing the force of male lust which is troubling when confined.[51] Literally, however, 'Wreke' means avenge and as such is a tellingly violent pun for the sexual act.[52] For Wit, marriage is concerned with transmuting the sharp violence of masculine desire into a more acceptable form. The Church had long taught that marriage could operate as a 'lightning-rod', releasing pent up and unruly sexual energy; Wit applies this more specifically to men.[53] The last line cited here warns men not to be wasteful and not to give their strength to prostitutes. This fear of male wastefulness is not matched by a similar injunction to young women to remain chaste until marriage. This betrays the dual assumption that it is both more necessary to conserve male strength and semen for legitimate relationships but also that men are more likely to be promiscuous.

However, Wit countervails these panicked assertions with a positive account of marriage that incorporates all of Augustine's three goods of marriage – offspring, fidelity and the sacramental bond – reminding the dreamer that marriage is an institution that 'God hymself it made' (B, IX, 117). Rather than contrasting marriage and virginity, Wit is concerned to juxtapose the rule of household with its terrifying antithesis: the chaos of sexual aberrance.[54] This serves to rehabilitate marriage, sanctioning it as a possible part of a spiritual life. In this way, as is often noted, Wit adopts the tone of a medieval marriage sermon, giving an affirmative account of wedlock.[55] Marriage performs two supremely moral functions that are specifically related to men and their moral lives. First, it channels male sexual urges into a legitimate and reproductive forum for their expression. Secondly, it provides men with helpmeets so that they can maximize industry and therefore production. In contrast, any offspring of extra-marital couplings or inappropriate marriages, according to Wit, is rotten, destructive and wasteful:

> Ac fals folk feithlees, theves and lyeres,
> **Wastours** and wrecches out of wedlok, I trowe,
> Conceyved ben in yvel tyme, as Caym was on Eve.
>   (B, IX, 119–21)

> *Bonum est ut unusquisque uxorum suam habeat propter*
> *fornicacionem.*
> That othergates ben geten, for gedelynges arn holden,
> And fals folk, fondlynges, faitours and lieres,
> Ungracious to gete good or love of the peple;
> **Wandren** and **wasten** what thei cacche mowe.
> Ayeins dowel thei doon yvel and the devel serve
>   (B, IX, 192–7)

This progeny make up the population of scoundrels who, elsewhere in the poem, Langland names as responsible for current economic and social ills.

Wastour is idleness personified in B-text Passus VI, in which Piers enjoins all to help him plough the half acre. Gluttonous and slothful, Wastour and his cronies not only refuse to work but also, as his name implies, waste the products of others' hard toil. It is no surprise, then, that 'wastours' – unproductive and rebellious individuals – should be the product of profligate and anarchic sexual unions. In the reckoning of Kynde Wit the inappropriately conceived are linked to an idle workforce through the vocabulary of waste.

The principal products, 'fruyt', of the ideal (re)productive husband and wife team are children, a subsistence living and, of course, ultimately salvation. The word 'fruyt' again shows Langland resorting to discourses of industry in a discussion of sexual reproduction and appropriating the use of agricultural imagery in Aristotelian medicinal writings. The use of Genesis and the problematic couplings of the offspring of Cain and Seth, most especially in the C-text, also exploit the imagery of agriculture and, particularly, crop rotation to discuss human impropriety and disobedience. Wit uses the word 'fruyt' ironically to describe the bad results of inappropriate marriages, playing on an assumed understanding that the 'fruyt' of a marriage should be children:

> It is an uncomly couple, by Crist! as me thynketh –
> To yeven a yong wenche to an yolde feble,
> Or wedden any wodewe for welthe of hir goodes
> That nevere shal barn bere but if it be in armes!
> In jelousie joyelees and **janglynge** on bedde,
> Many a peire sithen the pestilence han plight hem togideres.
> The fruyt that thei brynge forth arn manye foule wordes;
> Have thei no children but cheeste and choppes hem bitwene.
>
> (B, IX, 162–9)

The use of the word 'janglynge' here echoes the Prologue where 'jangeleres' are described as work-shy slackers:

> Ac japeres and **jangeleres**, Judas children,
> Feynen hem fantasies, and fooles hem maketh –
> And han wit at wille to werken if they wolde.
>
> (B, Prologue, 35–7)

The time wasting 'janglynge', which takes place in the marital bed of these indecent unions is akin to the grotesque entertainments – diversions from hard work – of those who would betray Christ himself. The idle workforce of Passus VI also 'jangle' (B, VI, 314). Thus, a parallel is drawn between these unholy marriages and sinful, ill-disciplined labour on the basis that both lack industry and are subsequently unproductive. A similar lexicon – about 'japeres', 'jangeleres' and 'wastours' – can be found in *Wynnere and Wastoure*, but Langland explicitly relates it to conjugal ethics and, by giving them less space to defend themselves, makes his assessment of such miscreants less ambivalent.[56]

The passage cited above from Passus IX is an emphatic critique of marriages of mismatched ages with a pair of outraged near tautologies in 'yong wenche' and 'yolde feble' that explore the physical and moral ugliness suggested by the word 'uncomly'. This is a disdainful attack on people who marry for economic reasons, and a similar indignation is also palpable in the arguments over the marriage of Lady Meed and False in Passus II, a marriage which is marked by the partners' inequality in terms of class, legitimacy and, ultimately, wealth.[57] Like other contemporary commentators, the *Wynnere and Wastoure* poet for example, Langland makes a kind of miscegenation out of disparities of various kinds, and his poem articulates disgust about the probable economic motivations behind these perverse couplings.[58] Marriages with an age gap are a post-Black Death phenomenon, according to Wit; a statement which runs counter to what historians tell us about rates of marriage after the pandemic. Below the aristocracy, marriages of mismatched ages were more common in the early fourteenth century.[59] At that time there was a land-hunger that increased the marriageability of widows with established holdings.[60] The availability of land after the Black Death has been shown to have reduced the prevalence of this, either because of a diminished desire on the part of young males to marry widows or alternatively because women may have found it easier to manage alone in the post-plague economy.[61] Despite the infrequency of these pairings, Owst has noted the regularity with which mismating was condemned in late medieval sermons; it certainly does not seem to have taken many of these alliances to alarm moralists; indeed, Wit complains about a minority practice as if it were commonplace.[62] In both Wit's sermon and the Passus II account of the marriage of Meed, anxieties about disaffected labour and economic self-betterment are displaced into a discussion of family and marriage: the standard object of conservatives' fears about social disintegration.

Whilst there is always a question about how authoritative Langland's personifications are, I think that the orthodoxy of Wit's sermon, its proximity to scriptural authority, contemporary medieval marriage sermons and preaching manuals, assure us of its reliability. Whilst Wit and Thought are closely affiliated with the dreamer himself, an affiliation

which may contaminate their judgement, Wit, in particular, is characterized elsewhere in Middle English literature as a rational faculty of some
trustworthiness; by the time of Hoccleve's verse Wit's presence within the
narrator's body has become the guarantee of his sanity. Although the
accounts of Do Well from Thought and Wit are not exactly supported by
those of others in the texts, they are not contradicted either. The attack on
Wit's sermon by his wife Study is an attack directed not at its content, but
rather at its being delivered to Will, a man whom she describes as both
ignorant and mad (indeed, a man in conversation with, and therefore
separate from, his own Wit).

THE TREE OF CHARITY AND THE NEW AGE OF MARRIAGE

Wit's version of Do Well never contradicts the comparative values given
to virginity and marriage in 1 Corinthians 7. However, and most especially in the B-text, Paul is read partially and strategically, redeeming
matrimony from some of his more pessimistic assertions. St Paul is always
reticent on the subject of children; Augustine, on the other hand,
nominates procreation as one of the goods of marriage. And Wit augments Augustine by identifying procreation, like industry, as a larger
social good as well as a good of marriage – the restoration of the
population of post-plague England is as crucial as, and related to, the
project of social and economic regeneration through hard work. There is,
though, a still more enthusiastic account of marriage in the B-text of *Piers
Plowman*, which is, in contrast to Wit's sermon, astonishing in its
reconsideration of the old Pauline hierarchy of virginity, widowhood and
marriage. In the 'Tree of Charity' section (B, XVI; C, XVIII) and
Abraham's speech just following it, this proclivity towards marriage
becomes part of a radical theology which is partially written out and
played down in the C-text, revisions which I suggest are made in
recognition of the uncanonical nature of the discussion of marriage in the
earlier version of *Piers Plowman*. Critics have made much of the poem's
altered economic politics in the C-text; it is telling and (given what we
know from the iconoclastic status-politics and domestic ethics of, say,
Chaucer's Wife of Bath) probably connected that its sexual politics are
also moderated and sanitized in the later version.[63] Indeed, it has been
suggested that the C-text excision of Wit's determined 'In this world is
Dowel trewe wedded libbynge folk' is evidence of Langland's alarm at
their 'revolutionary appropriation' by John Ball.[64] The beginning of
B-text Passus XVI, of course, has been much discussed particularly in

relation to Langland's precise theological position on the vexed question of grace and good works.[65] These arguments about Langland's possible semi-pelagianism have tended not to include the issue of marriage, despite marriage, reproduction and sexuality being intrinsic to the debates about original sin and traducianism.

The B-text, in a complex superimposition of trinities which is only partially reproduced in C, has Abraham, who is also identified with Faith, give this dramatic declaration:

> Might is in matrimoyne, that multiplieth the erthe,
> And bitokneth trewley, telle if I dorste,
> Hym that first formed al, the Fader of hevene.
> The Sone, if I it dorste seye, resembleth wel the widewe:
> *Deus meus, Deus meus, ut quid dereliquisti me?*
> That is, creatour weex creature to knowe what was bothe.
> As widewe withouten wedlock was nevere yit yseyghe,
> Na moore myghte God be man but if he moder hadde.
> As widewe withouten wedlok may noght wel stande,
> Ne matrimoyne withouten muliere is noght muche to preise:
> *Maledictus homo qui non reliquit semen in Israel.*
> Thus in thre persones is parfitliche pure manhede –
> That is, man and his make and mulliere hir children
>
> (B, XVI, 211–21)

There are three trinities being overlaid in this passage. First there is the conventional holy trinity of Father, Son and Holy Ghost; in both the C and B texts this corresponds to the familial trinity, seen at the end of this passage, of a man, his wife and their children. In the B-text, though, those two are contiguous with another that configures marriage as the Father, widowhood as the Son and virginity as the Holy Ghost. The connections which map one trinity on to another are contrived. Christ can only be figured as widowhood if his sense of having been forsaken by God at the crucifixion is read as bereavement. The relationship between virginity and the Holy Spirit is only implied by the symbolic connections made for marriage and widowhood. Indeed, Abraham seems entirely disinterested in the notion of virginity, and widowhood is also of less concern to him than marriage. The importance of this passage is in what it has to say about marriage and the pre-eminence of fatherhood – the usual hierarchy has been entirely reversed.[66] The speech of the patriarch recommends the rule of the father and householder, produced by the proper practice of marriage. The conviction conveyed by the word 'might' – the essential characteristic of marriage according to Abraham – is reinforced by its being powerfully placed in the alliterative line.

However, this speech is ascribed to the persona of Abraham, and his claim to authority on the subject of marriage is not straightforward. Several critics have seen the B-text account of marriage as confused and incomplete – not least because of its failure to include virginity fully in the triune figure.[67] This might, of course, be put down to Abraham's 'limited understanding' as a representative of the Old Law.[68] Abraham's example, Jerome made clear in his answer to Jovinianus, was obviated by the example of Christ.[69] Augustine also used the case of Abraham extensively in his response to the Pelagian heresy.[70] Augustine's over-determination of the example of the patriarch testifies to the strength that he leant to the anti-Catholic case. Augustine gives virginal men and women the answer they need to counter the question: 'What then, are you better than Abraham/Sarah?'; in this way he preserves the arguments of his opponents.[71] He argues not only that Abraham is of a different time, under a different law, commanded by God and driven by the need for a population increase, but also that Abraham should, on account of his obedience, be compared to the modern virginal rather than the married. Whilst moderns are, Augustine says, often motivated to gratify their lust, there are some righteous people who marry only to beget children. Abraham of course, was compelled only by God and never by personal lust. Further, Augustine reads Abraham's compliance with God's injunction to sacrifice Isaac as proof of his willingness to pass up the procreative function of marriage in order to be faithful to God. Augustine finds in that act a kind of chaste practice.[72]

Morton W. Bloomfield has suggested that Langland's figure of the three grades of chastity may be based on a combination of the arboreal figures in tracts on virginity – like the *Speculum virginum* – and Joachim de Fiore's extraordinary diagrammatic versions of time as a tree.[73] In the grades of chastity trees, a clear hierarchy made marriage – often represented by Abraham or Noah – into the root stock out of which the better, purer vidual (Anne) and virginal (Mary, Christ) fruit grew. In the Joachite trees, Abraham, Noah and other patriarchs are also figured as fruit, and together they symbolize the age of the father (the Old Testament), which, in turn, gives way to the age of the son (the New Testament); finally there is the projected future age of the Holy Ghost. In spite of the lack of a clear reception history for the Joachite *figurae* in the late fourteenth century, the similarities are striking.[74] Langland's image, though, is different from these two because of its interest in marriage and the example of Abraham, and not just as something to pass over in anticipation of a more valuable time or sexual identity. A true combination of these trees would project and yearn for a third age of perfect continence and would be very similar to those qualifications, from Jerome and Augustine, about the difference in the lives of the Old Testament fathers. There is, of course, also a temporal aspect to *Piers Plowman*; Abraham's speech occurs pre-incarnation so the distinction between the old and the new law is observed in the poem. Before Christ's incarnation, Adam, Abraham, Isaiah and others stand '*in Limbo inferni*' (B, XVI, 84), afterwards they are released, saved by Christ's harrowing of hell (B, XVIII, 249–71). The extensions made to the A-text to form B, constitute a discussion of the world before and after Christ's incarnation. However, this temporal structure *enabled*, as well as limited, a new exploration of the 'might' within matrimony.

Further, as David Aers has said of Langland's apocalypticism, *Piers Plowman* resists Joachite theology.[75] Although *Piers Plowman* is structured in such a way that Abraham's validation of marriage occurs pre-incarnation, this temporal structure is not consistently maintained, allowing Abraham's example to bleed into the values of the present.[76] Langland contradistinctively uses Abraham, in contrast to the way he is used in either the *Speculum virginum* or the Joachite trees, precisely because he is not interested in a possible future inhabited by the pure and chaste. In the B-text 'Might is in matrimoyne', Abraham does not set himself, in the way that Augustine does, aside from other married people; he doesn't qualify his own case with the difference of his day and his exemplary motivations. Numerous possible influences and sources have been suggested for the tree of charity figure; none is identical to Langland's.[77] While, for example, Andrew Galloway has identified an echo of the writings of St Bernard, he acknowledges that Langland transforms it, exhibiting a novel 'Bernadine Christology'.[78] Langland is inclined, in fact, to upend his greatest influences in both the vision of the tree of charity and Abraham's B-text speech.

Whatever protection the poem's diachronic structure and the Abraham persona (no longer an authority in a world transformed by Christ) gave to the B-text's claims about marriage, it was insufficient to satisfy the reviser of the C-text. In C, Abraham is given another trinity to describe instead: Adam, Eve and Abel; the order and method of their creation becomes a metaphor to elucidate the mad logic of the Holy Trinity. This is a refined version of the domestic trinity – man, wife and child – which, Tavormina has noted, is designed to be more precise than the B-text had been about

the generation and procession of the trinity.[79] Tavormina finds the C
rendition of the tree of trinities more successful because she is attracted to
the way that Langland uses marriage as a metaphor. In the C version the
concern is to shed light on 'one of the deepest Christian mysteries', the
Trinity; in B there is, I suggest, an interest in marriage and the generative
power of fatherhood for its own sake.[80] The later poem is much clearer
that Abraham's special association with fertility is a corollary of his being
a representative of the 'old lawe' (C, XVIII, 222).[81] There is still a vestige
of the B-text trinity – although it is now spoken by *Liberum arbitrium* –
in which virginity is likened to the Holy Ghost and so on, but its force is
reversed so that the central concern of the passage is to make exactly that
association; the tenuous bereavement link is virtually deleted but widows
are nevertheless still associated with Christ. Matrimony, though, is
demoted from its position of 'might' and becomes, instead, the avatar of
the 'flesche' (XVIII, 70–80).

In both versions of the tree of charity figure, the three grades of chastity
correspond to fruits of different qualities. Although *Liberum arbitrium*
speaks the corresponding lines of the C-text, this is Piers Plowman's
account in B:

> 'Heer now bynethe,' quod he tho, 'if I nede hadde,
> Matrimoyne I may nyme, a moiste fruyt withalle.
> Thanne Continence is neer the crop as kaylewey bastard.
> Thanne bereth the crop kynde fruyt and clennest of alle –
> Maidenhode, aungeles peeris, and arest wole be ripe,
> And swete withouten swellyng – sour worth it nevere.'
> (B, XVI, 67–72)

These six lines swell to almost fifty in C and, although there is a clear
vertical hierarchy in this passage in the B-text, C is much clearer about the
relative merits of these sexual distinctions. In the C-text, although
matrimony is still a 'moiste fruyt', widowhood is also said to be 'bettere'
and 'worthiore then wedlock'. Finally, 'Virginite' is both 'more vertuous
and fayrest' (C, XVIII, 86–9). On the other hand there is no decided
recognition in B that to be 'moiste' is necessarily worse than being the
'clennest'. In B, too, there is no overt difference in the taste of the fruit, so
that maidenhood is given a distinction of sweetness which is only dissimilar from matrimony or continence because it is achieved without
swelling. In contrast, in C we learn 'Ac somme ar swettore then somme
and sonnere wollen rotye' (XVIII, 60). In this phrase, though, there is an
equivocal failure to attribute the quality of sweetness, with its propensity

to rot quickly, to any of the three sexual states – an evasion that is entirely characteristic of this part of the C-text. If the reader supplies the connections based on their own notions of which might be 'swettore', they are quickly disillusioned by the second half of the line. The speed of decomposition is not a very attractive way to register ephemerality – sweet today, compost tomorrow – which might have been imagined more romantically and tragically.

Whilst this expansion in the C-text seems to be one of clarification, moving the B-text's non-committal valuations much more firmly towards the traditional medieval preference for continence, this tidying tendency gives way to a less innocent evasion in C, which is reluctant to reproduce that preference as a monologic truth. This is perhaps most quickly seen in the little parenthetical comment on the subordinate nature of marriage to virginity: '(ac bothe two ben gode)' that suggests unease about the relegation of matrimony to the lowly position it takes up in C.[82] Pearsall suggests that Piers Plowman is written out, and his speeches given away, to preserve his entry for later when he will have more impact; but he is also probably the most indubitably authoritative character in the poem.[83] Replacing this authoritative married man with a more difficult abstract persona, *Liberum arbitrium*, serves to complicate the authority of the C-text's resort to the traditional partiality to continence.

There is a similarly oblique discussion in the C-text that sets out the forms of respect that should be observed between 'the fayrest thyng', the 'furste fruyte/thyng', the 'clennest creature' (entities that are not plainly defined) and God:

> Hit was þe furste fruyte þat þe fader of heuene blessed,
> And bad hit be, of a bat of erthe, a man and a maide,
> In menynge þat the fayrest thyng the furste thynge shold honoure,
> And þe clennest creature furste creatour knowe.
>
> (C, XVIII, 91–4)

The fairest and the cleanest seem to be the same: the sexually continent. There are, though, several confusions: is the 'furste thynge' God – like the 'furste creatour' in the final line here – or the institution of marriage – as in the 'furste fruyte' of the first?[84] Are Adam and Eve, who are made out of earth rather than being conceived and born, being understood, then, as examples of the 'fayrest thyng'? What, in fact, precedes what? This question is crucial in exegetical debates about the implications of God's original commandment in Genesis 1.28 for the ethics human sexuality.[85] The penultimate line cited here is deeply ambiguous, the word order giving no clue as to which 'thyng(e)' should in fact 'honoure' the other. The C-text extensions and erasures are also disrupted by a number of other additions. Another deflecting comparison is introduced just after this passage: between the fruit that grows in the shade and that which grows in the sun; in ways that are never made clear, these distinctions correlate with the active and the contemplative lives. These extensions are as telling as the excisions; they are evidence of the fretfulness with which this re-evaluation is undertaken. The C-text interiorizes a clerical discourse about the inferiority of secular household ethics and yet never categorically negates them.

CONCLUSION: BEING MARRIED, BEING FAITHFUL

Langland's citations, on close scrutiny, reveal his often unspoken interest in marriage to be an enduring preoccupation. We have seen how Langland imports the discussion of marriage in the Epistles into his discussions of labour and Do Well; he is similarly drawn to Augustine's discussions of marriage, and cites them in ways which are not always forthright about their purpose. Several critics have looked for sources for the dreamer's vision of 'Myddelerthe', where the birds and animals mate and bring up their young so much more *reason*ably than people do.[86] It is clearly, though, partly in dialogue with a passage from St Augustine's *On Marriage and Concupiscence* in which Augustine posits marriage as a way that people can replicate the moderate but unreasoned behaviours of the birds and the animals. This is Langland's version:

> Reson I seigh soothly sewen alle beestes
> In etynge, in drynkynge and in engendrynge of kynde.
> And after cours of concepcion noon took kepe of oother
> As whan thei hadde ryde in rotey tyme; anoonright therafter
> Males drowen hem to males amornynge by hemselve,
> And femelles to femelles ferded and drowe.
> Ther ne was cow ne cowkynde that conceyved hadde
> That wolde belwe after bole, ne boor after sowe.
> Bothe hors and houndes and alle othere beestes
> Medled noght with hir makes that mid fole were.
> Briddes I biheld that in buskes made nestes;
> Hadde nevere wye wit to werche the leeste.
> I hadde wonder at whom and wher the pye
> Lerned to legge the stikkes in which she leyeth and bredeth.
> Ther nys wrighte, as I wene, sholde werche hir nest to paye;
> If any mason made a molde therto, muche wonder it were.
>
> (B, XI, 334–49)

And this, I think, is its source:

Copulatio itaque maris et feminae generandi causa, bonum est naturale nuptiarum: sed isto bono male utitur, qui bestialiter utitur, ut sit ejus intentio in voluptate libidinis, non in voluntate propaginis. Quanquam in nonnullis animalibus rationis expertibus, sicut in plerisque alitibus, et conjugiorum quaedam quasi confoederatio custoditur, et socialis nidificandi solertia, vicissimque ovorum dispertita tempora fovendorum, et nutriendorum opera alterna pullorum, magis eas videri faciunt agere, cum coeunt, negotium substituendi generis, quam explendae libidinis.

[The union, then, of male and female for the purpose of procreation is the natural good of marriage. But he makes a bad use of this good who uses it bestially, so that his intention is on the gratification of lust, instead of the desire for offspring. Nevertheless, in sundry animals unendowed with reason, as, for instance, in most birds there is both preserved a certain kind of confederation of pairs, and a social combination of skill in nest-building; and their mutual division of the periods for cherishing their eggs and their alternation in the labor of feeding their young, give them the appearance of so acting, when they mate, as to be intent rather on securing the continuance of their kind than on the gratifying of lust.][87]

Just beyond this passage Augustine discusses marriage and faith as a combined solution to chaotic human sexuality. This is a heady association for Langland and no doubt it is that, along with its description of the way that the birds seamlessly combine their labouring and domestic responsibilities, which attracts him to this text. Marriage and faith are also the qualities embodied by the wedded Abraham – 'I am Feith' he says (XVI, 176). Indeed, Augustine tells us elsewhere that, because of his faith, Abraham resembles and is as free as the birds, which live without rational thought.[88] Marriage and faith are the unstated answers to the riddle posed by the dreamer about how human sexuality can be regulated; that the answer does go unstated says something about the dreamer's ethical ignorance but also reveals a longing within the text that resists supplying the answer to which it wishfully inclines. Only the reader versed in Augustinian teaching on marriage is privy to the way in which conjugality haunts Langland's poetics here, offering a solution to the narrator's itinerant, questing ignorance.

The dreamer is rebuked, though, by both Reason and Ymaginatif for his solicitous invective on the subject of immoderate human sexuality and the unflattering contrast he draws between the human and avian worlds. His outrage is seen as an importunate attempt to question nature, indeed

God and his creation (e.g. XII, 217–35). In this respect his interrogation of
Reason demonstrates that he is a man with too little faith and he fails – or
falls – in his attempt to imitate either the instinctive behaviours of the
birds or the faith of Abraham. Augustine is insistent in *On Marriage and
Concupiscence* that marriage is only a regulatory institution for believers,
for the faithful. The narrator's excessive scrutiny of Reason makes his
faith dubious and, because faith is so attended by marriage in *Piers
Plowman*, I suggest that the narrator again finds the propriety of his
marriage in question. The dreamer's search for Do-Well is desiring, akin
to Adam's libidinous desire for God-like knowledge in Genesis 3, and
reveals his tragic lack of faith. Nicolette Zeeman has discussed the connection between inquiry and sexual desire, both in the writings of
Augustine and in *Piers Plowman*.[89] And yet in the lesson the narrator
receives on the ethics of enquiry, it is particularly the guilt of *married* sex
that upsets his quest; indeed, the guilt of married sex that is at the heart of
the poem's compulsorily heterosexual and specular masculine ethics.[90]
Glenn Burger has written about marriage as a 'hybrid' identity in his
account of *The Canterbury Tales*; in *Piers Plowman*, too, marriage can
only be recommended when it is hedged around with conditions and so
offers a difficult, troubled sort of resolution to the problem of sexual
desire.[91] Indeed, Will, a misfit who fails to find ethical accommodation
within the poem he narrates, looks a little sadly at the birds in their nests,
unproblematically and automatically fulfilling their domestic roles.[92]

CHAPTER 2

Them and Usk: writing home in the Middle Ages

INTRODUCTION

The narrator of Thomas Usk's *Testament of Love* prefaces a detailed and defensive account of the turbulent events surrounding the struggle for the office of London mayor in 1383, and his own part in them with this affecting account of the disruption of his home:

> also the cytie of London, that is to me so dere and swete, in whiche I was forthe growen – and more kyndely love have I to that place than to any other in erthe, as every kyndely creature hath ful appetyte to that place of his kyndly engendrure, and wylne reste and peace in that stede to abyde
>
> (I, 6, 86–90)[1]

This sentimental appeal assumes that an affection for home – the place of one's birth and childhood – is both innate and universal. The repetition of the word 'kynd(e)ly' places an inordinate stress upon this shared 'natural' sentiment which is typical of Usk's larger project. Representing London's factional in-fighting as devastating violations both of the city and of his own inalienable interior attachments, Usk's narrator makes a special petition to his reader's homely instincts and their experience of being, or their longing to be, loved children. This demonstration of civic loyalty is a sentiment which can also be found in another auto-biographical text written by the same author, his 1384 *Appellum* (Appeal, 89, 162–3, 168–9 and 192), a text which denounced his one-time master and the former mayor of London, John of Northampton, for 'confederacie, congregacion, & couyne' amongst other things.[2] This kind of cross-reference between the two texts has been crucial for those critics assessing the claims which are made in the *Testament* about its narrator's, and therefore nominally its author's, relationship to truth and treachery. While Usk's narrator's claim that he is a peace-lover and a good London

38

citizen is taken at face value by Gary Shawver, most other critics see *The Testament*'s narrative voice not just as unreliable but as fundamentally dishonest and as evidence for its author's notorious perfidy.[3] These critics are, of course, right to be sceptical about the narrating voice, just as all the narrators of life-written texts should be seen as partial commentators on their author's experiences. However, Shawver is also right to attack the pejorative tone of some of Usk's critics who make judgements about the motivations behind *The Testament*'s rhetorical strategies that are ultimately unknowable. I intend in this chapter to maintain an agnosticism about whether Thomas Usk was a good or bad man, servant, citizen or, indeed, writer. I am less interested in finding further duplicity in *The Testament* with which to confirm Usk's contemporaries' estimation of him as a 'traitor' – the defining and unifying feature of his life, or *bios*, in the related record – than in assessing the conflicted, anxious and fragmented representation of the subjective self, or *autos*, and its relationship to the society within which it was produced.

The critical mistrust of *The Testament* has led to a neglect or dismissal of, or attack on, several of its formal and rhetorical aspects. For example, Paul Strohm has argued that to see it as 'philosophic treatise' or 'erotic allegory' is ultimately a misreading of *The Testament*.[4] The language of the text has been described by Michael Hanrahan as an attempt at the reader's seduction and by Marion Turner as a 'shroud': both conceptualize language as a disguise on the surface of truth.[5] The 'real meaning' of *The Testament* is, it is said, its political agenda: its justification of its author's past actions and his future bid for royal preferment. 'Seeing through' the textual strategies in this way is, of course, a sophisticated way to read a text which is clearly concerned to settle some scores and present a favourable view of its narrator and therefore its author, who are related through the coincidence of the name Thomas Usk.[6] However, this critical distaste at the self-interest with which language is deployed in *The Testament* is disingenuous about the nature of writing in general and life writing in particular, which is always, surely, put to subjective use.

The Genesis narrator writes self-delusion and the deceptiveness of language into the Christian creation story: Adam blames Eve before admitting: 'comedi' – 'I did eat'; Eve charges the serpent before making a similar confession. Not only extenuating, these originary, first-person admissions are also incomplete: unwilling to speak an insolent desire to be Godlike, the pair develop concealing linguistic strategies which parallel their covering of their sexual bodies. The condition of fallen man is to obfuscate his libidinous desires with language; those desires then become the subject of confession. Life-written texts are always a subjective representation of experience, when experience is already an interior interpretation of social event or praxis. Life-written texts often suppress the more outrageous aspects of private desire. However, within Usk studies, the slipperiness of reflexive writing is seen as peculiar to Usk's narrator in readings that carry fourteenth-century allegations about the author into analysis of his literary productions. The element that critics 'see through' – the form of *The Testament* – deserves more examination because it reveals the troubled construction of the narrating Usk, whose language and imagery are organically related to his meanings. These meanings are, as Anne Middleton has recently argued, in 'plain view'.[7]

In particular I shall investigate the imagery of, and interest in, the home, the household and both familial and conjugal affectivity. I do this not to argue that *The Testament* is a humanist and transcendent work of philosophy, nor that it is apolitical; rather, I maintain that the choice of imagery betrays ingrained contemporary convictions about social relationships, which may also be textually significant, may also be considered a part of a text's 'real meaning'. In a seminal 1979 article, Middleton identifies Usk's *Testament* as a bourgeois text concerned with public and civic values rather than private and interior processes, common profit rather than erotic love. In doing so she implicitly suggests that the public, political self, a civic identity, is more historically constructed than the interior self and its private desires, which somehow transcend culture.[8] Her suggestion that erotic desire is not a part of the construction of the social being incorporates an intriguing assumption that the sexual and emotional is of less moment than, and indeed extricable from public politics. She dismisses the fiction of the Margarite Pearl with the assertion that Usk's 'destiny as a public man, not the cruelties of an indifferent mistress, informs his somewhat clumsy effort to be a vernacular philosopher of love'.[9] Of course, Thomas's search for his pearl lady, just like his dialogue with Love, is not literally true. However, many of the allegorical features of the work have quirky and tangential details that are unnecessary in the terms of the political narrative. Such eccentricities demonstrate an interest in familial and romantic things for themselves, revealing the centrality of the same to the discursive formation of the subject; they are not just cloaks for topics of greater import.

Indeed, the ethics of love, marriage and the household are, in this period, at the centre of cultural debate about social entitlement, authority and power. The nascent bourgeois communities in the urban centres were closely implicated in the administration of metropolitan trade and manufacture, at a time when the organization of labour and retail practice was a legislative priority, producing the kind of inter-guild tensions which surrounded the 1383 London mayoral election. Indeed, we might consider the importance of houses as rewards and settings within the narrative of these factional struggles.[10] Middleton has carefully positioned Usk's text, that is the hypothetical autograph manuscript, within the bureau-cratic communities of 1380s London, arguing that it was intended to 'participate in a larger conversation among men of letters', those iden-tified by R. L. Storey in the generation just after this one as 'gentlemen bureaucrats'.[11] The economic and political advances of this middling stratum were accompanied by a singularly devised household ethos.[12] Whilst furniture, fixtures and fittings glamorized domestic space and articulated economic power, conspicuous consumption of this kind was only accommodated in moral and religious terms by an increased emphasis upon domestic piety and sophisticated affective relationships. This was in part an aspirational fashion that adopted the purportedly more refined sensibilities and imitated the aesthetic conceits of the gentry and aristocracy.[13] It was also, however, innovatory and, in particular, asserted an ideal of romantic love and companionate marriage – not just as an attractive literary fiction, but as a possible, even a realistic option – much more confidently than in aristocratic quarters, where marriage partners were still being chosen with a mind to land-based wealth and the larger dynastic needs of the family.[14] The dual use of space, for both living and working – another feature which was more associated with, indeed, the preferred paradigm for middling, urban households – required a thorough-going rehabilitation of manufacturing and retail work as decent, dignified and compatible with the emotional lives and relation-ships of the occupants of that space.[15] The vocabularies and ethics of service and employment relationships came to influence and structure the ways in which families cohered; thus the affective and economic functions of the household coincided. *The Testament of Love* grapples with these themes ostensibly as metaphors, setting up a concept of 'home' as an allegorical amalgam of various wished-for things. Thomas's ambitions are posed in social and domestic terms; his pretensions are made equivalent to those amongst his ascendant peers and his social challenge is mitigated by the same sentimental and pious discourses that inflected their social and political achievements.

THE ALLEGATIONS

— against the man

Strohm's inspirational and nuanced work on Thomas Usk has set the tone for modern research on this fascinating author and his textual productions.[16] Although latterly his writing on Usk has become forgiving, in his harsh early assessment Strohm portrays the *Testament* as obsessed with its author's self-preservation and self-promotion. The work is, in that early view, a grubby postscript to Usk's betrayal of a populist cause made up of small craft groups which temporarily challenged the dominant mercantile oligarchy of late fourteenth-century London. This conclusion is based on Ruth Bird's account of the contest for office of Mayor between the incumbent John of Northampton and Nicholas Brembre in October 1383.[17] She saw these men as leaders of two distinct social groups: on the one hand, the merchant-capitalists, represented by Brembre, who made up the city's oligarchy and, on the other, Northampton's party, made up of the 'small masters of various crafts' who did not hold office and power to the same extent. The more privileged stratum, she found, was made up of those belonging to the five main guilds – fishmongers, vintners, grocers, mercers and goldsmiths – while the other group she identified was, in contrast, representative of the smaller trades. According to Usk's deposition, Northampton, leading an alliance of various, mainly non-victualling, mysteries, planned a four-stage programme of constitutional amendment which would undermine the economic interests of the richer trades in favour of those that were less advantaged:

> that aldermen sholden be remoued fro yer in to yer, & that the comun conseyl sholde kome be craftes, & that ther sholde no vitailler bere office judicial, & that al strang[e] vitaillers sholden with thair vitailles frelich kome to the Cite, to selle thair vitailles as wel be retaile as in other wyse, hauyng no reward to the Franchise.[18]

Others have noted that Northampton's term in mayoral office was characterized by apparent social scruple; his attempt, for example, to cap the price of food for the poor during his term of office suggests that Northampton was a man with a strong sense of social justice.[19]

Pamela Nightingale has, however, cast doubt on Northampton's reputed egalitarianism and Bird's reading of events.[20] She argues that the contentious 1383 mayoral election was a power struggle between

Northampton's party and those exporting wool through the official staple. Nightingale, considering the evidence over a much broader time-frame than Bird, characterizes Northampton – a man known to have ill-treated those in his personal employ – as an opportunist whose attempt to widen the base of government and whose populist appeal were cynical empire-building strategies, which would enable him and his faction to win control. She argues that these struggles were not

class conflicts between the oligarchy of merchants and the commonalty of small retailers, craftsmen and the unenfranchised. John de Northampton was not a radical leader fighting for the destruction of the merchant oligarchy and for its replacement by a more broadly based civic government. He was a member of that oligarchy, and Walsingham depicts him as 'an hardhearted man, astute, puffed up by his riches and proud' – a verdict echoed by Northampton's secretary, Usk ... Northampton was pursuing, first, the narrow sectional interests of his own mystery, and secondly, his own personal power.[21]

Notwithstanding the somewhat unreliable evidence of Usk and Walsingham, Nightingale puts forward a powerful case that London's problems, which came to a head during the 1383 mayoral contest, were part of an ongoing struggle for control of the City's policy relating to the wool staple and foreign trade and as such, as Strohm himself admits in a footnoted aside, a dispute between groups which were not socially that distinct.[22]

Usk was recruited by the then mayor, Northampton, as a scribe in the months before the October election.[23] However, his service was not limited to secretarial work and he became active in gathering support for Northampton and his agenda in the run-up to the October contest. If Usk received the type of training that was being given in some scriveners' shops at this time, then he would have been a versatile employee with a range of transferable administrative skills.[24] After Northampton's defeat at the poll, it was Usk and other supporters who were sent to the duke of Lancaster to acquire his help in seeking royal permission, which they were refused, to repeat the election process. Frustrated by the political process in this way, Northampton resorted to raising riots round the city; he was arrested by royal order in February 1384.[25] Usk's support for his master continued until his own arrest in the summer of the same year. It was during his imprisonment that Usk broke rank with the group and, in his 1384 *Appellum*, accused his previous employer of conspiracy and confederacy. Northampton was tried and sentenced to death, although he was later pardoned.[26] Usk was also pardoned and in time – time in which he probably wrote *The Testament of Love* – his fortunes began to rise as he acquired office as under-sheriff of Middlesex and the king's sergeant-at-arms.[27] These positions, however, were to serve him badly when, in 1387–8, the Lords Appellant accused the king's main supporters of treason.[28] Usk was arrested once more; he was tried, sentenced and put to death alongside Brembre, erstwhile rival of his old master. It is often observed that the earlier denunciation of Northampton was considered pertinent to Usk's second trial and that its implications followed him to the scaffold.[29] To betray one's master at this time was to violate a central taboo of a society that relied extensively on personal credit and fidelity.

The timing of Usk's 'turn' is clearly highly suspicious and suggests nothing so much as self-preservation in the face of fear. In the conclusion to his more moderate response to Usk's work, however, Strohm wisely cautions against judging Usk negatively from the comparatively secure position enjoyed by the modern critic.[30] It is speculative to imagine either the rewards that Usk hoped to garner, the threats he feared or the state-sponsored torture he experienced at the hands of the Brembre faction; such fillips are now hypothetical. It is impossible, too, to know whether Northampton *et al.* were champions of the people, friends to Usk and deserving of loyalty or, alternatively, corrupt and self-serving, seeing nothing beyond their own political ambitions. The 'facts' of Usk's case are now unrecoverable from a collection of stories about him, which testify only to what Hanrahan tautologically describes as his 'well-known notoriety', doubly enunciating the only constant in the case: his treacherous reputation. Strohm is right: who are we to judge what is socially impudent or politically shabby? I shall neither pity Usk for failing to be a revolutionary hero nor use the language of betrayal and infamy, which perpetuates his medieval reputation in his modern. Rather than condemning Usk's rhetorical strategies and textual ambitions I shall show how these are configured in ways which parallel coeval social trends, demonstrating that the persona and protagonist of *The Testament* are not copies of the 'real historical character' Usk but rather social and linguistic confections which respond to the discursive practices of his place and period.

— *against the text*

Whilst latterly critics have been prepared to rethink the life writing of marginalized and minority figures and, in particular, have rehabilitated

the autobiographies of women like Margery Kempe from the inter-
pretations they were given by some earlier critics, the reflexive compo-
sitions of the 'traitor' Usk have clearly proved more problematic.[31]
Kempe's strategic search for authorization and her astonishing textual
ambitions may well have seemed suspicious and impertinent to a patriarchal clergy, but are now celebrated as a brave challenge to iniquitous
assumptions about gender and social agency. Kempe's critics are concerned to analyse rather than condemn her rhetorical manipulations; it is
now rare for Kempe scholars to seek either to authenticate or to disprove
any of her assertions or to make a judgement about the literary merit of
the *Book*. On the other hand and understandably, the ambitions of a
'traitor' cannot be so readily reread. Whilst critics are keen not to per-
petuate the medieval marginalization of women into modern criticism,
the modern and medieval responses to traitors and their treacherous acts
are not so polarized; traitors are the ultimate marginals whose acts can
never be accepted, whose words can never be given credence. I suggest
that, although the textual ambitions of *The Testament of Love* may be
'worldly', they need not to be reproached but should instead be decon-
structed in the same ways as are Kempe's.[32] *The Testament of Love* should
be considered, like *The Book of Margery Kempe*, as life writing which
questions social identity and self-definition, even where it is self-deceiving
or ideologically unpalatable.

The identity position of 'traitor', of course, problematizes the already
complex genre of life writing in exactly those places where it is already
unstable. Life writing necessarily raises the question of motivation: why
and for whom was it written? Although ostensibly addressed to God,
St Augustine discounts the possibility of an omniscient being as the
reader of his *Confessions*, concluding that he must be writing for an
audience of contemporaries, setting an example for others in the story of
his conversion.[33] The anxiety with which Augustine's narrator searches for
that audience, though, and his surprise upon its discovery testifies to the
insufficiency of this conclusion: the *Confessions* is also a self-scrutiny,
made sincere by the surveillance of a panoptic God, in which the implied
reader is yet another version of the author himself. The apparent lack of
motivation – effected by addressing an all-knowing deity – establishes
Augustine's autobiography as an affecting account of the fragmented
subject and, therefore, the autobiographical impulse.[34] Furthermore,
through an interrogation of the self, the *Confessions* seeks a better
understanding of God; introspection is also a spiritual enterprise. These
are noble motivations that can be respectfully read as plausible and

consistent with their author's identity as Bishop of Hippo. In contrast, the motivation for *The Testament* seems all too obviously social and political rather than interior and spiritual. Whilst critics have argued about who the intended readers were and what political or legal influence they may have enjoyed, I suggest that *The Testament* also presents Thomas as a reader both of his text and himself.[35] To read Usk's autobiographical motive as wholly public and never personal is to suggest that political animals have no capacity for sincere self-reflection, to imply an integrity of the self which is fallacious and to assert a singleness of purpose for Usk which is belied by *The Testament*'s idiosyncrasies.

This fiction of the holistic self is, notoriously, an epiphenomenon of the autobiographical form, which seeks to represent a life as a sequential narrative in which every episode is a marker in the story of how the narrated protagonist becomes the narrator. Whilst usually this illusion of order partially disguises the chaos of the self and the haphazard nature of experience, conversely, in the case of *The Testament of Love*, critics who reject the authenticity of the form impose an order on the content and therefore its representation of self. Blatant in this citational text, which is a jumble of registers and influences, is a representation of the heterogeneous and socially interpolated individual; the form resembles the errancy both of memory and the subjective nature of lived experience.

Most crucially *The Testament of Love* destabilizes the definitive feature of autobiography: the autobiographical pact – the illusion of a correspondence between the authorial, narrating and narrated 'I's. The narrator's relationship to truth and authority is made tenuous in a genre whose traditional *raison d'être* is to persuade the reader, through the construction of a reliable narrator, of its verisimilitude. In *The Testament*, Thomas is compromised by the reputation of Usk as 'faux & malveise'.[36] In some ways this ought to be of assistance to the critic: the semblance of authenticity is exploded from the start. In other ways, though, it is a hindrance: the narrator's unreliability, a feature that is common to all autobiography, becomes distended, displacing other aspects and meanings of the text. Skeat's early assessment of *The Testament*, that it is 'vague, shifty and unsatisfactory' – which, Hanrahan notes, confuses Usk the author with his text – still predominates, despite the deployment of a critical vocabulary that disassociates the author and the persona from each other.[37] Although ostensibly reading against the text and distrusting its narrator, *The Testament* is described as unwittingly exposing the 'truth' of political ambition behind the false, philosophical form. The critical response is thus bifurcated: on the one hand it acknowledges the impossibility of discovering the 'real' Thomas Usk and discusses instead his persona in the text but, on the other, the autobiographical pact is upheld by those wishing to find a shared duplicity in the author and his textual avatars.

The opening of *The Testament*, an extended *diminutio* which justifies writing in vernacular prose, has been the place where critics have begun locating evidence of falsity. As most admit, this is a standard motif in medieval literature, in which the speaker, as does Thomas, professes to have little understanding of rhetoric or learning and to be telling a 'rude' narrative that is coloured not with sophisticated 'red ynke' but with more 'natural' and rudimentary markers: 'cole' and 'chalk' (I, Prologue, 12–13). Natural and agricultural imagery is juxtaposed with the language of art and manufacture. Of course, as many have pointed out, this trope in itself both demonstrates a knowledge of the rhetorical arts and deploys them ostentatiously, with florid images contrasting organic and mechanical forms, to make a claim about the simplicity and earnestness of the text's content. In this way, the form of the text contradicts the 'sentence' (I, Prologue, 3), illustrating rather than repudiating literary artifice and doubleness. Turner has suggested that this renders the narrator 'slippery' and 'sophistic', and Hanrahan has argued, similarly, that 'Usk's strategy of distancing his project from duplicity nevertheless inadvertently backfires'.[38] However, *diminutio* is a trope that is inherently desirous, manipulating an implied reader into an authorization of the narrator that is apparently unsolicited. Julian of Norwich and Margery Kempe both insist on their lack of learning and yet demonstrate in their life writings a thorough understanding of scripture and other exegetical and hagiographical texts.[39] Julian, in particular, contradicts her own assertion of female ignorance with a sophisticated, cerebral theology in a rhythmic and artful prose style that reveals a self-confidence and a writerly ambition which do not respect the supposed limits of the female intellect. Similarly Thomas, deferring to 'al the grettest clerkes' (I, Prologue, 83), affects a pose of humility which is actually an assertion of the self as a literary artist in terms and traditions that were culturally sanctioned.[40] Whilst writing is an ambitious act, medieval authors, responding to a culture which valued moderation more than enterprise, couched it in 'duplicitously' humble terms.

Although the opening of *The Testament* is indeed ornate, the anxiety of the *diminutio* is accounted for by the necessity for a defence of vernacular writing at a time when French and Latin composition still had more cachet. Although Chaucer was certainly leading the way, and although writing in the vernacular may well have been another means by which

Usk inscribed himself into the Chaucerian literary community,[41] *The Testament of Love* is singular and original, being life-written, English prose describing allegorical, rather than mystical revelations. The disjunction between the prose form and the poetic tone – cited by Hanrahan as evidence of Usk's attempt to seduce his readership – is surely suggested by Chaucer's 'degraded' prose translations of Boethius's Metra, which are similar in their, perhaps jarring, fusion of a poetic register and a prosaic form, and which demonstrate the problem faced by the late medieval translator of the *Consolatio*.[42] George Sanderlin has ascribed the awkwardness of Usk's style to the 'limitations of the English philosophical vocabulary of the Fourteenth Century'.[43] Stephen Medcalf, who is appreciative of the textures of Usk's prose style, describes *The Testament of Love* as 'not only the first book of original philosophy in English, but also the first book in which English prose is made to have something of the pattern, gorgeousness and poignancy of poetry'.[44] Comparing Usk's florid prose style with that of mystical texts like the *Cloud of Unknowing*, Medcalf acknowledges the pioneering nature of Usk's work. Indeed, Usk created a new text by collecting established forms of life writing into a bricolage, which owed much to Boethius, St Augustine, the practice of Christian confession, and mysticism. What is more, it is hard to think of a literary model for the plain-speaking political defence which Usk's critics might consider genuine. Lacking a firm template for his project, in a literary culture that valued authority, Usk's text is a fretful compromise of different styles. This agonistic relationship with his literary peers and forebears is also a dramatization of the individual's negotiation with his social world: emulation may also be rivalry; private ambition may also be couched in terms that imply cultural conformity.

Another suggestive comparison for the use of *diminutio* comes from Chaucer's *Franklin's Prologue* and *Tale*. In the *Prologue* the 'colours' of Ciceronian rhetoric, of which the Franklin says he knows nothing, are contrasted with the 'colours as growen in the mede' (*FranP*, 724).[45] The Franklin, of course, is satirized in Chaucer's *Canterbury Tales* as a man with both social and literary pretensions that are inextricably intertwined. His *Tale* is at once conservative – observant of courtly, literary conceits – and novel, asserting a new set of cultural priorities with accents on conjugal affection and the bourgeois capacity for largesse, recommending a social restructuring which attends to moral and educational merit rather than natal privilege. His disavowal of rhetoric is a device that is designed to draw attention to his auto-didacticism and powers of articulation, in fact to encourage his readers to read against the text and to see, not its humility and plainness, but rather its sophistication and its deliberate use of educated and literary traditions. *The Testament,* too, by purporting to be constructed in plain, vernacular prose, pointedly and transparently enunciates an obeisance for, but also a mastery of, not only a learned and Latinate culture but also the codes of ideal, courtly behaviour: the elegant discourses of love, the rhetoric of social etiquette and the syntax of gift-giving.[46]

The Franklin, with his use of romance tropes and his spurious Breton lay source, interrogates contemporary anxieties about the consumerism of the 'gentil' community. The Franklin is characterized as an urbane man but one who is looking for acceptance amongst his social betters on the basis of his appreciation of courtly aesthetics but also of his superior claim to a morality that is exhibited primarily in the domestic realm. In *The General Prologue* he is described as a 'housholdere' (*GP*, 339). His interest in household hospitality and the power relations within marriage are shown not as distracting stylistic froth but as crucial to his social and political ambitions.[47] He is portrayed as a *nouveau riche*: as a man appropriating and adapting *passé* feudal discourses to apply a patina to a novel and self-interested ideology. There is a critical assumption that bourgeois writing ought not to demonstrate the abstraction of courtly literature and that the dynamics of the bourgeois household are more appropriately represented in fabliau form.[48] Both *The Testament of Love* and *The Franklin's Tale* are texts that adopt supposedly high-status forms in ways that contemporaries may have considered impertinent and which Usk's critics see as incongruous. In Usk's text, the romance-style quest, the search for the Margarite Pearl, resembles the decorous dynamics of courtly literature, informed as it was by the clean aesthetics of Marian devotion. Rather than representing a satire, *The Testament* offers a eulogy on a social ethic of marriage and an ideal affective household, beautified through the use of romantic and devotional registers. Late-medieval vernacular writing is often a reading of earlier texts in a manoeuvre that feigns passivity and humility whilst all the time making original and audacious bids for authority and prestige. Of course, the Franklin is himself a satire on this kind of social boldness; Chaucer's sharp comedy relies on contemporary discomfort at current social restructuring. I suggest that there is a similar and lingering distaste in critical readings of Usk's political aspirations.

In the process of assemblage, medieval authors consistently sought to cover up their inventiveness, piecing together a disparate range of real or fictive authorities, translating them into, or adjusting them to fit a new text with a new purpose. It is this feature of medieval art that has been compared to the eclectic and recycled art forms of post-modernism, which similarly shatter the fantasy of completeness: the whole person and her ability to speak in language outside of culturally supplied discourses.[49] At the same time an individual's use and manipulation of space and language, the central media for authority and convention, continually demonstrate the capacity for customisation and self-expression. Not only influenced by forms of life writing, Usk also uses, magpie-like, various other kinds of texts and narratives. He deploys, to name only the most obvious: the Bible, St Anselm's *De concordia*, the poetry of Geoffrey Chaucer, Marian devotional verse and romance narratives to form a *Bildungsroman* – the narrative of the protagonist's socialization in the household of Love.

Although often faithful to fragments of other texts, *The Testament of Love* is in no way a sustained translation of any one of them. Of course this is highly manipulative, colonising as much as imitating in a way that exacerbates the tendencies already inherent within translation.[50] Further, it encourages a critical emphasis upon the language that has traditionally been used to assess translation, language about fidelity and betrayal, truth and falsehood. The use of source material in *The Testament of Love* has been denigrated as self-interested and as inattentive to the meanings and ideas in those appropriated texts. The charge is one of intellectual theft or vandalism; *The Testament* is seen as an impudent redaction of literature that is deemed to be of more technical merit. In particular, in criticism from Skeat to Turner, *The Testament* has been said to 'lift' material from Chaucer, misreading, plagiarizing and attempting to outdo an author whose literary reputation is, of course, impossible to rival – a fact acknowledged in *The Testament* itself.[51] Whatever Usk the author might privately have thought about Chaucer, whether he was envious, admiring or both, Love speaks this compliment:

> Certaynly his noble sayenges can I not amende; in goodnes
> of gentyl manlyche speche, without any maner of nycite of
> storieres ymagynacion, in wytte and in good reason of
> sentence he passeth al other makers.
>
> (III, 4, 236–9)

No author is likely to come out of a comparison with Chaucer well; Usk is no exception. As Turner argues, Usk will never escape these kinds of comparative assessments, given his use of Chaucer's work and his undisguised efforts to anchor himself to this distinguished and politic poet.[52] In particular, she has identified Usk's excision of the erotic in his use of *Troilus and Criseyde* as a pointed attempt to sanitize and reproach Chaucer's poem and demean its emphasis upon sex and passion. This correction, his attempt to 'amende' Chaucer, is, Turner suggests, 'unconvincing' and evidence of Usk's 'overreaching', a word which implies distasteful pretentiousness and impertinent self-aggrandisement.[53]

Reading, of course, is already a rhetorical act, involving improvisation and self-insinuation; use produces 'innumerable and infinitesimal transformations of and within the dominant cultural economy'.[54] Chaucer too, in the *Troilus* and elsewhere, was a reader and reformer of other texts and creates his own startling and fresh renditions that are not necessarily respectful. Whilst Strohm has detected a 'non-Boethian' aspect in Usk's appetitive use of the *Consolatio*, Chaucer's translation of the same was also a, possibly 'non-Boethian', political act of rivalry, furthering the fortunes of vernacular writing and, crucially, vernacular writers like Chaucer himself.[55] Chaucer's self-interest, however sophisticated and subtle, should not be underestimated. *The Testament* differs from *Troilus and Criseyde* in that it is not only a reading of prior text but also a reading of the self, which may explain the more overtly self-interested use of sources and influences. The tonal difference between the measure of Chaucer's work and the inordinacy of Usk's has been accounted for, too, by Strohm in his repeated reminders about the very different political and social fortunes of the two authors.[56] The overwrought representation of selfhood in *The Testament* would be better compared, I suggest, to the sometimes desperate quest for authorization in *The Book of Margery Kempe*. Leigh Gilmore has argued that critics conspire more readily with texts composed in ordered and restrained tones, only authenticating those which construct a reasonable, stable authorial voice.[57] This has certainly happened in Usk studies just as it has been an abiding feature of criticism on Kempe.

The Testament of Love demonstrates an instability that has been read as evasive and dishonest but might also be seen as tragically uncertain and lost. *The Testament*'s repression of sexuality and ambition, for example, has been read as a disingenuous and conceited claim about moral superiority but it is also a perturbed repression of the self, a corollary of an anxiety about exclusion from social, political and literary communities. *The Testament of Love* is an intriguing search for the appropriate masculine self, which often entails an agitated representation of the narrator as childlike, untouched by the stain of adult sexuality. However, this infantilization is at odds with the abundance of pseudo-erotic ideas that are often suggestively coupled with the imagery of weather, wilderness and water: the narrator and his immediate environment are in danger of being consumed by his interior desires.[58] The disquiet about social exclusion that these extreme impulses produce is everywhere written into *The Testament*, which imagines a body of negative opinion beyond itself, constructing rejection within its reader through its defensiveness:

> my corde is to short to let my boket ouȝt catch of that water, and fewe men be abouten my corde to eche. And many in ful purpose ben redy it shorter to make and to encose th'entre, that my boket of joye nothing shulde catch, but empty returne, my careful sorowes to encrese. And, if I dye for payne, that were gladnesse at their hertes.
>
> (III, I, 130–5)

The self-pity in this passage is palpable and produces this, some might say charming, some mawkish, image of the narrator attempting to draw joy from a well. The reader is asked to become part of an alternative community with the narrator that will be a substitute for those from which he is disqualified. Kempe, in a similar way, constructs her protagonist in opposition to a community of detractors who are either converted to her cause or rejected by Christ; however, giving space to opposition in this way enables a reader to see the protagonist as compromised and to refuse the authority of a defensive narrator who buries the 'truth' about the desiring self. The implausible renunciation of worldly and bodily desires, which takes place both within *The Testament of Love* and *The Book of Margery Kempe*, is an attempt to reach accommodation with those antagonized communities. This application for social acceptance on the basis of total self-denial, however, indicates an unstable social conscience that veers between the extremes of asceticism and self-assertion, which are related, contiguous and equally suspicious.

The interest in Boethius and Anselm, in their discussions of fortune and grace respectively, is induced by this interior negotiation over social rights and status. There is a constant questioning about whether it is possible to strive for rewards – whether there is free will – or whether they are distributed arbitrarily or mysteriously. Traditionally, medieval culture dispensed entitlement on the strength of inherited social privilege. In some quarters this was also an ideal of the holistic community that necessarily generated and glamorized a doctrine of endurance and obedience, a doctrine that was increasingly and nervously reasserted in the late fourteenth century, when many were beginning to question their natal entitlements. At the same time, though, those same conservative discourses of endurance and renunciation were adopted and used to contextualize and authorize social, political and economic challenge. New economic power was legitimized by an emphasis not upon acquisition and pleasure but on affectivity and moral propriety. New mercantile wealth was neutralized by the production of sentimental and pious household ideals that played down – or repressed – the importance of sexual and material appetites and which seemed – although in fact they weren't at all – removed from the arena of public and civic politics. These are the same discursive strategies that are used in *The Testament of Love* to legitimate the narrator's desires, desires that are dramatized in familial and emotional terms, using the imagery of domestic and private space to articulate a preoccupation with social and political access.

THE HOUSEHOLD AND HOME

Property and home

Love assures Thomas that she cannot find accommodation in well-stocked homes:

And yet, sayne some that they me have in cellar with wyne shet, in gernere there corne is layde, covered with whete, in sacke sowed with wolle, in purse with money faste knytte, amonge pannes mouled in a wyche, in presse amonge clothes layde with ryche pelure arayed, in stable amonge horse and other beestes, as hogges, shepe, and nete, and in other, many-wyse. But Thou, maker of lyght (in wynking of thyn eye the sonne is queynt), woste right well that I, in trewe name, was never thus herberowed.

(II, 2, 23–30)

This provisioned and spacious property is made inaccessible to Love because of its proliferation of internal boundaries: each thing is contained, honeycomb-like, within an excluding space. Usk includes the grain-store and livestock in an attempt to make the parsimonious, loveless and excessive household enviably self-sufficient. This is an image of comfort and sufficiency from which the imprisoned narrator, like Love, is excluded. Although this is a negative assessment of properties with specialized and subdivided space, there is a palpable fascination with, even a hankering after things in their purpose-made boxes or rooms, of the cupboards and chests dedicated to the exclusive storage of, say, clothes or kitchen utensils. Love's insistence that material goods, no matter how neatly stored, displace redeeming emotional relationships is designed as consolation for an excluded narrator, morally devaluing the attractive things he can never acquire. Asserting that she favours an isolated island-home over these well-stocked houses, she accompanies Thomas in his alienation:

Trewly, therfore, I have me withdrawe and made my dwellynge out of lande in an yle by myselfe, in the occian closed.

(II, 2, 15–16)

If Love is never read as other than a personification, this eremitical instinct is plausible, but the idea that love is more likely to abound in unpopulated places is surely deluded.

In contrasting the household and the island, *The Testament of Love* measures society – imagined as exclusive and excluding property – against the exiled self – a representative of familial and conjugal affection – and removes consumptive domestic practice from the indemnifying emotional significances which countervailed it in legitimizing contemporary discourses. The wealthy London houses of this period were at the vanguard of a new trend where household space was increasingly compartmentalized so that particular rooms could be adapted and dedicated for particular uses.[59] An epiphenomenon of that reticulation was a greater level of privacy; indeed, privacy might be seen as the ultimate acquisition, signing the economic worth of the family that enjoyed it. Further, although *The Testament of Love* considers it exclusive and emotionally cool, this privatization of space coincided with the production of ideals about familial and conjugal intimacy that offset material acquisition and consumption. That is not to say, of course, that these households *did* necessarily house more loving relationships than their rural or aristocratic counterparts, but that these institutions were underwritten by an ideology that stressed uncommon affectivity. *The Testament of Love* continually denigrates literal domestic property whilst appropriating the edifying meanings with which it was increasingly associated. Things of moral significance are venerated and kept safe by being locked into Love's 'tresorye amonges my privy thynges' (I, 9, 88–9); Love offers Thomas – one of her 'privy famyliers' (II, 3, 113–14) – access to her private household spaces, which, unlike the private chambers of real houses, necessarily exclude the wicked and appetitive. Such metaphors conspire with the tendencies that they purport to reject, demonstrating the narrator's superiority through a snug portrait of personalized space and encased property. Things, even things in daily use, are put in their boxes in an effort to preserve them, to develop a permanence of living; *The Testament of Love* continually reasserts the ephemeral nature of property but uses the metaphors of encasement – 'in the occian *closed*' – to make emotional and spiritual impulses permanent, producing a stability of settlement that is exclusive to the narrator.

Sarah Rees Jones has noted that the increasing reliance on written leaseholds 'placed more emphasis on the design and value of the house, rather than the land on which it stood', a shift which effected an increasing conceptualization of the house as a 'home'.[60] Usk's text is deeply invested in the ideologies of home but also describes an affecting exclusion from an experience of the same. *The Testament* is structured as a search for a home, for things lost and hidden, things unreachable and locked off. Usk is keen to show Thomas's search for access to interior spaces and emotional intimacy as moral and moderate, not disfigured by consumerism and excessive desire. The search for the appropriate desiring self in *The Testament of Love* is mitigated and worrying, potentially anarchic desires are limited by the same redemptive ideologies which were generated by a culture making moral accommodation with new standards of living and increased consumer spending.

Putting aspiration in homely terms may well be an attempt to neutralize its social challenge. Romanticizing the idea of home, *The Testament of Love* aims to inspire pathos through a simple appeal to family values and domestic comforts. Thomas understands his present displacement as a corrupted fantasy of home:

Myrth is chaunged into tene, whan swynke is there contynually, that reste was wont to sojourne and have dwellynge place. Thus, wytlesse-thoughtful, syghtless-lokynge, I endure my penaunce in this derke prisone, caytifved fro frendshippe and acquayntaunce, and forsaken of al that any wode dare speke. Straunge hath by waye of intrucyoun made his home there me shulde be, if reason were herde as he shulde.

(I, 1, 12–17)

Here the narrator's personal misfortunes are conceptualized as two parallel usurpations of dwelling space. First, the places that 'Myrth' and 'reste' were accustomed to inhabiting are taken over by 'tene' and 'swynke'. Secondly, Thomas's old position has been appropriated by the pretender 'Straunge' who has, illegitimately, made himself at home. The word 'Straunge' could mean, in a general sense, an unknown person, but also suggests, more specifically, someone from outside of the known communal institutions of medieval life: the Church, the guild, the household and the town.[61] Outsiders of this kind were the *bête-noir* of medieval law-makers; in this personification Usk articulates his interior ferment in terms of the contemporary paranoia about social and, in particular, civic disruption by an external catalyst, reinforcing his perceived rights with an appeal to contemporary notions of communal belonging.[62] *The Testament of Love* continually deploys the imagery of dwelling and dwelling space, demonstrating its emotional interest in the home as central to psychological and moral order.

The Testament of Love begins with an enforced absence from the pleasures of home; homelessness and displacement are part of Usk's affecting domestic imagery:

whan I pilgrymaged out of my kyth in wynter, whan the wether out of measure was boystous, and the wylde wynde Borias, as his kynde asketh, with dryenge coldes, maked the wawes of the occian see so to aryse unkyndely over the commune bankes that it was in poynte to spyl al the erthe.

(I, Prologue, 105–9)

The hostility of nature is contrasted in this passage with his 'kyth' – which can refer both to the place of home and to the family.[63] This journey is described in further detail and a dichotomy is established which juxtaposes the perilous and comfortless wandering in the wilderness with the pleasures of home. Here, for example, Thomas nostalgically recalls the time when:

Octobre his leave gynneth take, and Novembre sheweth hym to syght, whan bernes ben ful of goodes as is the nutte on every halke, and than good londe tyllers gynne shape for the erthe, with great travayle, to bringe forthe more corne to mannes sustenaunce ayenst the nexte yeres folowyng, in suche tyme of plentie, he that hath an home, and is wyse, lyste not to wander mervayles to seche, but he be constrayned or excited. Oft the lothe thyng is doone by excytacion of other mannes opynyon, whiche wolden fayne have myn abydynge take in herte. Ofluste to travayle and se the wyndyng of the erthe in that tyme of wynter, by woodes that large stretes werne in, by smale pathes that swyne and hogges hadden made, as lanes with ladels their maste to seche,

(I, 3, 24–35)

These cosy descriptions of barns full of 'goodes', the glut of nuts and the promise of corn next year reinforce the reluctance of winter travellers. The third-person form is used to identify a group of homeowners who, as a general rule, do not choose to travel when their barns are well stocked. There is, however, a switch into the first person as the narrator describes his own plight and predicament. The lost paradises of Mankind become more specifically the personal misfortunes of the narrator. He describes the coercion that is needed to goad him to undertake his winter journey and to swap his 'abydynge', his staying at home, for a wilderness in which he is menaced by 'grete beestes' (I, 3, 36). Joanna Summers has shown the similarities between this passage and one from Gower's *Vox clamantis* but, while the emphasis in Gower's passage is upon the wilderness through which the narrator is forced to travel and the beasts that he encounters, *The Testament of Love* is more preoccupied with a nostalgic and sentimental description of the home its narrator has left behind.[64]

Travelling in November was notoriously inhospitable; by choosing this time as the backdrop to his metaphorical journey, Usk signals the difficulty of his experience and the 'transitional nature' of a moment in his life.[65] It also underscores the centrality of home as a concept in the work. This image of 'home', though, is as constructed as the wilderness that is its antithesis.[66] This bucolic rural scene was certainly not the personal experience of home for the Londoner, Usk. Indeed, this is the kind of landscape familiar from the iconography depicting the labours of the months, in which the nut harvest was a standard part of the November scene. The typical images of labours of the months show the peasantry working in the foreground at an agricultural task. The background often shows the opulent residences of the manuscript owners. The October and November images in the *Très riches heures du Duc de Berry*, for example, show, in the first instance, workmen tilling and sowing in the shadow of the Louvre and, in the second, pig-men knocking down acorns for their animals – perhaps the sort of pigs snuffling amongst the acorns in Usk's woodland scene – before a crenulated residence on the hill behind them.[67] Harvest plenty, like Mom's apple pie, is a symbolic vision of the idyllic comforts of home. This is an image of rural household sufficiency, one that might rival the household in which Love says she can find no room. Sufficiency, Love notes, ensures that an individual is no longer subject to the whims of a tyrant but lifts him free to be his own man: 'Is he nat riche that hath suffisaunce and hath the power that no man may amaistrien?' (II, 2, 57–8). The great country residences offer independence from the network of obligation and political credit that bind town houses together. If we do read the wilderness, the wild beasts and the threatening sea, as allegorical descriptions of Usk's experience in his political *milieu*, as Strohm suggests we should, the household that Usk devises as an alternative is an isolated haven where he is protected from potentially damaging interaction with others.[68] However, he imports into that fantasy all the intimacy and trust, piety and moderation, which are features increasingly associated in histories of the late-medieval household with the precocious development of ethical ideologies in urban centres and the metropolis in particular.

Labour and fosterage

Usk does not write a *Bildungsroman* of the kind we expect in autobiography after Augustine; he does not write his own parents into his *Testament of Love* nor construct a representation of the cap maker's household in which it is thought that he grew up. Instead he imports a filial and sentimental dynamic into symbolic labouring or service identities and relationships. Adolescents in the late-medieval town were disciplined and educated, but also cared for through their employment relationships.[69] Young men were encouraged to identify with their trainers and accept their authority as a son would a father's; in return, a master was expected to provide for his young charges as a father might his children. In this period we see household heads influencing their servants' and apprentices' social and sexual relationships as well as the specifics of their vocational and moral training. In preventing inappropriate matches or funding their charges' establishment of new households and workshops on marriage, masters demonstrated their paternal authority and patronage.[70] It is not uncommon to see, in the testamentary evidence, masters and mistresses leaving items of some value to those who were ostensibly in their employ but who were also evidently treated as loved and protected dependants.[71]

Suggestively, although the conventional ideal promulgated in the records of late-medieval urban trade was for male-headed, patriarchal and conjugal households, and although Love was typically a male deity (Cupid or Eros), *The Testament of Love* produces a household headed by Love, a benevolent and unattached woman.[72] Usk's Love has very little in common with the figure of Venus, the female deity of love that is used, for example, in Gower's *Confessio Amantis*. Whilst, of course, the sex of Love is dictated by her close ties to the figure of Lady Philosophy in Boethius's *Consolatio*, and whilst the service relationship between Thomas

and Love is partly modelled on ideas of courtly love-service, the combination of these influences generates a unique scenario in the literature of
this period in which Love is simultaneously a foster-mother, a household
manageress and employer. Medieval people understood fine distinctions
between different modes of service, and those distinctions were marked
with a complex and nuanced vocabulary.[73] I shall go on to show how,
whilst the terminology of household service in *The Testament* is informed
by a variety of traditions and fashions, Usk collates them in such a way as
to make them more redolent of the homeliness which was associated with
the bourgeois urban household. First, however, I want to consider Usk's
curious writing-out of the father and male household-head who was such
a lynchpin in other depictions of the ideal bourgeois household.

In the Prologue to *The Testament of Love*, the narrator traces an agnatic
lineage through a labour identification with the classical thinkers and
writers who are represented by Boethius. He describes their writings as a
bequest, 'to us leften' (I, Prologue, 62) in an authorization device that
names Thomas as the philosophers' heir and successor. Usk uses the
metaphors, which he found in John Trevisa's translations of Higden and
Bartholomæus Anglicus, of agriculture and manual exertion to describe
the labours of the *auctors* ('these noble repers') as good workmen:

Herfore, truly the phylosophers with a lyvely studye, many noble thynges ryght
precious and worthy to memory writen, and, by a great swetande travayle, to us
leften *Of Causes [of] the Propertyes in Natures of Thynges*.
(I, Prologue, 59–62)[74]

Usk regularly demonstrates this kind of masculine pride in writing and
philosophical writing in particular, investing it with a bucolic dignity that is
familiar from other romantic visions of rural labour in this period. Thomas
expresses none of the anxiety about the masculine propriety of intellectual
work which, as I show elsewhere in this book, is a regular feature of
contemporary reflexive writing. Middleton has claimed that Usk's 'bib-
liographical and metapoetic signs' demonstrate a pride and a mastery of the
'textworker's' craft.[75] There is a palpable confidence in *The Testament of
Love* about the moral and cultural value of being a writer and a thinker that
stands out in a text otherwise so beset with insecurity and self-doubt.

It is telling that *The Testament* specifies 'the noble husbande Boece'
(I, Prologue, 93) rather than following Higden's lead and writing more
generally of 'auctours'. It is not surprising that Usk chooses Boethius,
who had such a formative function in the late medieval schoolroom, as a

role model and provider for his 'chyldren'. In translating the *Consolatio*, Chaucer had recommended Boethius as a model for those composing in English. Just as Boethius admired and appropriated the philosophic traditions of the illustrious Hellenistic past, substituting Latin for Greek, so Chaucer effected a similar substitution of English for Latin. In these acts of 'translation', unequal languages and cultures are collocated in such a way that the younger both borrows and reinforces the veneration afforded to the older, but also so that they jostle and compete. This ambivalent relationship writes translators of celebrated source texts into a filial role characterized both by deference and contestation. Usk, in keeping with the practice of medieval – and indeed Roman – translation and literary imitation constructs himself in a similarly ambivalent relationship to his literary and philosophical forebears.[76]

The Testament describes the narrator's relative position to the 'great workmen' philosophers in masculinist terms. With reference to Trevisa's translation of the *Polychronicon*, Usk borrows an image of the small man – the 'dwerf' – to represent the contemporary writer and his assemblage of the texts written by literary 'geauntis'. The metaphor is about physical strength and mythical heroism:

> But nowe, thou reder, who is thylke that wyl not in scorne laughe to here a dwarfe, or els halfe a man, say he wyl rende out the swerde of Hercules handes; and also he shulde set Hercules Gades a myle yet ferther; and, over that, he had power of strengthe to pul up the spere that Alisander the noble might never wagge; and that, passynge al thynge, to ben mayster of Fraunce by myght, thereas the noble, gracyous Edwarde the thyred, for al his great prowesse in victories, ne myght al yet conquere?
>
> (I, Prologue, 73–80)

In this passage Boethius takes on the fabled muscle of Hercules – again suggested by Usk's reading of Trevisa – and the military acumen of Alexander, and surpasses the victories enjoyed by Edward III, both innovations in Usk's text. Boethius's philosophical legacy is figured as the ancient symbols of masculine might: the spear and the sword. Usk's 'halfman' is somewhat different from Trevisa's 'dwerf' and 'pigmey', being underdeveloped and insufficient rather than fantastical and exotic. Usk's diminutive writer is a smaller, even a childlike version of those he intends to challenge. Whilst the *Polychronicon* already demonstrates a combative relationship between the 'pigmey' and 'Hercules', Usk augments the challenge posed by his puny contestant. Skeat was puzzled by the apparent confusion between Alexander and Arthur in this passage.[77] Alexander's heroic deed was to untie the Gordian knot and it was Arthur who was charged with removing a sword from a stone. However, when the reader hears about Alexander, a man of unquestionable ability, and the spear that he 'might never wagge' they are reminded, not of Arthur, but rather of the strong men in the same story who fail to lift the embedded sword. The narrator directly addresses the reader and asks him or her to recollect that, in spite of the censorious laughter of critics, sometimes the small man, like the child Arthur, can succeed. This passage of *The Testament*, then, amplifies the sense of its source, stressing the potential for the contemporary consumer of the philosophical greats to become a supplanter, as much as a humble worshipper of their authority.

In *The Testament*'s female-headed household, which is so absented by images of paternity and male authority, there is none of this intergenerational rivalry. Homosocial ambivalence is confined to the spheres of labour and battle, in metaphors that mimic acceptable and conventional treatments of literary authority. This distinction between public male space and private female space, however, runs counter to both the practice and ideology of medieval households, which were not only the preserve of women but also a place where men had agency and authority and where their generational struggles were enacted. Female authority is represented in Usk's *Testament* as benign and loving, as inclusive and frictionless. Whilst this is the period where male householders are increasingly being burdened with the task of maintaining order in the community by keeping watch over their own households and dependents, *The Testament* moves the contest for authority out of the home to insulate his narrator from its invasive effects.[78] In this way, the home represented in the text retains the emotional power but strips out the inevitable tensions produced by the negotiation of familial and household relationships. The relationship between Usk's narrator and Love is represented as similar to that between a son and his mother. Nevertheless their association is expressed in the language of service in a way that conflates the economic and emotional functions of the household. This is done in a very different way to other contemporary texts, many of which were also intrigued, indeed preoccupied by, the language of service or household. In particular, I shall contrast it with Chaucer's use of service imagery and terminology, especially in *Troilus and Criseyde*.[79]

There are two related ways in which Usk's narrator goes into the service of Love. First, Love commissions him to write up her words as *The Testament of Love*. This neatly reflexive moment is inspired by Philosophy's request to Boece to write an account of their dialogues, which is also related to the way in which the narrator of *Troilus* agrees to write up the experience of, or 'serve' 'Loves servantz' (*T&C*, I, 15 and 48–9). Whilst the recruitment of *The Testament*'s narrator as secretary may seem, given what is known of Usk's life, to be pertinent, Love's request must be seen as part of a Boethian tradition:

> I charge the in vertue of obeyence that thou to me owest, to writen my wordes and sette hem in writynges that they mowe as my witnessynge ben noted amonge the people.
>
> (I, 3, 164–6)

Usk's narrator's service as a writer, though, is a part of a larger debt of service to Love – and this is the second of his service roles – as a lover and suitor in her retinue. The *Boece* does not have a pronounced interest in the philosophy of love-service; the narrator of *Troilus and Criseyde* is explicitly distanced from Love's retinue as a servant of 'Loves servantz'. Indeed, in this respect, Thomas might be said to resemble Troilus himself, who pledges allegiance both to the God of Love and Criseyde (*T&C*, I, 421–34). Love-service in *The Testament* is similarly dual: owed both to Love herself and the Margarite pearl lady.

There is an approximation in traditional discourses of love-service between the romantic bond and the feudal relationship between a lord and a retainer. Andrew Galloway has argued that *The Testament*'s imagery of service suggests 'membership of a nobleman's livery and retinue'.[80] Crucially, of course, Love is not a noble*man*, but Usk's discussion of livery (I, 5, 98–100) clearly signifies that Thomas's position is intended to articulate the glamour of the traditional bonds of fealty and the kinds of courtly associations that *Troilus and Criseyde* also exploits in its aesthetics of service. Whilst Chaucer augmented the theme of service beyond what he found in Boccaccio's *Il filostrato*, these amplified meanings are very different from those in *The Testament*.[81] In particular, the narrator is imagined entering into household service in a way that is much more spatially specific than the service which Troilus undertakes. This is especially telling given Chaucer's embellishment of the household context presented by his Italian source; the English poem is palpably intrigued by the dramatic potential of the aristocratic residence, its staff and their domestic labours.[82] The industry of the peripheral household personnel, though, is always in ironic contrast to the romantic and erotic labours of the protagonist (e.g. *T&C* II, 935–52). Further, unlike the spatially abstracted labour of the hero, the labour of the 'meynee' in *Troilus and*

Criseyde is carefully situated in rooms with fixtures and fittings. Although the configuration of intimate space and its attendant hierarchies are central to Chaucer's poem, and although Troilus enters into the martial retinue of Love, nothing is said about Love's household and how its spaces are reticulated and used.

By contrast, in *The Testament of Love* the narrator is invited much more explicitly into household service, envisaged as a space as much as a social attachment:

'Nowe to the, thyselfe,' quod she, 'as I have ofte sayd I knowe wel thyne herte; thou arte none of al the tofore-nempned people, for I knowe wel the con-tynuaunce of thy servyce, that never sythen I set thee a-werke, myght thy Margaryte, for plesaunce, frendeshyp, ne fayrehede of none other, be in poynte moved from thyne herte. Wherfore, into myne housholde hastely I wol that thou entre, and al the parfyte privyte of my werkyng make it be knowe in thy understondyng, as one of my privy famyliers.'

(II, 3, 107–14)

Whilst Troilus's love-service is a means to an end – a way of attaining Criseyde in romantic and sexual terms – Thomas's entering into Love's household is evidently a special prize in itself. Whilst Troilus's soliloquies describe his love-service as an affected abjection and subjection (eg. *T&C*, I, 231 and 432–4), Thomas's hopes are far more positive, using the word 'famyliers' with all its associations of familial affection. The preoccupation in the above passage, and indeed in *The Testament* as a whole, with access and fidelity is effectively conveyed in the metaphor of household; contemporary records of household structure and organization foreground exactly these themes. Indeed, access – instruction and intimacy – represented the rights, and fidelity and discretion represented the duties, of young people entering into household service and vocational training. Apprenticeship indentures, for example, expressed this in contractual terms: whilst the young man or woman could expect to become acquainted with the inner 'werkings' of the household business and the trade it practised, they were expressly obliged to keep those same secrets and to conduct themselves in ways that caused no damage to that business, household or mystery.[83]

The narrator sees Love as the supreme householder who can give him access to a privileged and intimate space to which she holds the keys:

And than sayd I in this wyse. 'Nowe, wel of wysedom and of al welthe, with-outen the may nothyng ben lerned. Thou bearest the keyes of al privy thinges. In

vayne travayle men to catche any stedshyp, but if ye, lady, first the locke unshet.
Ye, lady, lerne us the wayes and the bypathes to heven;

(I, 5, 33–6)

Middleton has noted Usk's extensive use of the key as an image, showing
its textual tradition in the Psalms and the idea of the 'key of David'.[84]
Keys were also, however, the ubiquitous symbol of the female household
manageress. Bracton's *De legibus et consuetudinibus Angliæ* describes the
key as a marker of female adulthood, signalling an ability to orchestrate
the household routines and manage its resources.[85] Patricia Cullum and
Jeremy Goldberg have argued that the English cult of Sitha, the servant
saint, which created a central iconographic place for keys, was designed
for young women being educated in domestic administration.[86] *The Book
of Margery Kempe* also demonstrates the importance of keys as emblems of
female autonomy and authority (ch. 1, 178–83).[87] Thomas longs for access
to these female locked-off spaces, where provision will be made for him
and where an ideal household manageress will value him.

Whilst Love is a capricious and vengeful male deity in *Troilus and
Criseyde*, and whilst Criseyde's affections are variable and her motives a
cipher, Usk's Margarite is a symbol of constancy and his personification
of Love is a maternal figure who offers the protection of a home. Love
affectionately refers to Thomas as her 'nory', meaning not just a disciple
but also a fostered foundling whom she nurses at her breast. 'Nory' is a
borrowing from Chaucer's *Boece* and, in particular, his rendering of
Boethius's *alumne*. Blending the discourses of courtly love-service and
Boethian, maternal consolation produces a new combination in *The
Testament* in which the roles of adoptive son and servant are inextricable.
This is reminiscent of the contemporary ideals of household service that
placed employers in *loco parentis*, expecting them to nurture and provide
for the young people in their care. Indeed, it has been noted that young
people were entering into short periods of household service at around
the time when their own parents were dying; life-cycle service positions
absorbed adolescent orphans as well as those children whose places in the
households of others were negotiated by their parents.[88]

Usk develops the idea of the nursling into a sustained image in which
his narrator's political corruption is described in the arresting terms of
filial guilt. Love marvels that Thomas can ever have veered from her
motherly teachings:

O where haste thou be so longe commensal, that hast so mykel eeten of the
potages of foryetfulnesse and dronken so of ignorance, that the olde soukyng

whiche thou haddest of me arne amaystred and lorn fro al maner of knowyng?

(I, 4, 22–5)

The narrator is figured as a man who eats in company – 'commensal'. The strange and debilitating foods that he has imbibed are contrasted with the simplicity of his old fare, sucked from the breast of Love herself. This is a narrative that describes the persona's movement from a simple, natural and wholesome state into the world of cultured, contrived and degenerate practices. *The Testament* blames Thomas's society rather than his origins, his innate being, for his mistakes and moral decline.

The symbolism of nursing as spiritual counsel was common in the life writing models available to Usk. I have mentioned the direct reference to Chaucer's translation of Boethius's *Consolation of Philosophy*; the image of the consoling and educating woman perhaps inevitably becomes a maternal figure, who dries both Thomas's (I, 4, 31–2) and Boece's (I, pr 2, 25–30) tear-filled eyes with a fold of her dress. Nursing imagery was also common in medieval mystical works in which holy men and women were nourished at the breast of the Virgin, or sometimes Christ himself; in turn they were sometimes figured as nurses for their followers.[89] The mystic who was so cared for and so familiar with divinity, surely had visions which were true and which came directly from God? In Usk's text the breast-feeding imagery is used exactly in this way; by association with Love, Thomas claims a special relationship to a direct form of wisdom. Augustine in his *Confessions* also claimed to have sucked wisdom directly from his mother, Monica's breast (e.g. *Confessions*, III, iv, IV, i, and VII, xviii).[90] Such claims demonstrate a narrator's innate access to authority, and it is an authority that they are given through entitlement rather than on account of any solicitation on their part. As well as being an astute authorization strategy, the use of this imagery is sentimental and affecting; in Usk's *Testament*, an assertive claim about the narrator's privileged access to moral knowledge is simultaneously a portrait of a son who has lost his mother and an anxious admission of his isolation and vulnerability.

Maternal love, personified by Thomas's interlocutor, is juxtaposed with a false and inverted version of love. Love herself warns Thomas of her allure:

Proverbes of Salomon openly teacheth howe somtyme an innocent walkyd by the way in blyndnesse of a derke night, whom mette a woman – if it be lefely to saye – as a strumpet arayed, redily purveyed in turnynge of thoughtes with veyne janglynges and of rest inpacient, by dissymulacion of my termes, sayeng in this wyse, 'Come and be we dronken of our swete pappes; use we coveytous collynges.'

(II, 14, 5–11)

The vision of false love chosen to contrast with the true love of maternal affection comes from Proverbs 7, which also tells about the corruption of young men by a prostitute. Several critics have identified this 'strumpet' as a metaphorical manifestation of Northampton and his political faction. In a general sense, the story of the 'innocent' led astray clearly does represent part of a political defence. However, the metaphor is much more surprising than that and speaks not just of the machinations of political subornment, but also of the maternal body and sexual desire.

Usk's passage alters the text of Proverbs in crucial ways, cutting out all superfluous sensory detail. If this were simply an account of Usk's experiences in the Northampton faction the biblical story would have sufficed.[91] In Proverbs the woman's speech is enticing because it is lyrical. She promises an exotic setting and sensuous stimulants to enhance the sexual pleasure she offers:

Intexui funibus lectulum meum, stravi tapetibus pietis ex Ægypto; aspersi cubile meum myrrha, et aloë, et cinnamomo. Veni, inebriemur uberibus, et fruamur cupitis amplexibus.

(Proverbs, 7.16–18)[92]

Usk dramatically excises this speech; his prostitute simply says: '"Come and be we dronken of our swete pappes; use we coveytous collynges"' (II, 14, 10–11). By deleting the aromatic spices and luxurious textiles, the medieval passage comes to focus exclusively on the body of the 'strumpet'. In particular, what draws Usk to this Biblical text is the nursing imagery in the reference to *uberibus*, which he makes less abstract than the Biblical passage by the insertion of the possessive pronoun 'our'. The use of the plural forms, 'we' and 'our', to refer to the singular speaker is clearly suggested by the Latin *inebriemur* and *fruamur* but takes on the pejorative intimacy that they could carry in Middle English.[93] This new emphasis on the breasts accentuates the innocence of those she solicits, casting them as unweaned infants. In this sense the passage can be read, in terms of the political allegory, as a mitigation plea. However, the choice of this passage with its unusual imagery of sexuality and motherhood reveals an interest in such things for themselves and not just for the metaphorical meanings they might be made to carry. Love describes the 'strumpet's' methods as a 'dissymulation of my terms'; she is the antithesis of Love the mother, adopting and then perverting maternal behaviours. The temptations she represents are powerful because they exploit the narrator's vulnerabilities: his longing to be a loved and loving child.

Marriage and sexuality

The Testament expresses horror at the disruptive and anarchic power of desire both in others and in the narrator himself. Boethian water and weather imagery frequently present the fear of being engulfed and drowned by overwhelming appetites (e.g. II, 14, 35–9). Thomas laments the damage done to his world by the conflict of competing factional and personal desires – see, for example, the quotation with which this chapter began. The narrator is outraged by sexual desire in particular, shocked by the prostitute soliciting in the doorway and dismissive of the argument that marriages must necessarily be defined as sexual relationships. The repeated infantilization of the narrator is suggestive, pointing out rather than effacing, an anxiety about mature sexuality. The construction of the narrator as childlike necessarily creates a nursing temptress as its most disturbing moral challenge.

However, although the prostitute offering the 'Mylke of Fallas' (II, 14, 48) is in direct contrast to the Margarite Pearl – a proper object of desire and an elegant symbol of virtue, integrity and continence – *The Testament* does not create a crude dichotomy between virginity and sexuality, recommending one and condemning the other but, rather, constructs an ideal of marriage, informed by canon law, which is carefully poised in the abstinent middle ground between the two. In the reiterated images of keys and key-holders, of boxes, remote island paradises and enclosed female spaces is seen an obsession with tidy and restrained feminine sexuality. The narrator's preoccupation with obtaining access represents an abstracted expression of a masculine desire for heterosexual intimacy. These sanitized spaces and the ideal women who inhabit them, though, are moderate, and articulate the narrator's temperate masculinity. The pearl herself is a hygienic icon but she is also an object of great desire, a desire that is exacerbated by her inaccessibility and untouchable integrity. Hieronymus Bosch in his depiction of the half-obscured lovers in the mussel-shell in 'The Garden of Earthly Delights' understood the semantic slippage of this image.[94] Although appropriated from Marian devotion with its virginal associations, pearl imagery was also pseudo-erotic and equally derived from French love lyrics; enclosed in its shell, the Pearl is fetishized as a potentially carnal object within another tantalizing case.[95] For Usk, the Pearl emblem is not solely about chastity but about postponed and appropriate sexuality. Of course, Margarite and her potential union with the narrator are metaphors about entitlement and access, but their detail and consistency demonstrate an interest in conjugality in and of itself.

The Testament of Love expounds an Augustinian interpretation of marriage, which held that a marriage did not need to be consummated in order to be legitimate, and that while the main purpose of marriage was to have children, consent was the only basis for a valid marriage.[96] This was an uneasy position designed to accommodate the example of the Holy Family and the unconsummated marriage of Mary and Joseph. In his exposition Usk also uses the example of Christ's parents:

The aungel bade Joseph take Marye his spouse and to Egypte wende. Lo, she was cleped spouse, and yet toforne, ne after, neyther of hem bothe mente no flesshly luste knowe.

(I, 10, 92–4)

The example of Mary and Joseph was an important crux in the formation of the canon legal position on marriage in the twelfth century.[97] The special circumstances of their marriage and Mary's virgin conception were instrumental in determining the precepts of marriage law for the following centuries. In particular, the view expounded by Gratian, Peter Lombard and, later, Thomas Aquinas: that consent not coitus made a marriage, dominated the Church's logic on the relationship between marriage and sexuality.[98] The position was more flexible, however, when applied in practice. It was popularly believed amongst the laity that a marriage was only valid when consummated. Marriage litigants seeking to enforce an alleged marital contract would frequently claim *carnali copula subsecuta*, despite its supposed irrelevance in canon legal theory, to add greater weight to the contractual vows that were purportedly exchanged.[99] Consistory courts, reserving for themselves a certain amount of licence, would grant annulments on the grounds of impotence if the wife was of child-bearing age.[100] St Augustine's three 'goods' of marriage – *proles*, *fides* and *sacramentum* (that is children, fidelity and sacredness) – were, of course, fulfilled in the case of the holy family in spite of its representing a model of chastity.[101] It was considered normative in the later Middle Ages that young laywomen should want to be mothers – indeed, Mary herself was offered as a powerful maternal model for them – and this want was interpreted as a right by sympathetic consistory court verdicts which dissolved unconsummated marriages.

Mary, according to Augustine, implicitly consented to sexual intercourse, that is she committed her 'virginity to the divine disposition', on her marriage to Joseph;[102] this view accommodated the special case that their chaste union represented, without necessitating the enforcement of ordinary marriages where one of the spouses was incapable of consummation. In late medieval England, where most secular people married and had children, it may well have been considered extreme to enforce barren unions, and thus Christian ideologies were interpreted in ways that responded to cultural needs.[103]

Usk's account of marriage, however, is an accurate and strict interpretation of canon legal theory which is uncomplicated by popular belief and culturally adaptive practice. This accuracy reveals a pedantic concern for the intricacies of marriage in Christian doctrine and not simply as an arbitrary metaphor in his political defence. Love argues emphatically against the notion that marriages are formalized through copulation, stressing instead consent as the only proper foundation for a valid union:

and, if the lyste to loke upon the lawe of kynde, and with order whiche to me was ordayned, sothely, none age, none overtournynge tyme, but hyt herto had no tyme ne power to chaunge the weddyng, ne the knotte to unbynde of two hertes thorowe one assent in my presence togyther accorden to enduren tyl dethe hem departe? What, trowest thou every ydeot wotte the menynge and the privy entent of these thynges? They wene, forsothe, that suche accorde may not be, but the rose of mydenhede be plucked. Do waye, do waye. They knowe nothyng of this; for consente of two hertes alone maketh the fastenynge of the knotte. Neyther lawe of kynde, ne mannes lawe determyneth, neyther the age ne the qualyte of persones, but onely accorde bytwene thylke twaye. And, trewly, after tyme that suche accorde, by their consent in hert, is enseuled and put in my tresorye amonges my privy thynges, than gynneth the name of spousayle; and, although they breaken forwarde bothe, yet suche mater enseuled is kepte in remembrance for ever.

(I, 9, 76–91)

Usk's is a glamorous account of marriage, attractive enough to rival the standard medieval preference for chastity and providing a positive account of the canon legal position, which is elevated to the level of natural law – 'lawe of kynde'.[104] '[C]onsente of two hertes' interprets the austere precepts of the church's teaching in sophisticated emotional terms, stressing not verbal but inner intellectual consent.[105] The knot, which is an image used elsewhere in the work as a metaphor for bliss generally, here takes on the specificity of married happiness.[106] Although marriage, when contrasted with celibacy, was thought of as a sexual status, Love is keen here to eulogize marriage as an intellectual and romantic union, arguing not in favour of married sex but rather an ascetic kind of alliance which, whether or not it includes a sexual relationship, is not disfigured by excessive lust. The language which accompanied the discourses of virginity was often concerned with relative value, comparing the preciousness of chastity with the supposed richness of jewels and other superlative commodities. While that language is replicated here, it is subtly altered. Instead of chastity being like a valued gem, consent to marriage, which is of more value than married sex, is sealed in the lovers' hearts which are, in turn, locked up in Love's 'tresorye amonges my privy thynges'. In this way, Love manages the somewhat contradictory strands of Augustinian thought and legal theory: married sex is not abhorred but nor was it deemed strictly necessary.

The Testament often denies or passes over the sexual possibilities of its romantic fantasy, displaying a constant tension between erotic love and romantic or spiritual love. It is the elevated sense of a cerebral, sacramental union – uncontaminated by sexual desire – which gives marriage prestige and secures it a place in Love's 'tresorye', presumably a kind of reliquary or keepsake box. Of Augustine's three 'goods' of marriage, the third – its sacramental and spiritual nature – is augmented into a preoccupation with commemoration and ritualization. The passage cited above is in dialogue with Paul's writing on matrimony in Ephesians 5, a chapter that stresses the sanctity of marriage; as Penny Gold notes, Ephesians 5.32 was a verse that generated the later debate in the medieval Church about the sacramental nature of marriage.[107] The second *bonum* – the fidelity within and indissolubility of marriage – is also mentioned with a reference to the marriage ceremony in the Sarum manual: 'tyl dethe hem departe'.[108] The first – reproduction – is entirely excluded, revealing *The Testament*'s repudiating anxiety about sexuality which can be read in the palpable distaste of the flower-cropping metaphor, an image that articulates sexuality as the acquisitive divestment of fragile beauty.

It has often been noted that this passage contains a reference to Chaucer's *Troilus and Criseyde* – which Usk must have known in a very early version or even during its composition – and, in particular, to Antigone's speech:[109]

> For alle the folk that han or ben on lyve
> Ne konne wel the blisse of love discryve.

But wene ye that every wrecche woot
The parfit blisse of love? Why, nay, iwys!
They wenen all be love, if oon be hoot.
Do wey, do wey, they woot no thyng of this!
(T&C, II, 888–913)

In Usk's text, the 'ydeots' of Love's exclamatory dismissal are under the false apprehension that marriage must be constituted by a sexual relationship, whereas the 'wrecches' of Chaucer's poem, much less specifically, simply fail to understand the 'parfit blisse of love'. The word 'hoot', referring to the passionate physiological nature of those with a humoral balance dominated by blood, elliptically implies that the 'wrecches' are overcome by lust, as opposed to love.[110] However, there is no reference in this section of the poem to marriage. Indeed, any marriage between the two eponymous lovers in Chaucer's poem is conspicuously absent or rendered ambiguous. While some critics have argued that their union is intended to represent a clandestine marriage which is signed through an exchange of rings and words which resemble nuptial vows, these tokens and phrases in themselves would not have represented conclusive evidence of a contract within contemporary consistory courts.[111] Far more interested in the tragedy of failed relationships dramatized in the description of Criseyde's dark and empty household than conjugality and cohabitation, *Troilus and Criseyde* is evasive on the subject of marriage. Further, in several respects the rest of *Troilus and Criseyde* – with the exception of the Christianizing and destabilizing palinode – can be said to support the idea of sexual consummation as one of the defining aspects of a heterosexual relationship.

Turner has argued that Usk is here attempting to 'better' Chaucer by importing a 'greater moral "seriousness"' into his words.[112] He also, however, demonstrates a special and esoteric access to the complex logic of ecclesiastical marital law. What Usk extracts from Chaucer's poem is an intellectual and quasi-religious understanding of love as an exclusive knowledge, identifying himself with Chaucer by disassociating himself from the wretches and idiots who fail to understand the profundity of true heterosexual love. Usk also deploys Chaucer's text in a fresh way, producing a justification for a sexually frugal marriage and priding himself on his familiarity with the intricacies of canon law. He does so, moreover, in a way that anticipates Chaucer's interest in the ethics of conjugality in *The Canterbury Tales*. In the marriage debate of that later text it seems that Chaucer too has a touching faith in the idea of consent and its importance for the making of companionate marriages. Here I am not suggesting that Chaucer is an Usk imitator in *The Canterbury Tales*, clearly they are tonally very discrepant, but that they are part of a discursive community that is alert to the interconnections between companionate marriage and the political fortunes of the bourgeoisie.

Usk's discussion of matrimony does more than usurp the authority of his literary influences, it also effects a shift which parallels an amplification of the positive ethical possibilities of marriage in medieval, and especially urban society more widely. The doctrine of consent, with all its 'revolutionary' implications, was no longer only a part of a theoretical clerical debate as it was in the twelfth century; as Michael Sheehan has noted, by the end of the fourteenth century even very young people were fully conversant with their rights in marital law.[113] The institution of marriage was being systematically beautified in late-medieval cultural ideologies. Moreover, this discursive process appropriated the language and imagery that aestheticized chastity, placing these two sexual states in competition in pious estimation. Similarly, the courtly and devotional register which Usk borrows from Marian prayers and romance literature is attentively deployed for ends that are very different from those of those other genres, recommending neither celibacy nor eroticized romantic love. Instead he appropriates the rarefied spirit of those other kinds of texts to valorize and adorn a middle course: a measured and sober marriage. Thomas is never figured as the romance hero or knight errant who is represented in the chivalric manuals as a traveller even beyond his winning of a lady.[114] Usk's version of matrimony is part of a new discourse that advocated wedlock as a positive masculine life-style choice and which provided a hortative justification for what was a relatively novel option, but one being taken increasingly by those, like Usk, in a semi-clerical occupation.[115] Usk's experience within these occupational circles – circles which Middleton argues were Usk's intended readers – may well have encouraged him to produce a work that glamorized the lifestyle of secular professionals and married householders.[116]

It is telling that Usk does not use reproduction as a means of exonerating marital sex, given the readiness with which it was used elsewhere for exactly this purpose. If Usk did know *Piers Plowman* – a possible, although not a definite source for the arboreal imagery of Book III, 5–7 – he would have been aware of the claims that Langland was making for matrimony, partially on account of married people's roles as parents.[117] The only child in *The Testament* is the foundling Thomas, adopted and nourished by his parent, Love. The narrator's infantilization suggests him as modest and undesiring, as a young person who is betrothed in his minority to a suitably chaste lady by an authoritative familial figure. This was a model of marriage that was confined to the aristocracy and was most likely borrowed from romance narratives rather than any observation of social practice. Unlike Langland, Usk does not imagine the perfect married couple as a plough-team populating and feeding the world, nor does he recommend an ethical model that romanticizes the family of the peasant agriculturalist. Instead his version of marriage is an ethereal, unimpeachable but also aspirational union; religiously and socially it emulates the ambitious innovations within the bourgeois communities where the conjugal household and its ethical values were paramount.

Here Love describes the conventional move from the natal to the conjugal home but sees marriage as a potential social leveller:

Wherfore, the wordes of trouthe acorden that my servauntes shulden forsake bothe father and mother and be adherande to his spouse, and they two in unyte of one flesshe shulden accorde. And this wyse, two that werne firste in a lytel maner disacordaunt, hygher that one and lower that other, ben made evenlyche in gree to stonde.

(I, 9, 95–9)

The idea, translated from Ephesians 5.31, that husband and wife become one flesh on marriage, inspires Usk to write about the equality within marriage.[118] Of course, this is not a strident assertion of women's rights – which Ephesians 5 would not support – but rather consolation for Thomas, a disadvantaged man, courting a highborn mistress. *The Testament of Love* uses courtship and wedlock as metaphors to describe the nature and degree of the narrator's desires and measure them against his entitlements. There is, however, a curious contradiction within the discussion of matrimony. On the one hand, *The Testament* presents Thomas's marriage to Margarite as an intellectual, spiritual and romantic union, rather than a sexual one, and argues that it would demonstrate a restrained and moderate desire fully commensurate with canon law and the contemporary ethics of marriage. On the other hand, Love continually encourages Thomas to overcome his trepidation of courting above his social station, assuring him of the equality of people under God, pushing him to reach beyond his social entitlements. Even as a metaphor, these arguments are radical, confidently asserting the rights of a socially mobile narrator whilst always insisting on his moderation.

A palpable sense of alienation and exclusion produces this social audacity and testifies to the reflexive motivation for writing the Pearl as a superlative and unrealistic *telos* and a courtly and virginal lady. The text continually attempts to close the gap between the narrator and those things he desires, making them accessible, tangible and realistic, defending Thomas's right to his pretensions. Love keenly encourages the narrator to aspire for the Pearl despite his claim that she is of a different social rank, that his 'moeble is insuffysaunt to countervayle the price of this jewel' (I, 3, 116). Marriage imagery was often used to discuss economic and social advancement and, in his singular use of these metaphors, Usk can be seen engaging in challenging ways with a current debate about appetition and social entitlement. In chapter one, I discussed the way in which Langland condemns marriages of mismatched status and age. Langland does this on the assumption that such matches were based upon a pecuniary differential that was often indicative of the motivation for a marriage; love, rather than money ought to be the motivation for matrimony. Thomas's statement about his economic insufficiency is, of course, a standard humility topos that represents the narrator as undesiring and unassuming. It is, however, negated by Love's authoritative averment to the contrary, with which the reader, it would seem, is supposed to concur. Separating the narrator – a representative of course of the author – from an authoritative interlocutor is a strategy that enables the author to disown his most daring assertions. Love, not Thomas Usk, justifies marriage across social and economic boundaries; marriage ought to disregard, rather than observe the cultural impediments to marriage presented by money and social status:

Now than, why shuldest thou wene to love to highe, sythen nothynge is the above but God alone? Trewly, I wote wel, that thylke jewel is in a maner evyn in lyne of degree there thou arte thyselve and nought above, save thus.

(I, 9, 53–6)

Given leave by Love's radically levelling arguments to court above himself, Thomas is represented not as a consumer but as a man bestowed with social rights. This is a trope which is perhaps borrowed from romance narratives similar to those in Chaucer's *Clerk's Tale* of Griselda, for example. By inverting the gender dynamics of the Griselda motif, *The Testament of Love* thus develops a meritocratic masculine fantasy that is at once iconoclastic and aspirational, but not at odds with the political world within which it was composed.

This connection between social authority and marriage is clearly a very close one, preoccupying not just Usk but also the bourgeois and aspirational, late-medieval community. We might briefly compare what Usk does here to what Kempe does in the account of her narrator's marriage to the Godhead. Although Margery – represented by Kempe as a young girl – is reticent and bashful during the marriage negotiations, Christ, with the presumed backing of the implied reader, is adamant that the match is good and suitable.[119] Such authorization strategies are, of course, audacious and self-aggrandising but, by suspending their censure, critics have used Kempe's text in ways which move beyond assessing its authenticity. *The Testament of Love* shares with Kempe's *Book* a naked desire to at once disarm and impress a community of medieval readers but, in doing so, they use and expose the values and ideals of that readership. Whilst we evidently do well to avoid being massaged in exactly the way that the text hopes, reading those interactions for the cultural assumptions they betray does not necessitate a condemnation of their textual, social and political ambitions.

CHAPTER 3

John Gower's 'strange places': errant masculinity in the Confessio Amantis

INTRODUCTION: ENGLISH AND ERRANCY

Omnes quidem ad vnum finem tendimus, set diuerso tramite. [We all indeed strive to one end, though by a different path.]

(IV, 2245ff)[1]

In his first and more frivolous prologue to the *Confessio Amantis*, Gower imagines himself rowing up the Thames in imitation of Brutus come to found a 'new Troye' (Prologue, 37–8). The route that Gower's Prologue persona and Brutus take, the path of the river into the English capital, unites them, although they are distant in time. While it *is* possible that the poet John Gower, who lived in Southwark, may have taken such a trip up the river, this is, of course, a symbolic journey that describes the *Confessio Amantis* as an act of national foundation, a contribution to the project of producing a corpus of vernacular literature. Gower, then, connects a physical journey with writing, and here we see the associations between narrative and space that have been described by Michel de Certeau in his *Practice of Everyday Life*.[2] Whilst all literature, de Certeau says, is travel literature, having a trajectory (a plot), the Brutus story is also explicitly a travel narrative: a plot about a journey and settlement, a *leg*end (that which can be read) of landscape. The *Confessio Amantis* doesn't just describe this trajectory, it also re-enacts its symbolic significance through the act of writing in English. In alluding to the Brutus myth, Gower reproduces the etymologies of space – the study of the foreign derivation and historical development of Britain and, more particularly, London – which he found in the authoritative Latin histories, like Geoffrey of Monmouth's *Historia regum Britanniae*.[3] In this way Gower evokes a contemporary 'map' that locates London in temporal and geographical terms, in its relation to ancient Troy. Just as maps are a schematized and scientific representation of space, so the medieval

historians of national folklore offered an overview of all time that purported to be objective and all-encompassing. Gower, too, shows a penchant
for the totalizing map, seen for example in his interest in cosmological and
political science, those features of his verse that have left modern critics a
little uninterested.[4] For example, the Prologue of the *Confessio*, in both
versions, tackles synchronic (estates theory) and diachronic (the history of
empire) phenomena, homogenizing them onto a single plane. The *Confessio*, then, shares with the *Mirour de l'omme* and the *Vox clamantis*,
Gower's earlier poems, an interest in the 'encyclopedic *summa*'.[5] However,
in the *Confessio Amantis* this panoptic cartography becomes part of and is
disrupted by a conflicted autobiography; the trip up the Thames made by
Gower's narrator is a 'tour', a subjective account of the practice and poetry
of space, which jars with the comprehensive tabulation of the estates and
empires that it precedes – how does the narrator fit into the old social
orderings? The *Confessio* emerges as a dialectic between the 'two poles of
experience' – '"ordinary" culture and scientific discourse' – which de
Certeau has identified as alternative narratives of space.

Gower's estates theory, the 'scientific discourse' in the *Confessio*'s
Prologue, describes the body politic as a feature of the past, a past
inhabited by intrepid heroes like Brutus. What I am describing here is a
discrepancy, rather than an affinity between the Gower persona – an
inhabitant of the ordinary here and now – and Brutus – the Trojan
pioneer. Brutus is invoked as a figure separate from the narrator of the
Confessio's Prologue both in terms of time and also in the scope and
significance of his exploits; the narrator's parochial excursion up the river,
running just outside his front door, is a comic analogue in poor contrast
to Brutus' epic sea crossing to found a new civilization. Local and familiar
settings are mediocre in contrast to the exotic foreignness of classical
Troy, a discrepancy marked in both time and space. Contemporary
masculinity is homely in contrast to the adventurous masculinity of
the heroic past. At the same time, though, Brutus was not a wholly
uncomplicated figure, being a descendant of the traitor Aeneas and
part of the defeated Trojan diaspora. Troy itself, as Sylvia Federico has
argued, was not an uncontested precedent. Illium was at once a symbol of
past imperial glory and of doom, destroyed because of its inhabitants'
desirous excesses. Federico shows that this ambivalence was explicitly
understood in the English capital in the latter years of the fourteenth
century.[6]

Gower's narrator's identification with a somewhat cut-price hero, from
a culture destroyed by its own immoderation, associates him with flawed

masculinity and aberrant sexuality; Gower, thus, reveals his special interest in the imperfections of aristocratic manhood. The discrepancy comes not only between Gower's Prologue persona and Brutus but between those two – representatives in their different ways of compromised masculinity – and another group of intrepid travellers: the knights of medieval estates theory and the group described first in the estates taxonomy of the *Confessio*'s Prologue. In this chapter, I focus on Book IV and, in particular, its discussion of errant knighthood, a masculine model that Amans (Gower's narrator in the guise of a lover) rejects. I shall show that, in that rejection, Amans becomes 'errant' in another sense, being a representative of a new masculine modality: a dubious, homeless, undetermined and sometimes transgressive, indeed errant masculinity. The newness of social chaos – depicted in the Prologue – and the novelty of social and gendered categories conceived in that chaos, transforms this experiential, 'ordinary' and homely masculinity into something alien, foreign to the well-mapped categories presented by theoretical and holistic social models. However, in his critique of crusading and errantry, Amans also reveals the inadequacy of the old estates map drawn in the Prologue, questioning the universal relevance of the traditional gender paradigm of knighthood. Kurt Olsson has identified the homelessness of Gower's narrators both in the *Confessio* and his earlier work, the *Vox clamantis*, which Olsson argues is also concerned with 'place' (both geographical and social); I want to think about this errancy as a particular kind of vernacular masculinity that is newly confected in the altered social arrangements of post-Black Death England.[7] Elsewhere I have argued that Gower's in-between 'middel' spaces, to which he explicitly alerts his readership in an early manifesto in the Prologue and a summarizing coda in Book VIII, are the poetic expression of a cultural rite of passage in which traditional societal and gender categories were under review.[8] In particular, the demilitarization of the aristocracy and the laicization of England's central bureaucracy, processes which intensified in the period of the *Confessio*'s composition, abrogated the feudal estates taxonomy that was being anxiously revived and reiterated in the face of changes such as these. Gower himself, of course, has been located in those very nascent bourgeois and bureaucratic communities that were implicated in, but also commentators on, the discomfort caused by this perceived societal disruption.[9]

The transformation of late fourteenth-century England is at the heart of Gower's life writing. The *Confessio Amantis* is a travelogue of familiar places – the here, the self – made strange by cultural transition. It is appropriate that a bilingual text marks this introspective middleness; in the use of both Latin and English, the first-person narrator is fragmented by the unlike ways in which those languages were used, being sometimes written into a Latin gloss as a learned commentator, sometimes rendered a callow protagonist in the English narrative.[10] Further, if we see Amans' Confessor Genius – as James Simpson does – as 'Amans's own genius', their dialogue becomes a dramatization of the interior negotiations over the social conscience.[11] The subject of the *Confessio* is represented by a plurality of personae and protagonists, and it is in the spaces between them – 'strange' unmapped textual spaces – that I locate the autobiographical motive. It should be clear from this that I do not recognize the gulf, identified by critics like R. W. Hanning, between Gower's 'penitential poetic' and Chaucer's creative resistance to it as seen in, say, the confessional autobiographies of the Wife of Bath and the Pardoner.[12] Of course, Gower's subjective mode feels very different from Chaucer's, making little claim to verisimilitude; yet we know too that Chaucer's Wife generates, just like one of Gower's personae, only an illusion of authenticity. Gower's is a writerly kind of life writing that exposes the medieval conventions by which it is governed.[13] Gower explicitly strikes poses – as a lover, as a slothful man, as a conservative observer of social abuses – that simultaneously open experimental subjective space and place an indemnifying distance between the author and his personae. In this plural and knowing comedy is the urbanity of the bourgeois autobiographical subject. Whilst Hanning describes the Wife's 'symbolic identification with errant female sexuality, but also with the errant vernacular', I shall show that Gower's narrator, Amans, is similarly wayward in gendered terms and that his errancy disrupts the paradigmatic taxonomies that have so offended modern critical tastes.[14] My own view is most similar to that of Simpson, who has argued for the *Confessio* as a piece of life writing – he suggests *Bildungsroman*, I suggest travelogue – within which there is no stable authority figure and which is, as such, a much more interesting discussion of selfhood than is often acknowledged.[15]

The association between errant masculinity and the errant vernacular can be detected in the opening Latin verse of the *Confessio*:

> Torpor, ebes sensus, scola parua labor minimusque
> Causant quo minimus ipse minora canam:
> Qua tamen Engisti lingua canit Insula Bruti
> Anglica Carmente metra iuuante loquar.

[Sluggishness, dull wit, little schooling and least labour are the causes by which, I, least of all, shall sing of lesser things. Nevertheless in the tongue of Hengist by which the island of Brutus sang, with Carmentis' aid I will speak English verses.]

(Prologue, i, 1–2)

To occupy the same spaces as Brutus is as much as to use the same language as Hengist (another figure of not altogether creditable distinction, according to Geoffrey of Monmouth);[16] again Gower positions his Prologue narrator in a tradition of Englishness which is, although ancient, not altogether glorious. Nevertheless, the slothful vernacular writer stands in uncomfortable contrastive relation to these military action-figures and consequently his use of English – a language without the learned and aristocratic associations of Latin and French respectively – is duly accounted for with a humility topos whose sentiments are ubiquitous in Middle English literature. Yet whilst this kind of *diminutio* is common, Gower's particular use of this rhetorical standard is unusual, stressing not just a lack of learning but also of industry. The narrator encloses his claims about his intellectual incapacities and his poor education within the strangulating passivity and languid internal rhyme of 'Torpor ... labor minimusque'. However, the emphatic lethargy of the opening word 'Torpor' is oxymoronic and the spirited wordplay with which this verse continues – even where it is reflexively belittling – establishes the text's status not as the product of indolence but rather of hard *work*, exposing its craftedness along with the energy and skill of its creator.[17] Indeed, the language (Latin) in which they are composed playfully compromises the meaning of these lines and reveals the diligent application of the poet's erudition. In this way, although the narrator is presented, like the language he uses, as insufficient, he tacitly invites the reader to authorize him and his methods and to countenance, or at least entertain some of the social and poetical alternatives being proposed.

Not only does the narrator begin the *Confessio* with this avowal of his idleness, but Gower furnishes the work with an inert core: Book IV, in the middle of this eight-book work, also focuses on sloth. Further, sloth is Amans' central flaw and occupies the heart of his confession. Medieval poets often placed those things that were symbolically central at the physical heart of their poetry. Nicola McDonald has argued that this is true of Book V and I suggest that Book IV, being a related discussion of the economics of love, shares this distinction.[18] Book IV is conspicuous in other ways too. In this Book, Amans is at his most confessional; he is guiltier of *accedia* than of any other sin. At the centre of Book IV is its

longest section: a discussion of men-at-arms; again its literal placing hints
at its vital significance within the poem's cultural economy. Despite
having previously been circumspect about the legitimacy of crusading, in
Book III, in Book IV Genius proposes crusading and chivalry as
appropriate masculine ambitions and Amans refutes them; this is the only
place outside of Book VIII that the interlocutors come into a conflict of
this kind.[19] The *Confessio*, in adopting the dialogue format of Boethian
tradition, purports to split the first-person protagonist from any claim to
philosophical competence, apparently dividing the penitent from the
ethical code against which he is measured. However, the interlocutors'
falling out both exacerbates that split and also, crucially, discredits the
authority of both Amans and his confessor. The dispute over knighthood
reveals a narrator who is, unlike that of the *Consolatio*, unusually assertive
and partially convincing on the question of masculine ethics. Para-
doxically though, that assertiveness originates in his lack of valour, his
pusillanimity – the second branch of sloth.

It is in its discussion of sloth that the *Confessio* ever segregates male and
female error:

> Mi fader, as toward the Love
> Of Maidens forto telle trowthe,
> Ye have thilke vice of Slowthe,
> Me thenkth, riht wonder wel declared,
> That ye the wommen have noght spared
> Of hem that tarien so behinde.
> Bot yit it falleth in my minde,
> Toward the men hou that ye spieke
> Of hem that wole no travail sieke
> In cause of love upon decerte:
> To speke in wordes so coverte,
> I not what travaill that ye mente.
>
> (IV, 1596–607)

In turning his attention expressly to masculine indolence and industry,
Gower transforms the text, which is often implicitly phallocentric, into
one that is overtly about men and therefore the subjective concerns of its
male narrator. This gendered subjectivity is a new feature of the *Confessio*,
Gower's English work; an ostensibly similar discussion of sloth in the
Mirour de l'omme, for example, is not interested in the gendering of sin.[20]
It is no coincidence, in a culture experiencing a labour shortage, which
was universally preoccupied with questions of labour and social duty, that
this poem is most disrupted in those places that consider these same

questions. It is also no coincidence that Gower's life writing becomes most interior and subjective at the moment when it measures its narrator against culturally desirable models of masculine labour and finds him wanting. In a post-Black Death society, attempting to police a labour force that was increasingly mobile and self-confident, the narrator's nervousness about his occupation becomes as natural a subject of confession as sexuality;[21] indeed, anxiety about sloth and male sexual guilt are a cultural association not just in Gower's *Confessio* but in the London literature of the whole generation. Conservative responses to an invigorated work force were frequently couched in the language of sloth which was derived from sermon culture and penitential handbooks, the sort of manuals, in fact, that the advice form of the *Confessio Amantis* is designed to emulate.[22] The narrator is most verbose, linguistically energetic, when he is confessing his physical inactivity. Whilst Gregory M. Sadlek, who also thinks about the *Confessio* in terms of the late fourteenth-century labour crisis, has argued that Amans is an advocate of a new kind of proto-Humanist work-ethic based upon productivity, I shall argue that Amans is never so confident, the whole poem never so sure.[23] I shall show that, in this piece of 'travel literature', the narrator is repeatedly shown to be immobile and therefore outré (beyond the standard maps of masculine correctness) but that this opens imaginative reflexive spaces of frenetic interior exploration.

THE KNIGHT-ERRANT AND THE CARTOGRAPHY OF ARISTOCRATIC MASCULINITY

The *Confessio Amantis*, like so much late-medieval and, indeed, post-medieval literature, is sentimental about the masculine model of the knight-errant. The endorsement of the knight in the *Confessio* can be seen, for example, in the commendatory Latin verse that prefaces Book IV's men-at-arms section:

> Quem probat armorum probitas Venus approbat et quem
> Torpor habet reprobum reprobat illa virum.

[Venus approves of him whom probity of arms commends and the reprobate man whom torpor possesses she reproves.]

(IV, vi, 1–2)

In the second of these symmetrical lines, Gower places the man, 'virum', far from the state of 'torpor' that possesses him. In this way Gower locates slothfulness and masculinity at alternative, alienated poles. The juxtaposition of the knight and the lazy man hangs on a web of Venus's approval and censure – 'probat ... probitas ... approbat ... reprobum ... reprobat'. Genius goes on in the English couplets to draw a similar binary distinction between the knight-errant – the crusader – and the slothful, unmanly man. There seems to be no 'middel waye' for Genius in this matter. Although the 1390 date of the original dedication in the *Confessio Amantis* – by which time at least a first draft of the poem must have been written – coincided with a truce in the war with France, it was this European war, rather than more distant campaigns, which dominated the military agenda of the fourteenth century.[24] However, Genius proposes the following itinerary for the ambitious fame-seeking knight:

> So that be londe and ek be Schipe
> He mot travaile for worschipe
> And make manye hastyf rodes,
> Somtime in Prus, somtime in Rodes,
> And somtime into Tartarie;
>
>   (IV, 1627–31)

Gower chose to concentrate on the campaigning grounds in Prussia, Rhodes and 'Tartarie' because they were further away and because the journeys to them were more risky and more expensive: because crusaders were more stellar than their counterparts fighting in the more local war.

Fourteenth- and fifteenth-century nostalgia about knighthood has made it difficult for historians to assess how far there was a late-medieval chivalric revival, that is, how far chivalry, or crusading, was an 'actual' aristocratic practice and how far a literary construct and a romantic celebration of a socially anachronistic, but aesthetically enduring practice.[25] Whilst there is some evidence that fewer men were going on crusading expeditions, which were increasingly reserved for the elites – those who could afford the passage, the necessary equipment, and to leave their estates vulnerable to litigious neighbours for extended periods – no doubt this exclusivity gave the crusading knight a rarity value that increased his symbolic potency.[26] Notwithstanding the debate about how relevant chivalry and crusading were in the late fourteenth century, the appeal of the knightly idea always lay in its connection with, and its promise to reinstate, a past 'golden age'. Part of the palpable admiration for the knight in the *Confessio Amantis* is as an emblem of a lost time of feudal certainty. In this guise, the knight becomes part of another of Gower's 'maps'. After a dedicatory preface, Gower's Prologue launches into a wistful lament for the passing of an ordered feudal age – 'Tempus

preteritum ... beatum' [a previous blessed time] – which begins with a
nostalgic longing for a time when the knightly class was respected and
obeyed. This nostalgia drives Gower's verse into what has been described
by Winthrop Wetherbee as an 'encyclopedia of current prejudices and
ideals', repeatedly offering the same invective on the discrepancy between
holistic models and imperfect social practice.[27]

Historians have rightly concluded that the idea of chivalry still had a
powerful hold over the medieval imagination, in spite of the lack of clarity
about how such emotional responses translated into military practice.[28]
Part of the problem is that the knight-errant was not just a character from
popular romance; he was also a ready-made model in terms of which to
write the aristocratic self. Richard Barber has described the ways in which
medieval biographers frequently wrote the lives of knights in the terms of
the contemporary ideals of the estate.[29] When Geoffrey Luttrell, for
example, commissioned his famous Psalter – which, as others have noted,
is no mirror for everyday medieval life but rather a high-status artefact
with all its aristocratic values on display – he had himself represented as
the knight-errant; he is shown leaving the considerable comforts of his
marriage, family and estate – which are also illustrated in the manuscript –
grandly equipped and mounted, embarking for some unspecified campaign.[30] No doubt we are also intended to see Luttrell himself echoed in
the image of the crusader, an invocation of a previous and glorious age,
jousting with a blue-skinned Saracen and admire him for his military
courage and enthusiasm for foreign adventure.[31]

The peripatetic knight is also, of course, a construct that is developed
in medieval courtesy texts and the standard handbooks of chivalry – a
literature that also purports, however dubiously, to have some association
with lived practice.[32] Travel to the battlefront is described as crucial to the
education of an aristocratic man and considered, in some manuals at
least, to be a more significant marker of knighthood than the ceremonial
dubbing that is said to have ritualized the taking up of the right to bear
arms (although again historians are divided about how often these vigils
were actually undertaken).[33] For example Geoffroi de Charny, in his *Livre
de chevalrie*, places a stress on travel, beginning his account of ideal
chivalric practice with a discussion of the relative merits of local and
distant military expeditions.[34] There is an implicit assumption in de
Charny's *Livre* that younger knights will prove their military worth
locally before travelling to a distant campaign; travelling marks out social
adulthood. In Chaucer's *General Prologue* to *The Canterbury Tales*, the
Knight and Squire, who are identified as representatives of different

generations, as a father and son, are also differentiated by the places to which they have travelled; whilst the Knight is defined by his part in far-flung crusades in North Africa, the Baltic regions and Asia Minor, the Squire has a more modest service record in the French war (*GP*, 51–66 and 86). The *Confessio Amantis* is even less interested in the question of ritual dubbing than the *Mirour de l'omme* (*MO*, 23641–59) and moves the perfected knight as far away from the home as possible, locating him in 'strange londes' and 'sondri place' (IV, 1611 and 1614), using language which replicates the fascination with variety and exoticism found in de Charny's *Livre* which is admiring of those who journey through 'pluseurs paÿs estranges et lointains'.[35]

Indeed, although there is no direct evidence that Gower knew Charny's *Livre de chevalrie*, the *Confessio* appropriates the discursive and didactic features of the literature of conduct.[36] Book VII, for example, takes the theme of 'advice to princes' and is comprehensive in adumbrating the Aristotelian curriculum suitable for a young aristocratic man. In a study of Book VII of the *Confessio* and the mirror for princes tradition, M. A. Manzalaoui has identified Gower's interest, although crucially not an unquestioning one, in the 'encylopedic *summa*'.[37] Systematizing and tabulating knowledge under the headings of the different disciplines, Gower shows the predilection for taxonomy and comprehensiveness that he demonstrates in all his principal works. In so doing, his seventh Book reproduces the medieval notion of the episteme of resemblance, or the microcosm, attempting to educate the hegemonic man to be a miniature version of a holistic universe.[38] Chivalric handbooks in a parallel fashion – although they offered a different kind of syllabus – taught the gentle-born man to incorporate the whole geographical world into his preparation for manhood. Just in the way that Chaucer's Knight is a map of the cru-sading lands, and his superlative biography a collation of the furthest places, this kind of conduct literature provides a cartography of the hegemonic and indivisible masculine subject.[39] What is more, crusading, with its proselytizing purpose, was thought to finish the knight's educa-tion, not by affecting any change within the knight himself, but by absorbing the crusading lands into a homogenous, Christian corporation and transforming the world to reflect the ethics and wholeness of the knight. 'Whatever early maps were for, it was not for finding the way'; medieval maps represented the world in relation to the body of Christ, with Jerusalem at its symbolic heart, articulating the subjective ideologies of Christendom.[40] 'Cartography . . . was always the "science of princes"'[41] the crusader, like the cartographer, assembles the exotic and heterogeneous on one plane: that of his martial and social schooling.

The unity that the imperialist crusader attempts to bring to a plural world is also reflected in his moral and bodily integrity; regularly, the knight's sexuality is described in terms borrowed from religious discourses that were inflected by the standard medieval preference for virginity. It is no coincidence that a central characteristic of the ideal peripatetic knight is his clean, even chaste, sexuality: another feature of his inviolability.[42] Just as he is removed in social and physical terms from profane political conflicts or the quotidian banalities of home, he is also elevated beyond the sexual body into a devotional realm, where the beautiful but hygienic tropes of Marian devotion typify his relations with women. Ideal knightly lovers are refined and decorous, their masculine sexuality potent because it is treasured and dispensed selectively; they court their ladies, not through (in the medieval hierarchies of the senses) the potentially contaminating medium of touch, but through fame and good report broadcast through the air.[43] As chivalric writers like Geoffroi de Charny observed, knightly honour was enhanced by foreign travel, and honour was crucial in securing the admiration of women.[44] Genius describes the journey of the knight's reputation from the battlefield to his lady's ear; the knight himself pays, with 'gold and cloth', for its passage back via 'heraldz':

> So that these heraldz on him crie,
> – Vailant, vailant, lo, wher he goth! –
> And thanne he yifth hem gold and cloth,
> So that his fame mihte springe,
> And to his ladi Ere bringe
> Som tidinge of his worthinesse;
> So that sche mihte of his prouesce
> Of that sche herde men recorde,
> The betre unto his love acorde
> And danger pute out of hire mod,
> Whanne alle men recorden good,
> And that sche wot wel, for hir sake
> That he no travail wol forsake.
> (IV, 1632–44)

A knight must be fêted in public opinion and his honour suitably broadcast via the feudal networks of social obligation before his lady's consent to a union is given. Whilst Chaucer's Knight's journeys are his life-narrative, here the story of military honour – 'tidinge of his worthinesse' – goes travelling on the exemplary knight's behalf, crossing both physical distance and feminine inhibitions – 'danger'. By acquitting himself well on the battlefield, the knight writes himself into public estimation and so into his lady's heart. Spatially transcendent, the faultless knight colonizes his lady's heart at the same time as, and with the same acts by which, he colonizes those places he takes in military action; like the territory he conquers, her heart is drawn on his interior map. Medieval discourses that glamourized the ideal of the soldier who was sexually reserved were no doubt convenient for the medieval authorities who – mindful of the prevalent notion that sexual intercourse was physically draining and reduced pugnacity in men, and observant of the disruptiveness of inter-male rivalry and venereal disease – made repeated attempts to regulate, or prohibit, prostitution in military camps.[45] The problem of controlling the sexual behaviour of soldiers presumably contributed to, and was ameliorated by, the generation of positive discourses of knightly abstinence and distanced married love. Simultaneously, the spatial distances and the symbolic interconnections between home and war were made peculiar to models of aristocratic manhood, and young men were encouraged, not just to tolerate but also to embrace this socially convenient dichotomy – aspects of a 'required masculinity' – on the promise of social renown.[46]

In the *Confessio*, the model knight's distance from, but devotion to, his lady is also his link to ancient legend, as he comes to imitate the narratives, the journeys of the heroes in the old books. The old books are pressed into the service of medieval ideologies just as surely as foreign places were colonized by the crusading hosts; as de Certeau notes: 'readers are travellers; they move across lands belonging to someone else, like nomads poaching their way across fields they did not write, despoiling the wealth of Egypt to enjoy it themselves'.[47] Ulysses finally accepts his obligation to respond to the Achaean draft 'be him lief or loth' (IV, 1889) despite his desire to 'duelle stille / At home' with Penelope; he is tricked into dropping his pretence of insanity through an appeal to his paternal instincts when Telemachus, his son, is placed in the furrow he has sown with salt and before the plough he has yoked to a pair of foxes.[48] In swerving to avoid the boy, he reveals his good sense and is forced to recognize his military obligations overseas; his inalienable domestic instincts are inextricably bound up with, rather than being alternatives to, his martial honour. Just as in the passage cited above, Genius says that women must understand that men's military roles are not a contrast to, but are rather a confirmation of, their domestic and romantic circumstances. Men must manage the competing claims made on them in order to replicate the ideal of knightly manhood, whilst women, in the *Confessio* at least, are not pulled in different directions in the same way; women are unified in place, remaining static in the home and their 'occupacion' in love is understood as a straightforward imperative to marry and to mother a dynasty. Aristocratic men are expected, Genius says, to forge whole selves by balancing the responsibilities they have in diverse places. By acknowledging the equality and interdependence of his domestic and foreign responsibilities, in spite of their spatial separateness, Ulysses shows that his madness is only feigned and that he is really right and whole.

Again, by way of illustration of this exemplary balance, when Ulysses' duties are done he is described as hurrying home to Ithaca without procrastination (Gower was unacquainted with the Homeric story of his meandering journey through the Aegean). Penelope's letter to Ulysses, which reaches him in Troy, urges him not to waste paper with writing and to return to her without a slothful delay. Whilst women, stationary in the household, are entitled to correspond with their husbands (providing that they don't, like Laodomie, unreasonably ask them to abandon their combat responsibilities), men must dispense with writing – never substituting words for their own selves – and make the 'viage / Homward', following, presumably, the active reports about them that have travelled back on the grapevine. There are two other *exempla*, those of Dido and Phyllis, in which women are permitted to correspond in writing, while their partners, Aeneas and Demephon, who are expected to respond in person, slothfully fail to do so, resulting in the suicides of both women. Men of arms are best represented by the spoken rather than the written word, by a proximate rather than a distant act of communication; there should be no discrepancy between the masculine self and the body, the knight's deed and his word.

TEARING UP THE MAP

It is curious that the *Confessio* does not consider the French campaign as part of an honourable military service record, particularly given the way in which that campaign is preferred to those in 'Prus' and 'Tartarie', or 'Espruce et Tartarie', in the *Mirour de l'omme* (*MO*, 23895).[49] The narrator of Gower's earlier poem describes the crusading knight and the man who will not take up arms as equally culpable of wicked practice, and he provides an honourable alternative in the knight who seeks honour in France (*MO*, 23671). Indeed, of the crusader he remarks: 'ainz a sojour / Assetz te valt meulx reposer' [indeed, I think you could better have stayed at home] (*MO*, 23927–8). Furthermore, Genius's notion of the crusading knight paying for his own publicity, giving garments and money to the heralds (which I cited above), is exactly that used in the *Mirour* to condemn the vainglory of the proud knight:

> Si tu d'orguil voes travailler
> Pour vaine gloire seculer,
> Dont soietz le superiour
> Des autres, lors t'estuet donner
> Ton garnement et ton denier
> As les heraldz, qu'il ta valour
> Et ta largesce a grant clamour
> Facent crier; car si l'onour
> Ne voet celle part aider,
> Lors je ne say quoy ton labour
> Te puet valoir

[If you will work in pride for worldly vainglory, whereby you may be superior to the others, then you must give your garments and your wealth to the heralds, so that they may proclaim with great clamour your valour and largess. But if honour is unwilling to aid you in this, I do not know what your labours can be worth to you.]

(MO, 23917–27)

Already, Gower's earlier poem is thinking of knighthood as a kind of labour – 'travailler', 'labour' – and thus prepares it for inclusion in the sloth section of the later *Confessio*. However, in Book IV of the *Confessio*, Amans is not given the option of identifying himself with the more moderate figure of the knight fighting in wars countenanced by the *Mirour* – wars in France, Lombardy and Spain (*MO*, 23714). Like the narrator of the *Mirour*, and indeed Genius of Book III, Amans rejects crusading, although on slightly different grounds. The *Mirour* narrator complains, more in the spirit of chivalric manuals written by clerics like Raimon Lull than soldiers like de Charny, that the desires to win honour and a lady's heart are worldly rather than godly concerns; he is also perturbed by the exploitative plundering practised by the conquering, errant knight, which was a widespread fear of moral commentators.[50]

Amans contests the rectitude of crusading on both romantic and religious grounds. First, he argues against the logic of leaving home in order to win a lady; he is unconcerned about the worldliness of the romantic ambition in itself. Secondly, and on similar lines to Genius's own critique of crusading in Book III (2490–515), he contests the notion that pacifist Christian doctrine can be disseminated by violent means. Thus he disputes the whole logic of crusading rather than, as the *Mirour* narrator does, the motives of individual, glory-hunting knights. Amans' pacifism has been taken seriously by a generation of modern critics and historians who have concentrated on his lucid objections to religious warfare.[51] Amans' protestation that killing the infidel is no way to further the philosophy of Christ is a much quoted example of the kind of reassessments that were being made about warfare and what it could achieve. Indeed, Amans' reasoning has been identified as the view of John Gower himself, an identification in part achieved, as Elizabeth Siberry has shown, by homogenizing the arguments set out in the early poems the *Mirour de l'omme* and *Vox clamantis*, in the *Confessio*, and in the later English ballad 'In Praise of Peace'.[52] The ballad, for example, sets itself against the French war and suggests that knights who really cannot contain their energies ('sholde algate wexe wrothe') should direct it against 'The Sarazins, whiche unto Crist be lothe' (PP, 249–50); this is a begrudging tolerance, not the outright denunciation of crusading that appears in the *Confessio*. There is a debate, full of contradictions, both between and within Gower's poems, about war and peace. It is that debate, rather than a straightforward pacifism, which establishes Gower, along with Chaucer, as part of an urbane, bureaucratic and literary group that questioned foreign policy from their knowledge of domestic administration.[53] The historiographical discussion about whether or not chivalry was an outmoded practice in this period must surely reflect the equivocation of contemporary commentators, like Gower, who are at once enamoured by the idea of knighthood and yet sceptical as to the rectitude of any particular and actual campaign.[54] Certainly, critiques of the Hundred Years' War and its effects on domestic society and institutions had, since the composition of the *Mirour de l'omme*, become keener; perhaps the silence on the subject of the French war of the *Confessio* expresses this growing doubt about that campaign, but it is a doubt that leaves the question of knighthood much more contested than it is in the *Mirour*.[55]

Amans does not see how the immediate religious and military successes of crusading can deliver a romantic prize:

> For this I telle you in schrifte,
> That me were levere hir love winne
> Than Kaire and al that is ther inne:
> And forto slen the hethen alle,
> I not what good ther mihte falle,

So mochel blod thogh ther be schad.
This finde I writen, hou Crist bad
That noman other scholde sle.
What scholde I winne over the Se,
If I mi ladi loste at hom?
(IV, 1656–65)

Amans separates out military and romantic conquests in a way that his Confessor does not, and expresses a desire to concentrate his energies on love without undertaking a heroic physical journey. Amans rejects the glamour of errantry in favour of a unity of place. However, whilst Amans puts a forceful case when he measures the treasures of Cairo, won through un-Christian and brutal means, against his potential winning of his lady's affections, his argument is expressed diffidently; the narrator, in emphasizing the word 'schrifte', draws guilty attention to his feelings of inadequacy and the model of the perfect knight is rejected in favour of a less glamorous recourse to static courtship.

Because Genius sets up a simple dyad of crusading knight and slothful man, by rejecting crusading Amans becomes identified with the cowardly, errant man who is just as sharply condemned in the *Mirour*. In particular, the earlier poem is scathing about those amongst the gentle-born who stay at home to keep themselves safe and yet still use their social position to get themselves an advantage in law, in business and in legal office (e.g. *MO*, 23701–6); those, the narrator makes clear, ought rather to be occupational sidelines that are complementary to a traditional knightly, martial role. In short, the critique in the *Mirour* is concerned about the corruption of traditional estates:

Ce sciet cascuns en son endroit
Par tout le monde, quelq'il soit,
Qui tient estat en ceste vie,
S'il a son point ne se pourvoit,
Ainçois s'esloigne et se forsvoit,
Qant il ad fait l'apostazie,
Ja puis n'ad guarde de folie

[For everyone knows throughout the world – whoever he may be – that whoever has an estate in this world and does not prepare himself for his estate but rather separates himself and wanders away from it, when he has committed the apostasy he never afterwards keeps himself away from folly.]

(*MO*, 23809–15)

The reluctant knight's rejection of his natural place, his wholesale adoption of a tertiary sector occupation, is imagined as a religious error and physical straying – 'l'apostazie', 'esloigne'. In Book IV of the *Confessio*, Genius makes the lazy man into the antithesis of the perfect crusader, an example that the *Mirour* had earlier condemned. In this way, Genius remakes the crusader as an indubitably positive masculine model, cleansing him of the mud thrown at him in the *Mirour* and overruling the moral objections raised about him in the previous book of the *Confessio*. In rejecting the standard ideal put to him by Genius and with no mid-way alternative, Amans is compromised by exactly the same errancy of which the passage from the *Mirour* above complains. In this way, Gower represents his narrator as inadequate in contrast to a reformed masculine idea, and gives him none of the authority of his previous narrator in the *Mirour de l'omme*, even, by so doing, compromising his objections to crusading that critics have so admired and assumed to be so close to Gower's heart.

At odds with the anxieties of the *Confessio*'s Prologue, Amans confesses to being quite unlike the model legendary knight; Lachesse, a personification of procrastination, the first branch of sloth, continually tempts him, Amans says, to write to his lady rather than approaching her directly:

> He [Lachesse] seide, 'An other time is bettre;
> Thou schalt mowe senden hire a lettre,
> And per cas wryte more plein
> Than thou be Mowthe durstest sein.'
>
> (IV, 37–40)

In this way Lachesse attempts to drive a physical space between Amans and his written representation of himself, a space inadequately substituted for that which divides the two balanced halves of the good knight's identity. Procrastination falsely convinces Amans that he might write himself quite 'plein', sending him to fret over the inevitable variance between the self and language, a discrepancy that never troubles a knight like Ulysses who curtails it with his immediate, embodied approach to love-communication. Amans' anxiety about semantic slippage is represented as a lack of valour in the word 'durstest', which again contrasts the physically immobile and emotionally divided narrator from the peripatetic but internally intact soldier. The divergence between Amans and the masculine model of the knight is tellingly couched in the discourses of sloth; Amans weakly represents himself as a symbol of compromised masculinity. In debased times – described in the Prologue as the transition from a golden head to feet of clay in the *exemplum* of

Nebuchadnezzar's dream – troubled by widespread idleness, it is appropriate that the narrator's insufficiency is founded on his slothfulness.

While some critics have described Amans as effeminate, and while Amans may seem to resemble many of the spatially and emotionally rigid, letter-writing women in Book IV (like Dido and Penelope), I suggest that Amans is, rather, a representative of an alternative kind of masculinity which Gower wryly poses as a puny rival to the authoritative and established image of the knight-errant.[56] I shall suggest in the rest of this section that this alternative – a kind of *urbanitas*, a city-based and middling masculinity – while it appropriated, although not without parody, some of the courtly aesthetic traditions, was also self-fashioning, devising new ethical possibilities with new 'masculine plots' that were expressed in a new medium: English poetry.[57] Amans' rejection of knighthood is not singular in this period but conforms to changes taking place within both military ranks and the higher echelons of English society. The number of knights in the English army declined with some rapidity, a process that was mirrored by a steadier trend in society more generally.[58] The financial and administrative burdens of knighthood have been described as deterring men of good families from undergoing the formalities of dubbing.[59] This failure to seek admission into the orders of knighthood is accounted for by the economic pragmatism of a social group that was under increasing financial pressure, in the later fourteenth century, especially as the price of land fell in response to the demographic shifts of the previous decades. The demilitarization of the gentle-born was also indicative of a financial realism about the potentially sizable losses that might be incurred by those going to war, for which loot from Cairo or anywhere else could not compensate. Furthermore, there is also evidence, from distraint cases for example, to suggest that others who might have qualified for knighthood on the basis of their landed wealth were careful to evade the honour.[60]

Gower's *bios*, which has been pieced together by John Fisher, gives us a speculative, alternative 'masculine plot' of the kind that might have been open to the men who were unwilling to apply for the right to bear arms.[61] This exploratory life narrative suggests the plasticity not only of social category but also of the use of space. This is instructive, not necessarily in terms of locating the 'real' John Gower in order to identify him definitively with his narrator Amans (indeed, it is rather in the dialogue between Amans and Genius that I locate the autobiographical motive), but rather in locating the wider social and cultural conditions in which the *Confessio* was produced. Fisher assembles evidence that the poet, despite having a background that would have qualified him for knight-hood, preferred to remain an *esquire*, the title given him on his tomb at Southwark cathedral. Gower, Fisher speculates, came from a Kentish gentry family. His near relative Sir Robert Gower, with whom he may have lived as a child, was a retainer to the Earl of Atholl and married to Margaret Mowbray, the daughter of Sir Philip de Mowbray, the ancestor of the later dukes of Norfolk. Many of Gower's associates and business contacts, with whom he appears in the documentary evidence of his life, were of aristocratic stock. It has been suggested by Fisher that Gower's eschewing of knighthood was a conscious refusal of a crucial medieval rite of passage, a choice that seems to accord with a trend amongst other men socialized in similar ways at this time. It is thought that Gower was a lawyer of sorts; his poetry certainly exploits the effect of using legalese, and especially the language of property law, in unusual ways and at surprising moments.[62] The expansion of the central administration and the tertiary sector evidently supplied alternative livings for men loath to follow the routes that their fathers had traditionally taken.

These alternative occupations were quasi-clerical; they were jobs that had previously been undertaken by clerics, who were still largely responsible for the training of newer recruits. During the late fourteenth century there was a period of laicization that saw an influx of secular men into the central administration. As Glenn Burger has noted in his study of Geoffrey Chaucer, these positions, being neither fully clerical nor wholly secular, produced a novel, hybrid identity, an identity that he finds articulated by the many bourgeois Canterbury pilgrims and made man-ifest in their queer relationship to orthodox gender paradigms of the period.[63] Burger might have added that the curious aspect of these middling bureaucratic identities, in terms of medieval social theory and category, was the disparity between occupational and sexual identity; whilst these literate professions had previously been classified as those of the chaste religious (although in practice no doubt there had always been a body of secular clergy), married or, perhaps more confusingly, never-married bureaucrats looked as if they ought to be classed with the first estate on account of their occupation but with the second or third on account of their sexual or marital status. It is thought that Gower insisted on apartments in the priory at St Mary's Overie in Southwark after financing its restoration in 1377. As Fisher has noted: 'one might suppose that Gower would not have chosen an apartment in a priory if he wanted a normal domestic establishment'.[64] It is also thought that Gower was either a widower or, more likely, a never-married man at the time of the writing of the *Confessio*, although he was later to marry Agnes Groundolf in 1398. As an unmarried but secular man in a monastic house located in one of London's most notorious red-light districts, Gower did not replicate the standard pattern of contemporary residency.[65] Instead, in the speculative narrative of his life, Gower is an architect of individually determined and 'middel' spaces just as he is, as we shall see, the author of figment architecture in his poetry and a producer of a liminal poetic tone.

In the *Confessio Amantis* Gower is, of course, explicit about his 'middel waye' between, he says, 'lust and lore' and 'earnest and game'; in opening up strange indeterminate, intermediate and unmapped textual spaces, he constructs within the poem the autobiographical motive: the social indeterminacy of his bureaucratic *milieu*. Anne Middleton, along with other critics, has characterized Gower's halfway world as 'bourgeois moderation': a satisfactory and comfortable median.[66] However, this is a period in which middling ethics were still being formulated and Gower's 'middel waye' is rather the uncertain space between 'tuo stoles' (IV. 627), falling between the fixed points of the holistic social taxonomy, the map, which is set out in the Prologue's estates theory. Estates theory, as Ruth Mohl has noted, was being anxiously restated in a time of labour crisis; numerous legal and cultural productions – *Zeitgeist* texts like, for example, the Statute of Labourers and the *Vision of Piers Plowman* – asserted the importance of natal estates and their concomitant occupational categories in the restoration of social order.[67] Gower himself was a sharp critic of the commons, most especially in the first part of *Vox clamantis*, and joined with many of his contemporaries in asserting the need for a disciplined workforce. But elsewhere this invective against labour disruption was not only directed at the ordinary workers: it was also a critique of their employers and of the failure of traditional forms of authority to maintain order. In the context of a culture obsessed by the necessity of labour to economy, society and polity, pre-existing discourses that used the language of work and idleness took on new meanings. This heightened sensitivity deepened, for example, the ironies in the portraits of idle, aristocratic aesthetes; ironies that became so understood that satirists needed only to gesture at them superficially in order to hit their mark. When Langland, for example, depicts a knight 'courteisliche' (C, VIII, 161) and therefore ineffectively requesting that Waster and his cronies get back to their labours, he encapsulates in one word a bitter appraisal of an aristocracy enfeebled by its refined sensibilities and codified forms of etiquette. The figure of the *lovesick* aristocrat, more particularly, embodied these failures, and Amans is certainly in dialogue with his literary precursors of this type. Indeed, as Sadlek has noted, the aristocratic love literature traditions, which stressed idleness as one of the lover's main qualifications, threatens to destabilize the whole of Book IV's premise: its investigation of the sin of idleness in love.[68]

The ironic play that this enabled is nowhere more evident than in the figure of Chaucer's Troilus, who is a clear antecedent to the figure of Amans; indeed, the narrator fantasizes about reading *Troilus and Criseyde* with his lady (IV, 2795). Sadlek has shown the ways in which Chaucer augmented the lexicon of sloth and labour – words like 'werk', 'business', 'service' and so on – beyond what he found in Boccaccio's *Il filostrato*, the main source for *Troilus and Criseyde*.[69] Here Troilus is given the speech that most profoundly challenges his own construction:

> 'Allas,' quod he, 'thus foul a wrecchednesse,
> Whi suffre ich it? Whi nyl ich it redresse?
> Were it nat bet atones for to dye
> Than evere more in langour thus to drye?
> 'Why nyl I make atones riche and pore
> To have inough to doone er that she go?
> Why nyl I brynge al Troie upon a roore?
> Whi nyl I slen this Diomede also?
> Why nyl I rather with a man or two
> Stele hire away? Whi wol I this endure?
> Whi nyl I helpen to myn owen cure?'
>
> (*T&C*, V, 39–49)

Georgia Ronan Crampton has argued that with these words Troilus becomes a forerunner of many modern critics who, railing against Chaucer's passive protagonist, describe him as slothful and inordinately *langour*ous.[70] Whilst these critics find Troilus an impotent and effeminate hero, others have argued that Troilus is a model of courtly grace, whose affectivity and cultural finesse prevent him from displaying a pronounced masculine sexuality.[71] Troilus is, of course, somewhere between these two critical models, indeed between 'game and ernest' (*T&C*, III, 254), between satire and tragedy and, in fact, in the same middle ground occupied by Amans.

Amans delivers a long justification of himself in Book IV (1122–224), defensively proving his diligence in love, of which the following is a small excerpt. It is characteristic of the whole section from which it comes in its deployment of the language of labour and idleness:

> Thus hath sche fulliche overcome
> Min ydelnesse til I sterve,
> So that I mot hire nedes serve,
> For as men sein, nede hath no lawe.
> Thus mot I nedly to hire drawe,
> I serve, I bowe, I loke, I loute,
> Min yhe folweth hire aboute,
> What so sche wole so wol I,
> Whan sche wol sitte, I knele by,
> And whan sche stant, than wol I stonde:
> Bot whan sche takth hir werk on honde
> Of wevinge or enbrouderie,
> Than can I noght bot muse and prie
> Upon hir fingres longe and smale,
> And now I thenke, and now I tale,
> And now I singe, and now I sike,
> And thus mi contienance I pike.
>
> (IV, 1164–80)

This speech can be seen to share something with Troilus's cited above, echoing its agonistic repetitions and reproducing those heavily patterned rhythms that vary just slightly for most emotive impact; for example, the way that the recurrent phrase 'And now I . . .' flattens into 'And thus mi', might be likened to the way in which the anaphora 'Whi nyl I . . . ?' is exchanged for 'Whi wol I . . . ?' in the passage from *Troilus and Criseyde*. Just as Troilus's is sometimes, Amans' love service is hyperbolic and absurd. Whilst musing, watching and mimicking his lady's gestures, Amans claims to be hard at work. His attentive industry is an inversion whose irony is deepened by the lady's needle*werk*. The traditional maxim 'need hath no lawe' was conventionally used to justify those crimes committed for survival and is found prominently in texts – like *Piers Plowman* – which were invested in contemporary ideologies of labour; in the *Confessio* it is used flippantly to convey a sense of melodramatic earnestness.[72] These histrionics are summarized in the rhyme on 'sterve' and 'serve' and are only compounded by the reiteration of the word 'nede' and its adjectival and adverbial forms.

Although Amans has often been compared to Troilus, and although he shares many of his attributes, his rejection of crusading and, therefore, of knighthood makes him considerably more problematic.[73] He takes from his Chaucerian precursor the indolence and heightened affectivity of the aristocratic lover (along with Chaucer's topography of the household), whilst leaving behind the military identity (along with the siege setting).

Whilst Troilus's knightly countenance riding back from battle intoxicates Criseyde (*T&C*, II, 651), Amans has only one mode: at his lady's heel, paralysed by his desire for her. If critics like Arlyn Diamond have argued that the ideal of the lovesick aristocrat was already an archaism by the time of Chaucer's writing *Troilus and Criseyde*, how much more out of time it looks in the later poem, the *Confessio Amantis*, in which the protagonist can no longer lay claim to a chivalric identity of any kind, however contested.[74] For Amans rejects, in a way that Troilus does not, the martial identity that would ameliorate and contextualize his amorous sensibilities. His love service is never, as Troilus's is, counterbalanced by a political or martial part in an epic siege; unlike Troilus he is not Mars-like – who is, of course, both a bellicose and amorous deity. With no public duties or patriotic responsibilities, Amans describes himself as static within his lady's household, entertaining her servants and pets while she, who does have alternative work, 'besien hire on other things' (IV, 1183). Indeed, I suggest that Amans is much more reminiscent of Chaucer's Pandarus, the prototype of the industrious bourgeois man who, in spite of all his 'busyness', never gets the girl.[75] Amans becomes, then, a parody of an aristocratic lover who, in rejecting Genius's call to arms and without any other kind of occupation outside of his love service, is a pathfinder in a way that Troilus is not, exploring new modalities, having cut himself free from, or at least rejected orthodox social categories.

Sarah Stanbury has charted the 'movement to privacy' in Chaucer's *Troilus and Criseyde*, arguing that Troilus's retreat from the temple, in Book I, into the 'inner redoubt' of the household, chamber and bed, is matched by his recoiling into himself, depicted with the memorable image of Troilus as a snail retracting his horns. This retreat is, she says, exacerbated or caused by Troilus's being an object of the gaze of the other – the Trojan crowds and, of course, Criseyde.[76] Amans' interior drama in Book IV moves in a similar trajectory: from the 'chapelle' (IV, 1137) to household space, first the lady's, and then, when he is ejected, his own chamber and bed. However, Amans' emotional experience is not produced by his objectification and Amans has no interactive other: the lady is disinterested and his public non-existent.

Whilst the reader of *Troilus and Criseyde* is regularly privy to a secret space (a space we shall also find in the construction of Amans) between Troilus's face and his heart, in him the face of knightly equanimity and a masquerade of self-control consistently cover the tumult of his interior desires:

But Troilus, though as the fir he brende
For sharp desir of hope and of plesaunce,
He nought forgat his goode governaunce.

But in hymself with manhod gan restreyne
Ech racle dede and ech unbridled cheere,
That alle tho that lyven, soth to seyne,
Ne sholde han wist, by word or by manere,
What that he ment, as touchyng this matere.
From every wight as fer as is the cloude
He was, so wel dissimilen he koude.
(T&C, III, 425–34)

The rather beautiful simile of the distant cloud expresses the difference between Troilus and Amans: whilst Troilus has some absurd moments, Amans never countervails his absurdity with such dignity. Without a loyal servant like Pandarus, Amans is subject to the day-to-day humiliations of love service. Further, Amans' affections are never requited, whilst Troilus achieves some success, albeit tragically ephemeral. In the *Confessio Amantis*, Gower's authoritative, caustic attack on the commons from the *Vox clamantis* is replaced with a somewhat sheepish comedy of aristocratic fecklessness; this substitution articulates the difference between the confidence and the subjective errancy associated with composing in Latin and English respectively.

WANDERLUST

For overal, where as sche goth,
Min herte folwith hire aboute.
(IV, 670–1)

After a Prologue which treats all social categories of men and all human history – both the synchronic and diachronic, although phallocentric world – Book I opens with an admission from the narrator and confirmation from the marginal gloss that he is ill placed, being rooted to the ground, to provide an account of the universe:

I may noght strecche up to the hevene
Min hand, ne setten al in evene
This world, which evere is in balance:
It stant noght in my sufficance
So grete thinges to compasse,
Bot I mot lete it overpasse

And treten upon othre thinges.
Forthi the Stile of my writinges
Fro this day forth I thenke change
And speke of thing is noght so strange,
Which every kinde hath upon honde,
And wherupon the world mot stonde,
And hath don sithen it began,
And schal whil ther is any man;
And that is love, of which I mene
To trete, as after schal be sene.

(I, 1–16)

This is a self-conscious passage that is ostensibly about writing 'Stile', charting a transition from writing about the *world* to writing about *love*. However, the passage imagines 'writinges' in metaphors of the writer's body. The narrator describes his previous poetry, the Prologue perhaps, as a vain attempt to reach into the sky and right a world askew, ordering and homogenizing its imbalances. Just as his poetry cannot be about everything, so he cannot, himself, incorporate everything within his own skin. In contrast he proposes to continue by writing about love, a more mundane thing, a thing that is at hand, can be held in the hand or is, perhaps, manifest on the skin itself. In the image of the 'thing . . . noght so strange' held in the hand, the narrator limits himself to those themes which he *can* map and miniaturize, the familiar experience of love that is common to all 'kinde'. The narrator's previous ambition, his attempt to be like God – or, perhaps, the ideal crusader – and increase his own stature in order to embody the universe, transmutes only into another, newer ambition to domesticate that universe; although pocket-sized, love represents the whole of nature, 'every kinde', and history from creation to apocalypse: 'And hath . . . / And schal'.

In his capitulation over the 'grete thinges', the themes of the Prologue, the narrator acknowledges his masculine incapacity (his in*sufficance*). This is where his theme of love originates: in a community capsized and the narrator's own concomitant interior disruption. For love is no contrast to, but rather an interiorization of this mayhem and a state 'In which ther can noman him reule, / For loves lawe is out of reule' (I, 17–18), reinforced with the recycled word 'reule' in the rhyme position. Although, as the Prologue testifies, the experience of social imbroglio causes no small anxiety, it provides the narrator with a pretext for exploring the rhizomal possibilities, the erotic and romantic fantasies it presents. The *Confessio Amantis* experiments with poetic geographies, new ways of mastering the environment, new ways of being powerful and masculine which might rival traditional masculine paradigms. At the same time, though, those attempts at dominance and masculine authority, attempts at a new cartography, are predicated upon the divided and subjective self, producing 'tours', accounts of urban space as it manifests itself in the narrator's fantasies.

In the section of the Prologue on the decline of the knights' authority, Gower's narrator finds that in the heroic past the interior self and the body were an indivisible whole and that there was no discrepancy between language and its intent:

> Of mannes herte the corage
> Was shewed thanne in the visage;
> The word was lich to the conceite
> Withoute semblant of deceite
> (Prologue, 111–14)

In contrast, the present phonier times are characterized by widespread hypocrisy:

Nuncque latens odium vultum depingit amoris,
Paceque sub ficta tempus ad arma tegit
[And today hidden hatred portrays a face of love, and an age at arms is hidden beneath feigned peace.]

(Prologue, ii, 7–8)

The passage of time has effected the physical separation, the insertion, of a space between the face and the heart, representation and reality, the persona and the self. Gower recounts, with some suspicion, an increasing 'movement to privacy' within the self. Given his suspicion of interior privacy and dissimulation and, especially, the impersonation of love, it is curious to find Gower's reflexive writing adopting a similar pretence. The Latin marginalia to Book I, for example, declares:

Hic quasi in persona aliorum, quos amor alligat, fingens se auctor esse Amantem, varias, eorum passiones variis huius libri distinccionibus per singula scribere proponit.

[Here the author, imagining himself to be the Lover as if in the character of those others whom love binds, proposes to write about their various passions one by one in the various sections of this book.]

(I, 59ff)

The narrator takes on the 'persona' of a *romantic* lover, but the Prologue's social invective, cited above, defines love in its broadest terms (as Christian peace and harmony, contrasting them with hate and war). This common love comes to be conflated with *eros* and, as such, the complaint seems to compromise the author's pretended representation of himself as a lover.[77] In the adjective 'ficta', cited in the passage from the Prologue above, is an echo of the participle 'fingens', used in the Book I marginalia to describe the narrator's adoption of the guise – 'persona' or 'vultum' – of love. The narrator becomes a representative rather than just an observer of contemporary disruption and, splintered into several personae who commentate at a number of different levels, he makes no claim to have a 'visage' which reveals his 'corage' like the knights of old. Gower makes little claim to the verisimilitude of his personae, whether a knowing glossator, a naïve lover or conservative decrier of contemporary ills, and similarly shatters the usual purported correlation between the author (the 'corage') and the version of himself (the 'visage') he presents to the world through the text.

Slothfulness makes a space for this experimentation, creating an intriguing dislocation between a body ('visage') in stasis and a heart ('corage') loose in a fantasy cityscape in which it is confined neither by gravity nor by architectural impediment. Various trance-like and torpid states punctuate this poem and the narrator describes them as a divergence between his body and his wits, his outer and inner selves:

> And thus thenkende thoghtes fele,
> I was out of mi swoune affraied,
> Wherof I sih my wittes straied,
> And gan to clepe hem hom ayein.
> And whan Resoun it herde sein
> That loves rage was aweie,
> He cam to me the rihte weie,
> And hath remued the sotie
> Of thilke unwise fantasie,
> Wherof that I was wont to pleigne,
> So that of thilke fyri peine
> I was mad sobre and hol ynowh.
> (VIII, 2858–69)

This is an intriguing spatial representation of the relationship between the body and the self that deploys the image of the narrator standing at the threshold of a 'hom' calling in his errant 'wittes' as if they were a lost pet or a child. It also reflects the multivocality of Gower's reflexive voice; there are at least three personae present in this passage: a physical bodily self; a stray, fantasizing self and another with the power to unify the two. This latter 'self' may also be related to the somewhat Langlandian figure of Reason in this passage: an external personification of an interior faculty and yet another version of the narrator. Reason polices the return of a truant, idle and errant self. The poem's ending, of which this passage is a small excerpt, professes to effect a unification of the multiple narrators and the author in the single figure of 'John Gower' – 'I was mad sobre and hol ynowh' (VIII, 2869) – whom Alastair Minnis discerns as the *auctor* of the Latin marginalia.[78] But we might read the ending, in which the narrator is refused entry to the Court of Venus and drops his inappropriate romantic suit, as a palinode rather like that in Chaucer's *Troilus and Criseyde*; Troilus's objectivity in the eighth sphere turns the world into a totalizing map which unconvincingly obviates the moving appeal of the fragmented sexual subject, the living Troilus.[79] The narrator's discovery of his old age in Book VIII of the *Confessio* is a convenient one; his retirement mitigates the narrator's admission of his sloth and his romantic failures. Indeed, as Manzalaoui has shown, the ending of the *Confessio* is written in 'the spirit of *retraccioun*', of the kind that is familiar, of course, from Chaucer's poetry.[80]

However, this ending does nothing to efface the daring explorations of the truant heart. It is in Book IV and also some sections of Book V – that other midway Book – that the reader is shown the wanderings of the absent self (often referred to as the heart), while the physical self, incapacitated by sloth, becomes a static and vacant 'hom'. In particular Amans confesses to being fearful, to being guilty of the second branch of sloth: pusillanimity. This is the kind of sloth that the Confessor says is most incommensurate with 'manhed' and most confounds 'mannes werk'. Words associated with manhood and manliness are as much about virility as nobility in the Middle Ages and, as such, they convey a heady combination of associations in Gower's verse.[81]

In a confession which anticipates (and probably provides a source for) T. S. Eliot's J. Alfred Prufrock, Amans says that he is scared by the strength of his own desires and the reception that they might receive, asking 'Do I dare / Disturb the universe?':[82]

> Mi fader, I am al beknowe
> That I have ben on of tho slowe,
> As forto telle in loves cas.
> Min herte is yit and ever was,
> As thogh the world scholde al tobreke,
> So ferful, that I dar noght speke
> Of what pourpos that I have nome,

> Whan I toward mi ladi come,
> Bot let it passe and overgo.
>
> (IV, 355–63)

This fear of rupturing the world leads Amans into another kind of idleness: forgetfulness. His fear of speaking makes him forget what he would have liked to say and, even though he writes it down, still he forgets:

> So sore I am of hire adrad.
> For as a man that sodeinli
> A gost behelde, so fare I;
> So that for feere I can noght gete
> Mi witt, bot I miself foryete,
> That I wot nevere what I am,
> Ne whider I schal, ne whenne I cam,
> Bot muse as he that were amased.
> Lich to the bok in which is rased
> The lettre, and mai nothing be rad,
> So ben my wittes overlad,
> That what as evere I thoghte have spoken,
> It is out fro myn herte stoken,
> And stonde, as who seith, doumb and def
>
> (IV, 572–85)

Amans' fear-induced amnesia creates, of his desires for his lady, dead letters, phantom texts that hint at his missing motives and his absent self, the latter likened evocatively to a page in which the copy has been erased. Written and spoken language, an incorporeal shadowy medium, is alienated ('out . . . stoken') from the narrator's body – an impassive, inexpressive carcass with its heart empty and silent. However, the dead weight of the narrator's lifeless and fearful body is counterbalanced by the busyness, the energy of his unspoken fantasies that supply substitute texts – dreams and daydreams – that imagine a new, disembodied way of touching. This incorporeal courtship and consummation rivals the knight's courting of his lady through martial honour, another ghostly sort of lovemaking.

The somnolence section is almost as long as that which deals with men of arms, and in it Amans hesitates between denials and acknowledgements of his guilt. He details his insomnia, which is also an extended daydream, and all in the subjunctive mood, of what might be if 'I mighte come and duelle / In place ther my ladi were' (IV, 2774–5) or:

> . . . if sche thanne hiede toke,
> Hou pitousliche on hire I loke,
> Whan that I schal my leve take,

> Hire oghte of mercy forto slake
> Hire daunger, which seith evere nay.
> (IV, 2809–13)

He is explicit too about his unwillingness to wake from the erotic dreams (which he describes as journeys) that he has when he does finally sleep:

> For otherwise, I you behiete,
> In strange place whanne I go,
> Me list nothing to wake so.
> (IV, 3144–6)

This envisioned 'strange place' rivals the 'strange londes' and 'sondri place' (IV, 1611 and 1614) that are the stamping grounds of the crusading knight. The 'strange place', though, is just a more intimate space – the chamber or the bed – in his lady's household, which is otherwise familiar to Amans; the 'strange place' resembles those spaces that are the setting for Amans' waking life but is made foreign by virtue of the unfamiliar experience of unrestricted physicality with his lady.

> Thus ate laste I go to bedde,
> And yit min herte lith to wedde
> With hire, wher as I cam fro;
> Thogh I departe, he wol noght so,
> Ther is no lock mai schette him oute,
> Him nedeth noght to gon aboute,
> That perce mai the harde wall;
> Thus is he with hire overall,
> That be hire lief, or be hire loth,
> Into hire bedd myn herte goth,
> And softly takth hire in his arm
> And fieleth hou that sche is warm,
> And wissheth that his body were
> To fiele that he fieleth there.
> (IV, 2875–88)

There must surely be an echo here of Amans' earlier 'collacioun' when he, 'that mai noght fiele hir bare', imagines the feeling of his love's naked skin:

> ... 'Ha lord, hou sche is softe,
> How sche is round, hou sche is smal!
> Now wolde god I hadde hire al
> Withoute danger at mi wille!'
> (IV, 1146–50)

Imagining his lady to be diminutive and yielding, Amans also adds that she is 'round', a curious word that implies a self-containment and a wholeness which perfects her as a miniature doll-like version, a mapped and encapsulated version, of her real, intransigent self.

The honourable knight sees his lady's inhibitions, her 'danger', over-come by good report of his martial prowess; Amans surmounts the same obstacle through the power of imagination. In the daydreams, Amans wishes for the dissolution of his lady's 'danger' – her coyness – along with the clothes that separate him from her; in the dream he dispenses with the niceties of polite courtship – 'Danger is left behinde' (IV, 2903) – along with the barriers of domestic architecture, as the heart becomes an unstoppable penetrative force and a sinister symbol of sexual aggression. '[B]e hire lief, or be hire loth', a phrase used twice elsewhere in the Book to describe the good knight's self-effacing response to his martial duty, is employed here to construct a world which conforms to a new set of rules devised by Amans himself. In this 'strange place' the narrator's power violates and takes possession of his lady but also surpasses that of the knight who, like the lady, is *enforced* (albeit by his military obligations). Although Troilus has some terrifying rape fantasies, these are more temporary than Amans' and they are offset by the affective mutuality of his relationship with Criseyde, his ultimate desire to govern by consent.[83] Troilus rejects Pandarus's suggestions for taking Criseyde by force, con-firming his sophisticated understanding of the delicate interconnections between power and love, rejecting the vulgarity of tyranny in favour of the poetry of disappointment and mutability.

In the *Confessio Amantis*, the synecdochic heart behaves a lot like Pandarus who also has access to all areas, however intimate, overcoming the architectural boundaries which Criseyde relies on to protect her sexual reputation.[84] Amans has another of these erotic dreams in Book V and it works in a very similar way, again spiriting away the obstacles of physical architecture. This time Amans describes the bird's eye view he has over the city from his lodgings; seeing it in this way gives him the totalizing power of the cartographer (the voyeur god/godlike voyeur):

> Whan I am loged in such wise
> That I be nyhte mai arise,
> At som wyndowe and loken oute
> And se the housinge al aboute,
> So that I mai the chambre knowe
> In which mi ladi, as I trowe,
> Lyth in hir bed and slepeth softe,

> Thanne is myn herte a thief fulofte:
> For there I stonde to beholde
> The longe nyhtes that ben colde,
> And thenke on hire that lyth there.
> And thanne I wisshe that I were
> Als wys as was Nectanabus
> Or elles as was Protheüs,
> That couthen bothe of nigromaunce
> In what liknesse, in what semblaunce,
> Riht as hem liste, hemself transforme:
> For if I were of such a forme,
> I seie thanne I wolde fle
> Into the chambre forto se
> If eny grace wolde falle,
> So that I mihte under the palle
> Som thing of love pyke and stele.
>
> (V, 6659–81)

Here the heart gains access to the lady's bedchamber by stealth rather than force but this passage is just as threatening a portrayal of male sexual desire. This passage is followed by two classical *exempla* – those of Leucothoe and of Hercules and Faunus – both of which are narratives about attempted or actual rape, confirming the sexual aggression in Amans' confession. As a shape-shifter, housebreaker and picklock, Amans conjures up dream bodies and buildings that look just like conventional ones but behave very differently, no longer exacting his social and sexual conformity but, rather, matching his illimitable fantasies. In Amans' fanciful buildings can be seen a fantasy of power which is alternative to the traditional forms of hegemony and its spatial manifestations. We might also productively compare this representation of the self with the depiction, as analysed by Federico, of the shape-shifting rapists, that is the 1381 rebels as Gower describes them in his *Vox clamantis*.[85] In the *Confessio* the insolence of the 'hypermasculine rebels', as Federico styles them, the peasant other, comes to characterize the subjective fantasy of the reflexive narrator. Again the narrator is implicated in the disrupted social topologies of the late fourteenth century, becoming himself a 'hypermasculine rebel' but becoming so, remarkably, on account of his slothfulness, stasis and diffidence. Hovering between self-assertion and self-denial, Gower writes a startling version of masculine interiority that undertakes impressive journeys even while being grounded in its locality, that finds an authoritative voice within the vernacular and which pits iconic masculine models against a new-found and psychologically complex, masculine *urbanitas*.

CHAPTER 4

'And of my swynk yet blered is myn ye': Chaucer's Canon's Yeoman looks in the mirror

INTRODUCTION: 'I AM NAT WONT IN NO MIROUR TO PRIE'

It is often noted that *The Canon's Yeoman's Prologue* and *Tale* share the subjective tone of *The Wife of Bath's* and *The Pardoner's Prologues* and *Tales*.[1] Critical comment has coalesced around the Wife of Bath and the Pardoner in part because of their interest as sites of 'gender trouble', constructions that articulate contemporary anxieties about transgressive gender identities.[2] These gender quandaries are written into, and exposed by the confessional style of their *Prologues*. The Wife of Bath's *Prologue* is just over twice the length of the *Tale* that it dominates and eclipses. In that *Prologue*, displaying what Glenn Burger has described as 'female masculinity', the Wife appropriates and manipulates the same gynophobic, patriarchal and clerical discourses of which she is also a victim.[3] Thus, her portrait both subverts and confirms the gender arrangements of the society of which she is a product; it both celebrates and demonizes exuberant female sexuality. The Pardoner's confessional *Prologue*, on the other hand, clashes with and cancels out his homiletic *Tale*. His description in *The General Prologue* and his treatment by the other pilgrims – the Host in particular – gives him a slippery and indefinable sexuality, a sexuality that indecently chimes with the hypocrisy that so compromises his clerical role.

Although he has not yet been considered in these terms, the Canon's Yeoman is also a site of 'gender trouble'. The Wife, the Pardoner and the Yeoman are a triumvirate; each of these narrators gives a subjective account of a different gendered dilemma. Whilst the Wife and the Pardoner originate in contemporary suspicions of those who cross gender boundaries, occupying no gender identity unequivocally, the Canon's Yeoman's autobiographical confession negotiates the contemporary ideals about moderate, obedient and industrious masculinity. Further, his narratives can be located within a new form of masculine life writing that places labour at the centre of the construction of the self, and reads tools as extensions of the desiring body. The late fourteenth-century preoccupation with the regulation of trade and industry, a corollary of the labour crisis of that period, was written into masculine ethical models that were designed to repair the perceived problems of social and economic disorder. Lee Patterson notes that while the word 'yeoman' has a wide spectrum of potential meanings, the Yeoman's account of his labour experience marks him out as an apprentice to the Canon; the Yeoman mentions, for example, a seven year contractual term – the standard term of an apprenticeship – and his grievances are structured just like the complaints of other disaffected apprentices in the period who claimed they were badly trained or abused.[4]

Contemporary concerns about the ethics of labour and service were never so acute as in the debates surrounding apprenticeship. I shall argue that male, more than female, apprentices were suspiciously regarded, that there was a popular prejudice about their potential for disruption and, in particular, on account of their immoderate sexuality. I shall suggest that the Yeoman represents himself in inconsistent ways. On the one hand he is keen to elicit sympathy, stressing his youth and his subordinate position, and assuming the petitionary pose that Cordelia Beattie has identified as a successful narrative strategy for servants to deploy in the medieval courtroom.[5] Yet, on the other hand, he is also subject to the myths and assumptions about servants, and male apprentices in particular, and duly displays a paranoia about his interior desires that demonstrates his internalization of the cultural suspicion of adolescent men. Just as equivocal as the Wife or the Pardoner, the Yeoman inhabits the uncomfortable middle ground between himself and his community's expectations. The apprentices depicted on the misericord with which this book began may well look mischievous – they are many, small, and may escape their master's scrutiny – but their master is also a potentially abusive and exploitative man – a solid, central mass in the carving. Whilst Chaucer's Yeoman has been seen as a challenge to the forces of urban labour control, I want to think about him differently: as a vulnerable apprentice whose narratives are, in fact, not about resistance but rather about the agitated and inappropriate conformity that is produced through his being systematically abused.

Like the Wife of Bath's and the Pardoner's, the Yeoman's gendered negotiations are inscribed in the structure of his *Prologue* and *Tale*. Whilst

most of *The Canterbury Tales* have a two-part – prologue and tale –
construction, *The Canon's Yeoman's Prologue* and *Tale* is in three sections,
and the boundaries between them are permeable; the Yeoman's accounts
of himself and his personal experience are not thoroughly demarcated
from the narrative he tells. The *Prologue*, in which the Yeoman joins the
pilgrim company, has often been read as an introduction; the *prima pars*
of the *Tale*, an account of the Yeoman's experience in his master's service,
is thought of as a prologue; the *pars secunda*, a narrative about a fraudulent alchemist, is considered as the *Tale* proper.[6] While the boundaries
between the *Prologues* and *Tales* of the Wife and the Pardoner are fairly
clear, the Yeoman's *pars secunda* replicates many of the features of his
'autobiography', effacing the distinctions he tries to enforce. Samuel
MacCraken has noted the confusion that this caused the scribes of the
manuscripts who found it hard to mark a division between the Yeoman's
memoir of his working for the disreputable alchemist and Canon of
religion and his hyperfictional narrative about the duping of a priest by a
fraudulent alchemist (yet another canon of religion).[7] The Yeoman
attempts to distance the two alchemists from each other with this
assurance:

> This chanon was my lord, ye wolden weene?
> Sire hoost, in feith, and by the hevenes queene,
> It was another chanoun, and nat hee,
> That kan an hundred foold moore subtiltee.
> He hath bitrayed folkes many tyme;
> Of his falsnesse it dulleth me to ryme.
> Evere whan that I speke of his falshede,
> For shame of hym my chekes wexen rede.
> (*CYT*, 1088–95)

The question in the first line nervously suggests ways in which the
audience might read against the Yeoman's words and his oaths add an
exclamatory excess that only serves to associate the 'two' canons more
closely than the rest of the passage would seem to allow. There is some
ambiguity in the final lines cited here: although the Yeoman is ostensibly
discussing the second, fictional and fraudulent alchemist, the third-person
pronouns blur his dissimilarity from the first – the Yeoman's own master.
The shameful acts of the second alchemist are inscribed on the Yeoman's
body: he blushes as he relates them. This passage has been hotly debated:
are the canons – who are related through their work, clerical identities
and itinerant lifestyles – really different, or the same and, so, how far is

the *pars secunda* about the Yeoman himself?[8] Chaucer leaves the question characteristically open and unanswerable. Joseph Grennen has ingeniously suggested that the *Tale* imitates the transmutations of alchemy, that the second canon is a 'multiplied' version of the first.[9] Progressing in the same way as the process of alchemical transformations, the narrative creates labour links between the inter-reliant *prima pars* and *pars secunda*. These are no casual associations but ones that accord with a growing fashion within late fourteenth-century male life writing, in which the narrator embodies the ethical conundrums surrounding the regulation of labour in the same period. The Yeoman and the priest are different but also linked by their work, in particular their blowing the fire, and the myopia produced by their excessive industry. The priest is tricked whilst he wipes sweat from his eyes (*CYT*, 1186–7); of himself the Yeoman declares: 'of swynk yet blered is myn ye' (*CYT*, 730). Through these coincidences the fiction of the *Tale's pars secunda* bleeds into the *prima pars* and the *Prologue* or, rather, it happens the other way around, and the subjective quality of the first-person account infuses the third-person narrative; feigning distance from his *Tale* does nothing to insulate the Yeoman from its implications. All of *The Canterbury Tales* though, just as much as the *Prologues*, are about their narrators, however indirectly. Indeed, the Yeoman, in making a new *Tale* as he, as Donald R. Howard so neatly puts it, 'gets a grip on himself and objectifies', deploys a distinctly Chaucerian strategy that apparently moves the narrative away from the self.[10]

Several attempts have been made to identify the characters and *personae* of *The Canon's Yeoman's Prologue* and *Tale* as versions of Geoffrey Chaucer.[11] The 'multiplicity' of this *Tale*, the portrait of the fractured *autos*, constructs the impression of the autobiographical impulse prior to the text. Certainly, the *bios* of Chaucer is closer to the circumstances of the Canon's Yeoman's narratives than, say, the Pardoner's or the Wife of Bath's. Whilst Mark J. Bruhn, detecting an equivalence between the processes of writing poetry and alchemy, equates Chaucer with the Canon. Patterson, on the other hand, identifies Chaucer with the Yeoman: both represent 'middleness'.[12] Their occupations leave them between secular and clerical identities. In this way, Bruhn and Patterson assume occupational connections, the Canon resembles Chaucer the Poet, the Yeoman is reminiscent of Chaucer the controller of customs – an indeterminate, bureaucratic status. A labour or status identification governs the connections between other authors and their narrators from the same cultural, literary and political *milieu*, and Chaucer builds a similar web of associations in *The Canon's Yeoman's Tale*, although he leaves those associations characteristically inconclusive.

Patterson notes that Harry Bailey, in his description of Chaucer the Pilgrim, uses the word 'elvyssh', a word which also appears in *The Canon's Yeoman's Tale*. The Host's sketch of Geoffrey is suggestive and notable for its comic self-deprecation:

> This were a popet in an arm t'enbrace
> For any womman, smal and fair o face.
> He semeth elvyssh by his contenaunce,
> For unto no wight dooth he daliaunce.
>   (*PThop*, *1891–4, 701–4)

Relating to women – immature, 'smal', women – only as a toy, the narrator embodies insufficient manhood. Although he is described as remote – in the word 'elvyssh' and in the antisocial implications of the last line cited here – the hypothetical 'enbrace' of the young women suggests that the other pilgrims might similarly adopt the poet-narrator as a dinky mascot. The Host's words pointedly depict Geoffrey as diminutive, and part of their point must be a demonstration of the Host's virility. However, they are also a self-representation; Chaucer presents his narrator as compromised with the familiar diffident wit that can be seen, say, in the portrait of Amans in Gower's *Confessio Amantis*. Usk too, with less humour, diminishes and infantilizes himself, attempting to elicit sympathy and avoid any rivalry between him and either his literary forebears, his political contemporaries or his readers. The Yeoman adopts a similar stance, stressing his youth and his trainee status, hinting at an apprenticeship contract, hoping to find protection within the pilgrim body by smoothing away homosocial competition. A central strategy within the masculine life writing under discussion in this book is to find social accommodation for the desirous self through pity and amused patronage, presenting both the tragedy and the comedy of fallible maleness.

Moreover, the Yeoman uses the epithet 'elvyssh' to describe, not himself, but the very practice of alchemy (*CYT*, 751). In this way the connection is made not between two characters – the Yeoman and the pilgrim-narrator – but between Geoffrey and the Yeoman's *labour*. In a similar way, as Grennen has noted, the Yeoman and the Canon are sometimes indistinguishable from the stuff – the apparatus and ingredients – of their craft.[13] Tools are extensions of the body in a *Prologue* and *Tale* that conclude: we are what we do and are identified by what we use. Certainly there is an equivalence between cerebral introspection and labour; the Yeoman's confession is substituted for his work. Describing his life working for, and learning under, the Canon, the Yeoman says he is unaccustomed to self-reflection; he has had no time to notice the physical injury caused by his labour:

> I am so used in the fyr to blowe
> That it hath chaunged my colour, I trowe.
> I am nat wont in no mirour to prie,
> But swynke soore and lerne multiplie
> (*CYT*, 666–9)

In his confession to the pilgrims, the Yeoman has his first opportunity for introspection and is first at leisure to look in the 'mirror'; his 'auto-biography' fills the vacuum left by his labour and training. However, rather than being wholly dissimilar, the Yeoman's unreflexive labour and his first-person account of it are a continuum. Indeed, his confession proves to be as difficult, painful – 'soore' – and quixotic as locating the 'philosophres stoon', mystifying rather than exposing the truth about himself. The word 'prie' (668) suggests not a casual looking but an inquisitive peering and reveals an anxiety about the propriety of reflexive observation that is commensurate with fears about the rectitude of alchemical inquiry. The anxieties about study and its desirous ambitions which Nicolette Zeeman has detected in *Piers Plowman* (and other contemporary Augustinian texts) are also in evidence here.[14] Tellingly, Pandarus is said to 'prie' under Criseyde's bedclothes in one of the most contested episodes in *Troilus and Criseyde* (III, 1571);[15] 'prie' is a word that implies an improper, libidinous *curiositas* within the Yeoman's confes-sion. The word is also used by the Merchant in *The Canterbury Tales*, who despairs of Argus (the many-eyed but blind guardian of Io) and by association January, who both 'pryen' but miss the truth nevertheless (*MerT*, 2112). Pandarus' prying uncovers Criseyde's sexual body; Argus and January, for all their prying, fail to uncover the sexual goings-on taking place on their watch; the Canon's Yeoman's narrated I – that is, the Yeoman of his historical, life-written narrative – has failed to look at himself, to see the damage caused by his aggravated industry, to uncover the truth about his own interior desires and the errors to which they have led him. His first-person narrative, though, is a peering into the self and, as such, an enactment of those desires: his surveillance is prurient, his self-policing flawed by its own inquisitive dynamic.

This is the narrator's unheard *alarum* to the priest: 'O sely preest! O sely innocent! / With coveitise anon thou shalt be blent' (*CYT*, 1076–7). The priest is represented here as an internal contradiction: as an 'innocent' victim of his own 'coveitise'. In creating the priest, though, the Yeoman attempts to protect himself against a charge of masculine immoderation (I shall show later that the priest's covetousness, unlike the Yeoman's, is explicitly associated with inappropriate sexual behaviour). At the same time the shift into the *pars secunda* provides a similar immunity for his master, who is described as foolish rather than wicked. In this way, the reputations of the Canon and his apprentice are still intertwined, despite the irrevocable collapse of their working relationship in the *Prologue*. While the pair are still confederate, when they first meet the pilgrim company, the Yeoman asks that the pilgrims 'trusteth' him (*CYP*, 601). It is clear from his later admissions that to have done so would have been unwise. Even beyond the breakdown of his working association with the Canon-alchemist, though, at line 889, the Yeoman asks to be trusted, and is yet untrustworthy. This time, the Yeoman tells the pilgrims to trust his advice on how they can spot would-be alchemists (*CYT*, 885–9). He talks here about alchemists in general – never talking about his own master in the specific – and deliberately segregates this off as a digression from his personal story with the dismissive: 'Passe over this; I go my tale unto' (*CYT*, 898). Although he repeatedly agrees to be candid – about his master and about the secrets of alchemy (*CYP*, 704 and 715–19; *CYT*, 749, 788, 819, 902, 990–1 and 1167) – his confession is cautious and disingenuous, slipping into abstract denunciations and jolting unnaturally into the 'fictional' story of the gullible priest.

Furthermore, the Yeoman draws attention to the limits of his knowledge, of the things that he cannot or will not tell, the things he has forgotten and the necessarily subjective aspect of his account:

> Yet forgat I to maken rehersaile
> Of watres corosif, and of lymaille,
> And of bodies mollificacioun,
> And also of hire induracioun;
> Oilles, ablucions, and metal fusible –
> To tellen al wolde passen any bible
> That owher is: wherfore, as for the beste,
> Of alle thise names now wol I me reste,
> For, as I trowe, I have yow toold ynowe
> To reyse a feend, al looke he never so rowe.
> (*CYT*, 852–61)

Again the Yeoman touches on the ethics of knowledge, holding back that which might trespass into 'Goddes pryvetee' – a phrase which punctuates *The Canterbury Tales* and is used, for example, by John the Carpenter, in

The Miller's Tale, of Nicholas' arcane studies (*MilT*, 3454).[16] The Yeo-man's confession cannot be fully open about the alchemical process, also stopping short of revealing himself, for fear of revealing God's secrets and exposing the 'feend' within himself. This reticence reproduces the terms of the Yeoman's apprenticeship contract in a new relationship with God. Thus the bonds that bind the Yeoman prove to be resilient – being transferred to a new master rather than being broken – and they continue to distort the Yeoman's reading of himself. We might compare these desultory incongruities, in which he veers between protection and exposure – of himself, his master, the secret of the alchemical process and divine knowledge – with the Pardoner's queer offering, alternately, of his own false and then Christ's true pardon (*PardT*, 906–45).[17] When are they performing? When are they sincere? Such inconsistencies demon-strate their internal contradictions and deepen their tragedies.

Whilst much of the criticism on the Canon's Yeoman successfully engages with the theory and textuality of alchemy, here I am interested in the ethics of labour, the cultural ideology surrounding the urban work-shop setting.[18] The Yeoman describes alchemy as an industry as much as a theoretical study, and his *Tale* is, as James Landman notes, inflected with the language used by the guild records of the same period.[19] Whilst many critics have seen the Yeoman as a symbol of a counter-culture, as a portrait of mutinous labour, I will argue instead, that the Yeoman is disquieting because he exposes the potential terrors of conformity and complicity.[20] Indeed, like the Wife of Bath or the Pardoner, the Yeoman hesitates between cultural corroboration and defiance, showing how societies are most devastatingly dismantled when those that understand and appropriate their terms challenge them from the inside.

'HE IS SO VARIAUNT, HE ABIT NOWHERE': THE TROUBLE WITH TRANSIENCE

The Yeoman confesses to the pilgrim body the dubious location of his master's workshop:

> 'In the suburbes of a toun,' quod he,
> 'Lurkynge in hernes and in lanes blynde,
> Whereas thise robbours and thise theves by kynde
> Holden hir pryvee fereful residence,
> As they that dar nat shewen hir presence;
> So faren we, if I shal seye the sothe.'
>
> (*CYP*, 657–62)

Gervase Rosser's work on the suburbs of London indicates that it was the place where the city's refuse – both literal and moral – was jettisoned and the site where new, unregulated and untaxable businesses grew up, serving those who moved in and out of the city gates.[21] Impermanent and autonomous, suburban concerns are represented here as illicit and secretive. In this malign, peripheral place the Canon and his Yeoman have set up a workshop that, in all other respects, replicates more conventional businesses. In particular, the master-apprentice bond is governed by the same rules that govern businesses within the walls, which are under the auspices of the trade guilds.

This mimicry is similar to the way that the Canon and his Yeoman attempt to join the pilgrim body, which has been watched and followed all the way to the outskirts of Canterbury from the Southwark inn. This at least is the disturbing admission of the Canon's Yeoman who, with his master, has raced to catch up with the pilgrims, aspiring to the spirit of jocularity that marks out their journey and their tale-telling game, exhibited in particular by the Host in *The General Prologue* (e.g. 757 and 759). This is the character reference the Yeoman gives the Canon in a bid to get him and by extension himself accepted into the group:

> Who, sire? My lord? Ye, ye, withouten lye,
> He kan of murthe and eek of jolitee
> Nat but ynough; also, sire, trusteth me,
> And ye hym knew as wel as do I,
> Ye wolde wondre how wel and craftily
> He koude werke, and that in sondry wise.
> He hath take on hym many a greet emprise,
> Which were ful hard for any that is heere
> To brynge about, but they of hym it leere.
> As hoomly as he rit amonges yow,
> If ye hym knewe, it wolde be for youre prow.
> (*CYP*, 598–609)

Their surveillance gives them the information they need to insinuate themselves by fraudulent replication. The Yeoman stresses 'murthe' and 'jolitee', imitating the conviviality he has observed in the group. During this speech though, the pilgrims' play is transmuted into 'werke' and 'emprise'. Whilst Harry Bailie is keen to know if the Canon can tell a 'myrie tale or tweye' (*CYP*, 597), the Yeoman increasingly stresses the economic contribution – 'prow' – that the Canon could make to the company that Harry leads. The alchemical businesses described in the Yeoman's stories are similarly external to the economic community, and yet the alchemists and their assistants in those stories are keen observers of, and fake a resemblance to, that community. The Canon's Yeoman threatens the play ethic of *The Canterbury Tales*, attempting to transform it into a discussion of desire and production. Rather than representing work as a moral force, however – like the closely linked *Second Nun's Prologue* and *Tale* – his narratives reveal the dangers of blind industry and misguided obedience.[22] Although the Yeoman, unlike his master, remains with the pilgrims, he is never integrated into the ludic aspect of the company: his 'Tale' is dark and tragic, not 'myrie'.

Bruhn has described the Canon and his Yeoman as 'interlopers', interrupting the pilgrimage plot.[23] Shadowy, suburban and peripheral, they seek, but fail, to ride 'hoomly' amongst the pilgrim group. *The Canterbury Tales*, though, is everywhere interested in interlopers, in transient communities and temporary residency. The stranger is often introduced who will shake up complacent and settled communities, creating the dramatic crux at the centre of many of the narratives. In particular this is shown at the household level, and despite evidence that many, indeed the majority of the migrants into the urban centres in the late-medieval period were women, the interlopers in *The Canterbury Tales* are male boarders, guests, students, servants and apprentices.[24] The quotation below is the Cook's comment on *The Reeve's* and *Miller's Tales*, and yet it might also have been written about *The Shipman's* and *Merchant's Tales*, the episode in *The Wife of Bath's Prologue* in which she describes her fling with Jankyn the apprentice and, indeed, the Cook's own *Tale*:

> Wel seyde Salomon in his langage,
> 'Ne bryng nat every man into thyn hous,'
> For heberwynge by nyghte is perilous.
> Wel oghte a man avysed for to be
> Whom that he broghte into his pryvetee.
>   (*CkP*, 4330–4)

In the word 'pryvetee', with all its intimate and sexual connotations, the problem of temporary residence is developed into the familiar triangulated patterns of homosocial rivalry.[25] This masculine competition is represented as normative in many of *The Canterbury Tales*, yet it is this that is conspicuously missing from the Yeoman's account of his damaging relationship with his master. Their split in the *Prologue* is precipitated when the Yeoman discovers a newfound oppositional position from which he can invade his master's 'pryvetee':

> And whan this Chanon saugh it wolde nat bee,
> But his Yeman wolde telle his pryvetee,
> He fledde awey for verray sorwe and shame.
>   (*CYP*, 700–3)

However, notwithstanding this promise of openness in the *Prologue*, the Yeoman ends his *Tale* with a final guardedness about divulging alchemical truths. This ending, as Patterson shows, acknowledges the insufficiency of language to locate alchemical truth accurately and unambiguously.[26] It also shows, though, a respect for a 'pryvetee' – God's and, incidentally, his alchemist master's – which he might otherwise violate. The word 'pryvetee', then, is a word that interrogates the ethics of entitlement, envisaging knowledge – trade secrets, divine truth – in intimate spatial terms like the sexual and economic territory of the male householder, which the Cook warns is threatened with invasion by temporary residents. '[P]ryvetee' connotes the spaces where masculine competition is staged. In negotiating the ethics of inquiry and invasion, the Yeoman fretfully seeks the balance between hubristic enterprise and crippling humility.

Gervase Rosser has argued that the populations of medieval London houses were often transient and that there was a strong culture of temporary letting and leasing, especially where property prices were low in the suburbs of the city.[27] High death rates in cities meant that businesses and households had to be staffed with immigrant labour.[28] Whilst the suspicion of the stranger was not new to the late fourteenth century, legislative attempts to control mobility and, in particular, mobile labour became more insistent in the post-Black Death period and this was undertaken at the level of houses and businesses.[29] The Yeoman's description of the second, fictional, Canon, 'He is so variaunt, he abit nowhere' (*CYT*, 1175), constructs him as the nightmare of lawmakers and enforcers attempting to immobilize labour.[30] Itinerant people, like the canons in *The Canon's Yeoman's Tale* and the interlopers in the other *Canterbury Tales*, had no investment in the well-being of the community in which they settled and, therefore, provision was made to supervise both their work and their social conduct. The spirit, if not the letter of the ancient system of frankpledge, which required all 'good men' to pledge to abide by the law and to regulate the lives of those resident in their houses, perpetuated, into the wardmote jurisdictions of the fourteenth century, a partiality to local policing and governance by male property owners. In turn these men were given privileged access to local office and legal redress.

These men were expected to police their households, answering for the offences of their dependant wives, children, servants and apprentices. The householder's authority was enshrined in the ordinances and contracts drawn up by their craft guilds, possibly backed by the municipal authorities who had a particular interest in seeing apprenticeship in particular – a route to the freedom of the city – controlled and restricted.[31] The responsibility of governing this youthful, urban population was thus increasingly devolved to householders who, as masters, managed this task through labour legislation and contract. Sarah Rees Jones has argued that the late fourteenth century was a period of transition: while adolescent men, who were renting or in service, had previously been accountable before public courts, increasingly they came to be disciplined within the confines of the household. Marjorie McIntosh suggests that this privatization of social discipline became a necessity as the legislative energies of the community were diverted to enforce the labour legislation.[32] Further, a late marriage pattern extended the disruptive period of dependent adolescence, retarding young people's participation in adult life and their assumption of households of their own.[33] The household was becoming the *locus* of moral and social policing and the householder a major instrument of urban control.

The Canterbury Tales regularly finds fun – or at least grotesque fascination, if we are circumspect about the dark and complex *Merchant's Tale* – in the comic scenarios presented by the householders' burden. Heather Swanson argues that the notion of the master-craftsman and householder perfectly in control of his business and home is an illusion constructed by the records, part of the authorities' wish list for 'a hierarchical and above all male-orientated order'.[34] Whilst guild and municipal records develop an ideal of a householding man able to restrain the appetites and behaviours of those under his aegis, and whilst male householders as a group were relied on to stabilize the urban economy and community, the inevitable discrepancy between this ideal and the practice of running a household and business, and negotiating the relationships within them, produced a cultural anxiety about masculine sufficiency. Many of *The Canterbury Tales* feature the device of the young male interloper, disrupting the supposedly ordered institution of the household and challenging the authority of the householder husband. Chaucer's *Tales*, though, usually celebrate the dynamism and vitality brought by those testing the forces of regulation with enterprise. The borders, servants or apprentices are disruptive but they are also irrepressibly inventive and rejuvenating. In this way, Chaucer's pilgrims transmute the deepest anxieties of the society of which they are a product into comedy – 'earnest into game' (*MilP*, 3186). There are very few stable households in Chaucer's *Tales*; those that there are – Griselda's, St Cecilia's or Melibee's perhaps – are sites of suffering that are grim, problematic or both. In contrast, in his household comedies, with a levity that is anomalous in its period, Chaucer continually reproduces a farce of the broken home. This home-breaking is effected by a male in-comer who embodies the myth of migrant manhood and the heroism of enterprise: comfortable with women, commanding good wages and driving fast carts.[35]

While the interloper of *The Shipman's Tale* is an exception to the regular pattern that I am outlining here, being a monk who is not necessarily younger than the merchant whom he cuckolds and robs, the merchant of the *Tale* is a paradigmatic version of a householding man. The merchant is twice identified as a 'goode man' (*ShipT*, *1219, 29; *1297, 107), a title which insists on his role as a householder, within a community of similar men, obliged to shoulder the burdens of social control. The householding man demonstrates his economic power and social worth by being hospitable and opening his house to guests. The merchant in *The Shipman's Tale* maintains a culture of hospitality suitable for his station but this practice also makes his household vulnerable to attack from the numerous guests he invites to enjoy it (*ShipT*, *1210–14, 20–24).

In only the second line of *The Miller's Tale*, John the carpenter is described as a man 'that geestes heeld to bord' (*MilT*, 3188). In John's case this is not a sign of his largesse – his guests are paying lodgers who ensure his financial security. The early identification of John as a landlord is a proleptic reference to his sexual humiliation. Nicholas, in *The Miller's Tale*, is a representative of the students of university cities, another transient and clerical population. It was common for students to be lodged in private houses, causing something of a headache for the university authorities attempting to regulate a 'sprawling academic population scattered throughout the town'.[36] Servants were also a temporary population; young people would usually undertake only one or two years of what is known as life cycle service during adolescence.[37] *The Merchant's Tale* analyses the profound paradox of the unfaithful servant: 'famulier foo', 'servant traytour, false hoomly hewe / Lyk to the naddre in the bosom' (*MerT*, 1784–6). Although Damyan has less energy than Nicholas, his status as a live-in household servant makes his rivalry with January ineluctable.

The guest, servant or lodger continually exploits the work of the householder husband, and the adultery tricks are often effected through the subversion of working practices. In *The Miller's Tale* Nicolas courts John's wife while John is engaged on a carpentry job at the abbey of Osney; John's great labour to construct a new ark, orchestrated by his young rival, leaves him exhausted and unable to prevent his cuckoldry (*MilT*, 3643–6, 3274, 3400 and 3657). The merchant in *The Shipman's Tale* is betrayed while on a business trip abroad. The interlopers – Nicholas and Daun John – have an inverted work ethic: they use their vocational knowledge and privileges to deceive, and their sexual promiscuity goes together with their clerical identity. These *Tales* continually and mischievously use the vocabulary of work ironically and euphemistically in the discussion of sexual play.[38] January in bed with May, for example, describes himself as a 'werkman' who 'laboureth' until dawn (*MerT*, 1832 and 1842). A businesslike Absolon objects to the teasing 'pley' of Gerveys the blacksmith, whose work – forging agricultural tools – he has interrupted to further his revenge in the sexual farce of the central plot line (*MilT*, 3761–86). Palpably and voyeuristically fascinated by fantasies of youthful male sexuality, pilgrims like the Miller and the Cook appropriate the interlopers' panache to glamorize trade deception. Perkyn the Revellor's master in *The Cook's Tale* is said – if we read it literally – to buy his apprentice's misbehaviour – his womanizing and gambling – in his own shop (*CkT*, 4393); the Cook's own sharp trade practices, detailed in his portrait in *The General Prologue*, identify him more with the rogue Perkyn than his duped employer in his *Tale*, for whom the Cook has very little sympathy.

In *The Canon's Yeoman's Tale*, however, confidence trickery never buoys up the narrative in the same way. The power differential between the tricksters and their victims is reversed. Now it is not the young underdogs that get one over their elders and employers, servants who, with the support of beautiful and closely-kept wives like Alisoun and May in *The Miller's* and *Merchant's Tales*, attack the complacency of established and parsimonious householders; the two alchemists, masters of workshops, with access to superior knowledge, exploit presumably younger men who identify with them as pupils and employees – an altogether more sinister scenario. The lexicon of labour is not ironic in *The Canon's Yeoman's Prologue* and *Tale*; that work is physically demanding is signed in the free-flowing sweat and the physical damage written on the Yeoman's body and face (e.g. *CYP*, 664). Whilst figures like Daun John and Nicholas in *The Shipman's* and *Miller's Tales* use their libidinous energies to advance themselves, the Yeoman complains that his desires and those of his fictional priest are points of susceptibility that expose them to the dangerous influence of the devilish canons. While the Miller uses Nicholas to humiliate John, a carpenter, and, through a trade association, his fellow pilgrim, the Reeve, the Yeoman is eager not to implicate other 'worshipful chanons religious' (*CYT*, 992–1011) and, in his lengthy exoneration of them, dissipates any potential homosocial abrasion that his *Tale* might generate. Indeed, whilst the 'real-time' story of the Yeoman's severance from his master introduces an element of competition, the history of their relationship, up to the Canon's flight at line 702 of the *Prologue*, is characterized by collaboration rather than contention. Even beyond this point, the Yeoman shows himself reluctant to define himself in direct contrast to his one-time master and, tragically, vestiges of his previous, ill-advised loyalty remain.

CHAUCER'S APPRENTICES

The homosocial tensions, missing from the Yeoman's stories but inherent in the other narratives of temporary residence, can also be detected in the contemporary attitude to, and characterization of, apprentices.[39] Masters were not usually of a different social status to their apprentices. Whilst this led to a shared outlook between a master and his charge, and a culture of support for younger by older men, it also indubitably introduced conflict into that relationship. The potential for friction between masters and their adolescent apprentices was predicated on the fact that masters had what their charges aspired to: workshops and households. The houses in which apprentices trained were the stepping-stones to houses and livings of their own. Masters were also in a position to frustrate or smooth this transition. This was not a private negotiation, however, and other interested bodies – especially the trade guilds and the municipal authorities – had an investment in ensuring that only those who had reached a particular vocational aptitude, and had demonstrated good moral behaviour, passed out and worked in the trade in their own right. In particular, the apprenticeship indentures stressed that the apprentice must be loyal, keeping his master's – and by extension the trade's – secrets; in return he was to be properly trained and made capable of maintaining the standards expected within the craft.[40]

Patterson has described the Yeoman's break with his master in the *Prologue* as an 'insurrectionary moment' on the basis that the Yeoman offends against two taboos 'central to the strict discipline of London society; that a man should not slander his superior, that an apprentice should not reveal trade secrets.'[41] Patterson finds it remarkable that the host sanctions the Yeoman's 'misconduct' and his transmutation into 'one of those vagabonds, those men without masters, who so disturbed the governors of late-medieval England'. Employment contracts of the period, and apprenticeship indentures in particular, certainly did enjoin apprentices to keep their master's confidences, as did the 1371 indenture of Nicholas, son of John de Kyghlay:

The Apprentice was to live with his master from the feast of St. Peter ad Vincula [1 August] 1371 for seven years, willingly perform his master's order and keep his secrets and counsel.[42]

The obligation to keep secrets infuses *The Canon's Yeoman's Prologue* and *Tale*. The Yeoman swears Harry Bailey to secrecy in his *Prologue* (643); the fraudulent alchemist asks the priest who, though not identified as an apprentice himself, is closely associated with the apprentice-narrator:

> 'Sire Preest,' he seyde, 'I kepe han no loos
> Of my craft, for I wolde it kept were cloos;
> And, as ye love me, kepeth it secree.'
> (*CYT*, 1368–70)

In his account of his own circumstances, the Yeoman insists, however, that he is no longer obliged to respect his master's secrets, that his contract with the Canon has already been broken, but not by him, by his master. Nevertheless he vacillates between exposing his ex-patron and preserving faith with him, trying, however ineptly, to disassociate his master from his narrative of fraud. The Yeoman does not throw off his loyalty to his master easily; his socialization as an apprentice creates an enduring anxiety about the master–servant bond which says more, I think, about conformity than insurrection.

The injunctions to apprentices to keep their masters' counsel and not to slander them were not unconditional. John de Bradley for example, the master of the 1371 indenture, had the following obligations towards his young charge:

John de Bradlay was to instruct and inform Nicholas, his apprentice, as well as he knew how in the bowercrafte, in buying and selling, without concealing anything, and was to provide him with food and drink, linen and woollen clothing, a bed, shoes and all necessities for all the said term.

The first lines of *The Canon's Yeoman's Tale* give the narrator's justification for leaving his master under the terms of such an indenture:

> With this Chanoun I dwelt have seven yeer,
> And of his science am I never the neer.
> Al that I hadde I have lost therby,
> And, God woot, so hath many mo than I.
> Ther I was wont to be right fressh and gay
> Of clothyng and of oother good array,
> Now may I were an hose upon myn heed;
> And wher my colour was bothe fressh and reed,
> Now is it wan and of a leden hewe
>
> (*CYT*, 720–8)

The shifting tenses, contrasting his past and current fortunes, stress that the Canon has offended, not only by leaving his trainee in ignorance but also by making no proper provision for his welfare. The implication is that the Canon is not a fit man to keep an apprentice, and yet it appears, from the fourth line cited above and the Yeoman's later description of their alchemical failures (*CYT*, 921–46), that he keeps several.

Only certain kinds of men were considered to be morally suitable to take on the responsibility of training an apprentice. Many London guild ordinances specified that only freemen of the city were entitled to keep an apprentice.[43] The 1355 London Braelers' ordinance went further; as well as having to be a freeman, a man could not keep an apprentice

if it be not testified by the good folks of the said trade sworn, that he is a man proper and sufficient to keep, inform, and teach, his apprentice;[44]

Men who took in apprentices were vouched for, and bound into a community that could provide supervision and prevent iniquitous practice, whereas the Canon's workshop is isolated and outside of a guild community. Situated in the suburbs, which was hardly the location for a legitimate business, the alchemist's laboratory is sited beyond the control of any proper supervising authority. Urban guild legislation consistently ruled to try to keep trades within certain spaces and the reaches of their jurisdiction.[45] What is more, while apprentices each swore to keep their master's trade secrets, the guilds were anxious to make urban trade transparent to themselves and to regulate both manufacture and retail. The arcane and esoteric space of the Canon's workshop is hardly the picture of good practice that would have satisfied a guild searcher of the late fourteenth century. It seems remarkable, then, not that the Host and the pilgrims countenance the Yeoman's departure from the Canon, but rather that the Canon's shady business dealings should have inspired the kind of loyalty in the Yeoman which lead him to protect his diabolic master.

The social explanation for this misplaced allegiance can be found in the conditions to which indentures bound apprentices, which articulate particular prejudices about young people and young men in particular. Just as the Wife of Bath interiorizes the misogynist discourses of a patriarchal clergy, the Yeoman demonstrates an anxiety about the aggressive desires of young male apprentices, a stereotype that can be seen in the contemporary record. A young man's apprenticeship indenture placed him in competition with his master in another sense: as a sexual rival. Whilst the apprenticeship indentures of women, of female embroiderers for example, stipulated that they should not contract matrimony without permission during the contractual term and forbade various sorts of misbehaviour, the indentures of young men went further and were more specific:

He was not to play at dice nor frequent taverns, the chess-board and brothels, nor commit adultery or fornication with his master's wife or daughter, under penalty of doubling the length of his apprenticeship. He was not to contract matrimony with any woman during his term of seven years, except with his master's consent.[46]

One might imagine that the injunction to refrain from sexual intercourse with the master's wife was one that, being beyond moral dispute, might have gone unwritten; the document does not guard against other equally self-evident offences: kicking or shoving the master's wife, for example, are not expressly forbidden.

This ordinance testifies to a stereotype of the promiscuous apprentice that is also invoked in *The Canterbury Tales*. Janekyn the apprentice in *The Wife of Bath's Prologue* is constructed solely in terms of his sexual flirtations with Alison. These are the dissimulating words of the Wife to her third husband about the attachment:

> And yet of oure apprentice Janekyn,
> For his crispe heer, shynynge as gold so fyn,
> And for he squiereth me bothe up and doun,
> Yet hastow caught a fals suspecioun.
> I wol hym noght, thogh thou were deed tomorwe!
> (*WBP*, 303–7)

The intimacy of the pronoun 'oure' is a telling indication that the Wife's audience should read against her protestations.[47] The second and third lines cited here are an unnecessary digression which work to undermine the rest of the passage, which she later admits is a lie (*WBP*, 379–83). Within that aside there is yet another – 'shynynge as gold so fyn' – which lingers lasciviously on Janekyn's hair. The phrase 'up and doun' is suggestive, euphemistic and well placed in this playful account of Alison's household affair. The Wife of Bath assures her husband that her flirtations with Janekyn would never be consummated even if he were conveniently to die. In this statement she hints at the presumption that an apprentice's ambitions were not just to be like his master, but actually to replace him. Perkyn the Revelour, the apprentice in *The Cook's Tale*, is similarly presented. Although Perkyn is not shown courting his master's wife, his promiscuity is an important part of his portrait, following only his physical description and his name.[48]

In contrast, in the Canon's Yeoman's life narrative, his apprenticeship is not characterized by sexual promiscuity nor an affair with the Canon's wife. Indeed, women are, in the main, conspicuously absent (the exception being the priest's landlady), as elusive as the secret of alchemy itself. It has been said by Helen Phillips that *The Canon's Yeoman's Tale* contains 'no sex' and that it is singular among *The Canterbury Tales* for this reason.[49] However, there *is* some 'sex': the Yeoman is fixated with teleological desire and libidinal economies. For example there is a curious parenthetical observation about the association between the priest's erotic desires and his yearning for the alchemical product near the end of the *Tale*:

> This sotted preest, who was gladder than he?
> Was nevere brid gladder agayn the day,
> Ne nyghtyngale, in the sesoun of May,
> Was nevere noon that lust bet to synge;
> Ne lady lustier in carolynge,
> Or for to speke of love and wommanhede,
> Ne knyght in armes to doon an hardy dede,
> To stonden in grace of his lady deere,
> Than hadde this preest this soory craft to leere.
> (*CYT*, 1340–9)

Quite suddenly this passage effects a shift from the London workshop setting into the pages of a popular romance, contrasting the priest with a bird, a lady singing and finally a knight-errant, winning his lady, a sexual prize, through martial adventure. In these dallying contrasts the narrator turns to the subject of love as if it occurred to him casually – 'Or for to speke of love and wommanhede'; this meiosis does not disguise a significant association between erotic and material desire. D. Vance Smith has discussed the promise of medieval alchemy to restore the male body to perfect virility and potency.[50] For the deluded, the pursuit of the philosopher's stone – this 'soory craft' – becomes a prestigious and daring quest for masculine sexual success. Many illuminating things are parenthetical in this *Tale*, which seems itself to be in parenthesis and outside the story-telling compact.[51] Here is another supposed digression, introducing the priest into the *Tale*:

> In Londoun was a preest, an annueleer,
> That therinne dwelled hadde many a yeer,
> Which was so plesaunt and so servysable
> Unto the wyf, where as he was at table,
> That she wolde suffre hym no thyng for to paye
> For bord ne clothyng wente he never so gaye,
> And spendyng silver hadde he right ynow.
> Thereof no fors
>
> (*CYT*, 1012–19)

Here again is some 'sex'. The last dismissive half line in this excerpt purports to undermine the importance of those that precede it and yet draws attention to them as a digressive aside. In a tale so absented by women, this interlude cannot be so easily passed over with the evasive phrase 'Therof no fors'. This passage contains the only living space and the only overtly sexual space in the *Tale*. The word 'servysable' is a euphemism that implies at least a sexual tension, if not a physical relationship between the priest and his landlady and, tellingly, also evokes the ethos of service. The kinds of service to which this priest is accustomed are inappropriate; he attempts to circumvent the proper processes of production and industry in an alternative and corrupt sexual economy. The priest's own proclivities make him vulnerable to the alchemist's improbable promises of quick riches.

In producing the second, fictional tale the Yeoman puts some distance between himself and the priest. After all, the priest is not an apprentice and, crucially, and unlike the Yeoman himself, he has lodgings outside of the alchemist's workshop. The priest's relationship with his landlady and his libidinous energies are not directed against the Canon–alchemist. Whilst one property serves for all the action – both sexual and economic – in *The Merchant's*, *Miller's*, *Reeve's* and *Shipman's Tales*, *The Canon's Yeoman's* proliferates and compartmentalizes spaces much more pedantically. The priest's 'chambre' is not, like Nicholas's study-bedroom in *The Miller's Tale* or Damyan's servant's quarters in *The Merchant's Tale*, a strategic space where a husband's humiliation is effected. Instead, the fraudulent alchemist approaches the priest as he lies in bed in his 'chambre'. This intimate setting and his vulnerable, prostrate position symbolize the weakness that his appetition represents; while, in *The Miller's Tale*, Nicholas's appetites are his strength, the priest's, in *The Canon's Yeoman's Tale*, are his downfall. In developing these new, cor-doned-off spaces in his *Tale*, the Yeoman can describe the relationship between twin desires – for the alchemical product and for women – locating them beyond his own household and without placing himself in competition with his master.

This suspicion of young men, and their supposed propensity to disrupt the households within which they lodged, was incorporated into the ways in which disputes between masters and apprentices were treated and resolved. Although some apprentices were successful in claiming breach of contract, the guild ordinances are biased in favour of employers and masters.[52] Where training contracts were broken, guilds may even have made it difficult for some apprentices to take up positions with new masters. The *Tale*'s shift, from 'autobiography' into a new, fictional layer, shows the Yeoman attempting to uphold the terms and conditions of his contract in spite of its irrevocable collapse, a collapse caused by his master's insufficiency. This is not just an admission that his part is unlikely to be taken by a community predisposed to assume the way-wardness of male apprentices, but also a demonstration of the way in which he has learned to accept, even concur with, this prejudice. The Yeoman repeatedly expresses guilt about his interior desires and, like so many other victims of abuse, tragically blames himself, seeing himself as implicated and complicit in his master's business practices.

The swing into the *pars secunda* disassociates the Yeoman's master from the worst allegations of fraud. Instead he describes the first Canon, like himself, as deluded and hopeful; although cursed, the Canon is also a victim of his own private aspirations and the failures they exact: 'we faille of oure desir' (*CYP*, 671), 'We faille of that which that we wolden have' (*CYT*, 958), the Yeoman says, with a stress on the first-person plural form. They *do* extract money from others with false promises but the Yeoman suggests that they also try to achieve the things they promise, signalling that they are an inept, rather than a fraudulent, outfit and that they impoverish themselves as much as their creditors:

> To muchel folk we doon illusioun,
> And borwe gold, be it a pound or two,

> Or ten, or twelve, or manye sommes mo,
> And make hem wenen, at the leeste weye,
> That of a pound we koude make tweye.
> Yet it is fals, but ay we han good hope
> It for to doon, and after it we grope.
> But that science is so fer us biforn,
> We mowen nat, although we hadden it sworn,
> It overtake, it slit awey so faste.
> It wole us maken begars atte laste.
>
> (*CYP*, 673–83)

Again, the first-person plural form repeatedly expresses a unity of purpose. The pair share 'good hope' towards which they collectively 'grope'
but, instead, they are beggared together. The Yeoman's own appetites
mirror and match his master's, and he exhibits the anxiety that accompanies the knowledge of his own responsibility and collusion. The Yeoman describes himself as a good servant who is contracted to his master to
practice avarice as if it were a trade like any other.

In *The Cook's Tale*, Chaucer shows an apprentice acting against his
master's interests in a much less ambiguous way. When Patterson
describes the Yeoman's break with his master as a moment of insurrection
he reads it as similar to the split between Perkyn and his victualler-
master. Perkyn is a rebel whose negative influence over the other servants
eventually leads to his early release from his apprenticeship contract:

> Upon a day, whan he his papir soghte,
> Of a proverbe that seith this same word:
> 'Wel bet is roten appul out of hoord
> Than that it rotie al the remenaunt.'
>
> (*CkT*, 4404–7)

In contrast, the Yeoman does not depict himself as a rotten apple, acting
against his master's interests and orders. In an atypical moment of
reflection on his individual part within the collective, and unusually using
the first-person singular rather than the plural, the Yeoman describes his
unease in the aftermath and analysis of each abortive experiment, about
his personal responsibility for the team's alchemical failure:

> Somme seyde it was long on the fir makyng;
> Some seyde nay, it was on the blowyng –
> Thanne was I fered, for that was myn office.
>
> (*CYT*, 922–4)

This devotion to his master and the project is also in evidence at the meeting between the Canterbury pilgrims and the master-apprentice pair; further, the Yeoman is never fully purged of his adherence, although his narrative becomes increasingly punctuated by denunciation. The shift into the *pars secunda* is a final and unconvincing attempt by the Yeoman to protect the Canon and repress his own complicity in his misdealings. His irresolution, about whether to break faith with his master, continually reiterates and re-enacts the fear, expressed above, about his 'office'.

Perkyn, on the other hand, is not 'fered', and *The Cook's Tale* is saturated with the language of play and jollity. Helen Phillips has argued that *The Cook's Tale* 'conveys a [...] generalized sense of social *fear*: street gangs of youths, rushing around the city, day and night, resistant to the control represented by masters' anger or short prison spells in Newgate'.[53] While I agree that the *Tale* might be expected to betray these sentiments, it is, in fact, tonally blithe; even where the narrative becomes a string of didactic saws, Chaucer's text does not carry the sense of moral urgency with which these debates were characterized elsewhere. Consider, for example, this excerpt, which is typical of the whole of Perkyn's description:

> Gaillard he was as goldfynch in the shawe,
> Broun as a berye, a propre short felawe,
> With lokkes blake, ykembd ful fetisly.
> Daunceen he koude so wel and jolily
> That he was cleped Perkyn Revelour.
> He was as ful of love and paramour
> As is the hyve ful of hony sweete;
> Wel was the wenche with hym myghte meete.
> At every bridale wolde he synge and hoppe;
> He loved bet the taverne than the shoppe.
> (*CkT*, 4367–76)

The last line here and the reference to the 'wench' at line 4374 may contain a reproach but it is tempered, indeed neutralized by the positive tenor of the rest. Jaunty and saccharine, this is a far remove from the fears of the contemporary authorities about youthful misbehaviour. The words 'Gaillard', 'fetisly' and 'paramour' contribute a courtly elegance that, coupled with the mellifluous imagery of 4373, connotes the warmth of innocent romance rather than the social problem of sexual incontinence. The disarming bird and berry imagery naturalizes his mischief: boys will be boys. No doubt there is some irony here, signalling the flippancy with

which Chaucer can make a burlesque out of his community's deepest
anxieties. Even where the Cook turns to the subjects of 'thefte and riot',
Perkyn is still given the epithet 'joly' and his energy – his hopping,
singing and leaping – make his story invigorating rather than threatening.
Before the text abruptly breaks off, Perkyn leaves his master's house and
moves in with his friend and his prostitute wife, a move that is not
accompanied by any disapproval from its narrator and is at odds with its
more conservative, fifteenth-century continuations.[54] This romp is also a
far cry from the Boethian anxiety of *The Canon's Yeoman's Prologue* and
Tale, a dramatization of an endless, bitter and unsated searching.

Perkyn's master's initial reluctance to let his apprentice go is in keeping
with the guidance that was given about how best to punish and manage
the misbehaviour of apprentices in this period. The indenture, which I
cited above, states that apprentices that violate the terms of their contract
do so under penalty of doubling their contractual term. As a punishment
for seducing the master's wife or daughter this seems to be somewhat
illogical: it certainly would not serve the interests of the master himself,
who might seek to eject his wife's lover, rather than continuing to put
him up in his property. This disciplinary measure would, however,
damage the prospects of the apprentice, delaying his progression into social
adulthood and a workshop of his own. What is more, it also profited the
trade who avoided having to accept members who were inappropriate in
some way; it also enabled the civic community to restrict membership of
the freedom of the city to those who upheld particular standards and the
rule of household. Further, keeping disruptive young people segregated
in private households, rather than letting them congregate as independent
communities and trade organizations, meant that their behaviours could be
more effectively policed and managed. An independent residence of
unsupervised young men precipitated the complaint of the mayor and
aldermen of London in 1415; they summoned the master and wardens of
the Tailors' guild to the Guildhall and asked them why

they allowed their serving-men and journeymen to occupy such dwelling-houses,
so as to live together in companies, by themselves, without any superior to rule
them, and to commit and perpetrate so harmfully such evils and misdeeds.

The mayor and the aldermen, concluding that the group was 'like a race
at once youthful and unstable', ordered that the men be evicted on pain
of a fine or imprisonment.[55] This record reveals the palpable alarm at the

prospect of a cohesive male labour group operating as an alternative to the established guild system.

The Cook, at the end of his *Tale*, manoeuvres his protagonist into an unorthodox residence beyond the regulatory influence of the masters of any trade. Whilst Craig Bertolet has argued that *The Cook's Tale* is not 'comic but cautionary', his evidence is only disbelief that the Cook might tell a tale which runs counter to the cultural distress that the question of mutinous apprentices arouses in the contemporary records.[56] However, the last lines of the unfinished *Cook's Tale*, set in Perkyn's new home, are not a retrospective of the victualler's losses but a comic exploitation of the fresh scenario. In stark contrast are the final lines of *The Canon's Yeoman's Tale*; here, transferring his allegiance to a new master, Christ, whose secrets he resolves to keep, the Yeoman holds to himself the 'roote' of the alchemical secret as Plato advises:

> The philosophres sworn were everychoon
> That they sholden discovere it unto noon,
> Ne in no book it write in no manere.
> For unto Crist it is so lief and deere
> That he wol nat that it discovered bee
>   (*CYT*, 1464–8)

He follows this with an affecting appeal that evokes the penalties of the apprenticeship indentures – extended contractual terms – as part of a metaphor about a life led in sin:

> For whoso maketh God his adversarie,
> As for to werken any thyng in contrarie
> Of his wil, certes, never shal he thryve,
> *Thogh that he multiplie terme of his lyve.*
> And there a poynt, for ended is my tale.
> God sende every trewe man boote of his bale!
>   (*CYT*, 1476–81)

Now this *is* a cautionary tale that supplies the Yeoman himself as a warning, rather in the way that the Pardoner advises his audience against his own sinful example. I don't recognize the emancipation of the Yeoman that Patterson and Robert Cook discover in the *Tale*;[57] affectingly, the Yeoman describes himself as perpetually bound to the same codes of discretion and the same terms of service that have always circumscribed him.

CONCLUSION: THE INFECTION 'AMONGES US'

> Ther is a chanoun of religioun
> Amonges us, wolde infecte al a toun
> (*CYT*, 972–3)

The cultural experience of pandemic was a significantly unsettling event that disclosed a social malaise with an unclear prognosis. With the Black Death came the conviction that the disease was a punishment for some moral failure that preceded it.[58] The Black Death and the social, ethical and religious discourses it prompted have been compared to AIDS and the way that it was discussed in the 1980s;[59] certainly, both instigated a reactionary Pauline discourse about death and illness being the wages of sin. However, although there is some historiographical and medical dissent about the exact nature of the medieval pestilence and how it was transmitted, we can be sure from the contemporary accounts of the contagion that it does not share a pattern of infection with the HIV virus.[60] While it is convenient for those on the religious right that prostitutes, their clients, homosexuals and intravenous drug-users make up the majority of those infected with HIV (in Europe and the USA), the 1348 plague, once it had spread from the Muslim East, did not claim its victims from groups perceived to be leading their lives in obvious error.[61] Instead it was contracted from family members, work colleagues, fellow worshippers and so on; the same bonds and associations that bound society together and made it strong became the fault lines making it vulnerable to collapse. In a culture sensitive to portents, the single parents, understaffed businesses and empty tenements must have appeared as glaring voids that, in the discursive tradition that described disease as punishment, exposed areas of moral disrepair. God had judged the way in which people married, worked and worshipped – those things that apparently glued society together – as reprehensible.

The Yeoman describes alchemists as a potential source of infection but one that threatens from the inside, from '[a]monges us': that is, our community, our town and even our selves. The Yeoman, discussing those who are tempted to sell everything they have to fund their pursuit of the philosophers' stone, makes very little distinction between the victims of alchemy and alchemists themselves, showing how one, by some alchemy, becomes the other in a smooth and imperceptible transition:

> That futur temps hath maad men to dissevere,
> In trust thereof, from al that evere they hadde.
> Yet of that art they kan nat wexen sadde,

For unto hem it is a bitter sweete –
So seemeth it – for nadde they but a sheete
Which that they myghte wrappe hem inne a-nyght,
And a brat to walken inne by daylyght,
They wolde hem selle and spenden on this craft.
They kan nat stynte til no thyng be laft.
And everemoore, where that evere they goon,
Men may hem knowe by smel of brymstoon.
For al the world they stynken as a goot;
Hir savour is so rammyssh and so hoot
That though a man from hem a mile be,
The savour wole *infecte* hym, trusteth me.
Lo, thus by smellyng and threedbare array,
If that men liste, this folk they knowe may.
                                        (*CYT*, 875–91)

In his unthinking masculinism, using the word 'men', this narrator demonstrates his concern with the masculine community. This passage begins by discussing with some sympathy 'men' as the pitiful victims of their future hopes; by line 885, though, it has become necessary to detect these men to delimit their polluting influence – expressed in the language of disease – over other 'men'. Beginning with honest hopes, these aspirants are transformed, as Grennen notes, into the foetid substances with which they dabble.[62] Elsewhere, too, the Yeoman describes this contagion and how those who lose out in alchemical scams 'exciteth oother folk therto', comforting themselves by seeing others suffer 'peyne and *disese*' (*CYT*, 744 and 747). The Yeoman attempts to immunize his audience, educating them to recognize the symptoms in others.

Being able to identify the telltale caprine odour of the infected, though, offers little protection; even at a distance of a mile and beyond any reasonable defences, this smell 'wole infecte' a 'man'. The reputation of the second alchemist in the *pars secunda*, like this evil stench, encourages 'men' to 'ride and goon ful many a mile / Hym for to seke and have his aqueyntaunce' (*CYT*, 987–8) and, in this way, he 'wolde infecte al a toun'. The 'rammyssh' 'savour', though, is not mentioned again: neither of the alchemists in the Yeoman's stories is noted for it – although their poor, threadbare clothes may give them away. We are told, however, that the canon of the *pars secunda* produces another kind of stink: 'Loo, how this theef koude his *service beede*! / Ful sooth it is that swich *profred servyse* / Stynketh,' (*CYT*, 1065–7). This is much less instinctively detected than the more conspicuous whiff of brimstone and goat with its more obvious assault on the olfactory sense.

Service, the defining ethic of the late Middle Ages, offers a route into an otherwise impregnable community.[63] In the Yeoman's warning about cold calling, there is surely an echo of the Merchant's histrionic concern about Damyan's 'profred servyse':

> O perilous fyr, that in the bedstraw bredeth!
> O famulier foo, *that his servyce bedeth*!
> O servant traytour, false hoomly hewe,
> Lyk to the naddre in bosom sly untrewe,
> God shilde us alle from youre acqueyntaunce!
> O Januarie, dronken in plesaunce
> In mariage, se how thy Damyan,
> Thyn owene squier and thy borne man,
> Entendeth for to do thee vileynye.
> God graunte thee thyn hoomly fo t'espye!
> For in this world nys worse *pestilence*
> Than hoomly foo al day in thy presence.
> *(MerT,* 1783–94)

Again the language of epidemic – 'pestilence' – is used to describe the interior threat posed by seditious labour. Disease is a striking metaphor, describing the way that the most devastating incursions come from the inside and present in the same patterns that structure forms of communal association. The passage above expresses horror – seen in the repeated use of possessive pronouns and the lexicon of familiarity – at the vulnerability of intimate spaces, those places thought to be safest and most unassailable. And at the heart of medieval private space was the bond between master and servant, which ought to brook no invidious and disruptive influence. In the *Canon's Yeoman's pars secunda*, the fraudulent alchemist, seeing that his victim is invincible in the company of his faithful servant, makes sure that this assistant is sent on a phoney errand, urging the priest to protect 'oure privetee' from his 'man', before attempting his sleight of hand (*CYT,* 1102–39). What is more, a false alchemist is better able to prey on his community when he possesses the concerted assistance of his own loyal servant. In the *Prologue,* for example, the Canon stands a chance of infiltrating the pilgrim body when his Yeoman stands with him. The Yeoman is keen to represent himself as a good servant, as a man unreasonably abused for his constancy; in doing so he shows the alarming, indomitable potential of partnership and communal action. Conservative commentators in this period continually stressed that social cohesion would come about only through the efforts of an industrious population, advancing not their individual interests but strengthening the ties – the labour links – between them and others. In contrast, while the enterprise of the population of male interlopers in *The Canterbury Tales* (while individualistic) is healthy and even communally advantageous – a new and necessary influx, filling the holes left by the dead – *The Canon's Yeoman's Prologue* and *Tale* offers a pessimistic account of concerted labour.

Whilst historians are divided about the exact relationship between the labour crisis and the Black Death, contemporaries certainly made a connection: the Statute and Ordinance of Labourers dated the problem of insubordinate 'servants' from the pestilence.[64] *The Canon's Yeoman's Tale* testifies to the paranoia of a community that related the two closely, dramatizing a period of confusion much more bewildering than, say, Langland's apocalyptic vision of a mutinous workforce in Passus VI of the B-text of *Piers Plowman*. Rather than rejecting the call to work like Langland's Wastour, rather than openly opposing correct modes of labour organization, exploitative labour parodies the composition and the affective power of working relationships. In Chaucer's story the rebel-servant is hard to identify as other to the self; the sinister predator turns out to have been corrupted by the same curiosities that his detractors share – the Host's curiosity and his careful questioning of the Yeoman may well suggest him as a man susceptible to infection. The word 'pestilence' in *The Canterbury Tales*, in *The Merchant's Tale* or *The Pardoner's Tale*, for example, is very often a discussion of interior corruption, of the way in which people delude and damage themselves. To return to the passage from *The Merchant's Tale* that I quoted above: its tone is a kind of mock sympathy. January is a monster who gets what he deserves; his private household is under threat because it offends against the moral order and every medieval ideal of marriage set out in contemporary sermons and other didactic literature.[65] May and Damyan may be the agents of his humiliation but its roots must be located within January's aberrant self. We might compare too, the way in which Death in *The Pardoner's Tale* exacts the ultimate punishment from the three protagonists, disbanding their 'compaignye' by discovering its interior corruption. These 'brothers' find what they are looking for – the source of the 'pestilence' (*PardT*, 679) – both death and their own wickedness. Similarly, in *The Canon's Yeoman's Tale*, the alchemists gain access to the inner resources and spaces of the individuals they menace by exploiting their victims' questionable and hidden fantasies.

The Canon and his Yeoman are introduced onto the pilgrimage as a dark and potentially destructive force that, like a disease, seeks acceptance through its modelling itself in the likeness of the pilgrim body. The curiosity – close to, but much more dangerous than suspicion – that is articulated by the Host, exposes the community to the infection. And yet curiosity is everywhere joyfully appreciated in Chaucer's work. Unusually here, in the Canon's Yeoman's contribution, Chaucer touches on its potentially tragic consequences, on the exterior manipulation of our interior lives. And, conversely, this tragically vulnerable narrator also simultaneously warns against the almost opposite dynamic: of the danger of interiorizing and embodying social, gendered and apparently authoritative expectations without question, of modelling the self on an *exemplum*. The Canon's Yeoman's subjectivity is located at the interface between curiosity and conformity and articulates a masculine anxiety – at least as troubling as the gendered anxieties of the Wife of Bath and the Pardoner – which is rooted in the ethics of the urban workshop and the intricacies of homosocial alliance.

CHAPTER 5

Autobiography and skin: the work of Thomas Hoccleve

Hoccleve, with his literary interest, his dining club, and his scruples, was probably more cultured but more *thin-skinned* than the average clerk.[1]

INTRODUCTION: 'WHAT DOES SKIN HAVE TO DO WITH AUTOBIOGRAPHY?'

Autobiographical writing, notes Sidonie Smith, sponsors intriguing overlaps between 'the body of the text, the body of the narrator, the body of the narrated I, the cultural body, and the body politic'. In this chapter I want, like Smith, 'to explore the politics of autobiographical skins', the boundaries between the bodies addressed by autobiography.[2] In this case I am interested in the skins and bodies of Thomas Hoccleve's auto-biographical poetry – 'La male regle', *The Regiment of Princes* and *The Series*.[3] Smith argues that autobiography is about seeking comfort, finding accommodation within the world, within the text, and ultimately within one's own skin:

the body seems to be the nearest, most central home we know, the very ground upon which a 'notion of a coherent, historically continuous, stable identity' can be founded.[4]

Hoccleve, looking for a Boethian home in his poetry about mental illness, financial insecurity and contemporary social disorder, finds no such rest and residence:

> This troubly lyf / hath al to longe endurid;
> Nat haue I wist / how in my skyn to tourne.
> But now myself / to myself haue ensurid

For no swich wondrynge / aftir this to mourne
As longe as my lyf / shal in me soiourne.

(Complaint, 302–6)

Here the narrator describes, with a pun on 'wondrynge', his previous
mental illness as a homelessness and exile within his own 'skyn'. This
spatial dislocation places a physical distance between the 'skyn' and the self
or animating 'lyf', displaying a Gowerian errancy of the kind that I
described in chapter three. But while in John Gower's *Confessio Amantis* the
splintered self is apparently repaired – 'I was mad sobre and hol ynowh'
(*CA*, VIII, 2869) – Thomas continues to make distinctions between different aspects of himself beyond his purported mental recuperation. These
different bits of the narrator converse with, make promises and live –
'soiourne' – inside one another. Here and elsewhere Hoccleve makes his
narrators plural, differently imagined in every autobiographical poem, in
fraught interior conversation amongst themselves; even Thomas's purported discussions with others – Health in 'La male regle', the old man in
The Regiment of Princes, the friend in 'The Dialogue' – are internal
dilemmas dramatized as spoken exchanges.

Any consideration of Hoccleve's reflexive voice is indebted to the
arguments made by John Burrow in his famous lecture on the subject. He
has corrected the assumption that literary convention and personal confession are incompatible, arguing that lived experience, just like the literary representation of the self, is always also shaped by conventions.[5] Just
as Eva M. Thornley has discussed Hoccleve's 'La male regle' in relation to
the conventions of the penitential lyrics it appropriated, this chapter will
consider other tropes and texts with which Hoccleve's account of himself
is in dialogue.[6] In particular I am interested in the ways in which bodies –
Christ's body, the text as a body – were represented, primarily in devotional lyrics, and the way in which they might have served as a model for
Hoccleve's representations of his own body. Hoccleve's choice and use of
inherited devotional discourses is clearly highly strategic and yet revealing
not perhaps about his ontological character but about his desires for the
integrity and cleanliness of his own body and the place he hopes to
discover for it within the social body. Anthony Hasler has also been
intrigued by the overlap between various bodies in *The Regiment*.[7]
However, whilst he focuses on the 'monarchic ideology' of the king's two
bodies and its relationship to the body of the subject and the body of the
text, this chapter is concerned, instead, to think about the body of the
clericus uxoratus and the vexed juncture of work and marital status therein

that has also been explored by Ethan Knapp; although I reach different conclusions and evoke different contexts for Hoccleve's verse, my thinking is clearly indebted to his groundbreaking and inspiring investigation of Hoccleve's bureaucratic poetry and identity.[8]

Several studies of the madness of Hoccleve's work have commented on Hoccleve's descriptions of himself as a fractured narrator and it is in that anxiety about dispersal and disassembly that the autobiographical motivation is located.[9] Hoccleve produces some intriguing imagery – of labour and homeliness – to describe the relationship between the interior and the exterior self. The narrator's body in Hoccleve's writing is regularly described as a home from which his soul or wit might truant or, alternatively, within which it might sleep or lurk malevolently (*RP*, 152–4, 274–7, 387, 1956–7, 1985, 'Complaint' 41–2, 50–1, 64, 144–5, 232–3, 247–9, 400). Off playing, sleeping, or on pilgrimage, the 'wit' / 'goost' leaves the body behind to labour in its absence. Jeremy Tambling has compared the '"nomadic" subject' of Hoccleve's 'Complaint' to the 'decentred and schizoid' subject depicted by Deleuze and Guattari.[10] Hoccleve may have seen and adopted the idea of the 'nomadic' nature of madness from his copying of Gower's *Confessio*, or from the discourses of medieval dualism (that he found, perhaps, in his reading of Henry Suso), but he also makes it a habitual motif, a veritable obsession in his poetry.[11] The narrator in *The Series*, of course, insists on his mental recovery: 'thogh þat my wit / were a pilgrim // And wente fer from hoom / he cam agayn' ('Complaint', 232–3). However, his work colleagues, he says, are still to be convinced. The home that Thomas professes to find in his own self is not replicated by an acceptance amongst his peers within the bureaucratic community to which he has belonged, but from which he now feels excluded. He describes the impermeable, complete body that he sees in the mirror and wonders at his continually being rejected by the 'prees' at 'Westmynstre' ('Complaint' 155–68, 183–91). The intellectual quandary of how to convince his colleagues of his recovered unity of mind and body, and his physical trudging of the 'pauyment' to curry support, recreate the agitated itinerancy of the mental illness that he wants to put behind him: 'O lord, so my spirit / was restelees // I soghte reste / and I nat it fond' ('Complaint', 194–5).

The home that he seeks, that would ratify his newfound sanity – his being at home in himself – is respect from his co-workers. The narrators of both *The Regiment* and 'La male regle' refer to the Privy Seal as 'hoom' (*RP*, 1486, LaMR, 188), a word that puzzled F. J. Furnivall, one of Hoccleve's earliest editors. He concluded that Hoccleve just meant 'back at the Privy Seal', rejecting the idea that the poet had lodgings actually at the Palace of Westminster.[12] It is the work community, though, that is homely and with which the narrator unthinkingly and intimately identifies. The homosocial world of the 'Westmynstre' 'prees' is at the emotional heart of Hoccleve's verse, is its home and *summum bonum*. Others too have noted the warmth with which Hoccleve describes the masculine communities surrounding the Inns of Court, a warmth that John Burrow notes is reproduced in the easy discourse between Hoccleve and his male friend in 'The Dialogue'.[13] Furnivall describes Hoccleve's pre-married life as 'Club life', reading Hoccleve's evocation of 'la Court de bone conpaignie' in his ballade to Henri Sommer, a little as if it were a nineteenth-century gentleman's club.[14] Whether or not such a club actually existed, the ballade claims a friendship with a potentially influential patron and draws a picture of congenial dining circles to which both Hoccleve and Sommer belong.[15] Hoccleve's autobiographical poetry often gives its motivation as a request for payment for work done. That 'petitionary pose', as Burrow has labelled it, produces, as in 'La male regle', comic descriptions of men together, working hard and playing hard; Judith Ferster has identified an Hocclevian appeal to a 'universal brotherhood' in his petitionary poetry.[16]

Several of Hoccleve's characters are converted from, and stand as warnings against fast living and youthful rebellion. Such confessions and their related petitions are often marked by an evocation of fraternal *bonhomie*. However, God has punished the narrators of 'La male regle' and *The Series*, and the old man in *The Regiment* for the trespasses of their past. Their experience of contrition and confession gives them the authority to speak in a homiletic and paternal tone, derived from medieval sermon culture, against contemporary ills: false flattery, the derelict state of modern fashions, coin-cutting and the like. These two positions are by no means incompatible: the second cancelling and legitimating the former, as Larry Scanlon has noted of the contrastive dynamics within *The Regiment*, which he describes as simultaneously a begging poem and *Fürstenspiegel*. They do, though, challenge any claim to a unified structure.[17] The paternal and homiletic voice in Hoccleve's poetry overrides but does not wholly erase the accounts of male homosociality. In 'La male regle' for example, the narrator worries about his past misdemeanours but in a way that recalls them with some nostalgia:

> But on the morn / was wight of no degree
> So looth as I / to twynne fro my cowche:

By aght I woot / abyde / let me see!
Of two / as looth / I am seur, kowde I towche.
I dar nat seyn Prentys and Arondel

Me countrefete, & in swich wach go ny me;
But often they hir bed louen so wel,
Þat of the day / it drawith ny the pryme,
Or they ryse vp / nat tell I can the tyme
Whan they to bedde goon / it is so late.
                                        (LaMR, 317–26)

Although written in the style of a contrite confession – 'I dar nat seyn' – this evokes the image of three young friends enjoying the tavern culture of London. The word 'countrefete' implies that Prentys and Arondel followed Thomas's lead, rather than instigating tavern visits themselves. Thomas carries into his apology a sense not only of his comparative fault but also of his superlative inventiveness as a prime mover in this homosocial world.

All male association is crucial not only to Hoccleve's petitionary pose but also to his notions of domestic comfort. In contrast to some of the other authors investigated in this volume, Hoccleve is not particularly attracted to the ideal of the conjugal household; the 'pore cote' (*RP*, 845, 940) that the narrator of *The Regiment* twice expects to have to inhabit with his wife also contains the friendlessness of retirement, the loss of the collegiate environment and his falling into 'homeless' wedded hardship. In contrast to the 'pore cote' is the hostel accommodation – 'At Chestres In, right faste by the Stronde' (*RP*, 5) – that (although Hoccleve claims to live there while married, presumably somewhat unusually and awkwardly) provided predominantly male companionship.[18] Whilst 'hoom' may seem an eccentric word to apply to one's workmates, this was a culture that understood the practice and homeliness of living and working in fraternal groups. The 'home' that Hoccleve's narrators seek, the place of rest that will settle the self, is closely bound up with work and clerical community. By Hoccleve's time – the early fifteenth century – labour and labouring communities have become the natural subjects of masculine autobiography: work defines the masculine self.

Intriguingly, work in Hoccleve's poetry often integrates the external and somatic with the interior, subjective selves of the narrator, elements that would otherwise fly apart. In this chapter I shall describe work as a kind of skin upon which the coherence of all sorts of bodies depends. In particular, work binds together social corporations; the health of the body politic is contingent upon the labours of its various members. The labour crisis with which Hoccleve would have grown up had produced a preoccupation with work as a social duty; it had also laid a stress upon the social necessity of agricultural and manual labour that was critically scarce. Hoccleve offers a defence of his professional writing by stressing its manual, physical aspects. He depicts himself, indeed, not as a cerebral writer-philosopher but instead as part of a clerical proletariat in solidarity with others like himself. The defensiveness of Hoccleve's tone testifies to an anxiety about what does in fact constitute appropriate and socially advantageous work. That disquiet about the nature of appropriate labour is deepened in Hoccleve's verse by the infrequency with, and unreliable way in, which it was paid. Knapp and Ferster have documented the changing remuneration systems within the Lancastrian bureaucracy in order to assess Hoccleve's repeated concerns about his financial security;[19] such uncertainties must also have appeared as a comment upon the value of bureaucratic work. It is now much observed, and most notably in relation to Hoccleve by Knapp, that the late-medieval and secular bureaucrat found himself in an odd position vis-à-vis the ethics of labour and social duty.[20] The bureaucrat's labour was clerical but jarred discordantly with his secular identity – so often demonstrated in his married status. Whilst we have seen the effects that this disjunction produced in the works of some of his literary predecessors, Hoccleve's response to his quasi-clerical status was to construct his narrator as much more unequivocally of the first estate. The narrator's identification with his work colleagues is even pseudo-monastic and, as I shall show below, he defines work in ways that originated from monastic negotiations of the philosophy and theology of labour. Hoccleve distances his narrator (in both *The Regiment* and *The Series*), and therefore nominally himself, from his marriage and indeed from women generally; I conclude that Thomas is constructed as inherently clerical, as a natural celibate and a man whose marriage is an aberration. The labour identifications in Hoccleve's poetry are thus even more crucial to the integrity of his body. The body is a source of pollution in verse that regularly produces an aggressive clerical antipathy to sexuality, which is again a marked point of difference between the work of Hoccleve and that of his contemporaries investigated in this book.

The authority in Hoccleve's verse is predicated upon this kind of clerical identity. Indeed, the old man that Thomas meets in *The Regiment* adopts a tone similar to that of Chaucer's Parson, who is, of course, an estate model, an icon of masculine labour. Whilst the old man is a construction that moves any impudent claim to authority away from the narrator, there is clearly a close relationship between these interlocutors;

the old man is an embodied warning, a projection of what the narrator might become – simultaneously an aged and poor *imitatio Christi* and a symbol of human sinfulness. Whilst the narrator is young and well dressed, his work-related injuries and his growing poverty show him transforming into his interlocutor. Further, the differences between these two personae allow the text to stand somewhere in between them, relying on their respective claims to humility and the rhetorical arts for its authority.

Whilst Hoccleve's social invective – that part of his verse that is most homiletic in its tone – has been described as an uninteresting 'blemish' on his work, I agree with Larry Scanlon that these seeming digressions are in fact central to the subjective concerns of Hoccleve's verse.[21] Hasler, too, has argued for the symbolic centrality of Hoccleve's digressions to his accounts of himself, considering the way in which they disrupt the body of *The Regiment*.[22] These tangents extrude awkwardly from texts that don't seem to contain them effectively enough for much modern critical taste. The perceived disorder of the body politic is replicated in Hoccleve's spilling narrative forms, skins that cannot adequately contain the fragmenting world or the fractured *autos*. Women – the narrator's marriage, the ethics of marriage and debates on anti-feminism – are often the subjects of these Hocclevian digressions. Whilst this might seem to marginalize the feminine, in fact it reveals its insidious destabilization of Hoccleve's masculine poetics. Women threaten the integrity of the chaste male body, and as such cannot be incorporated naturally into the text, striking off at tangents to the main sentence. In this chapter I shall show the way in which the textual body is sensitive to, and disrupted by, its intersection with the body of Hoccleve's reflexive narrator, his anxieties about women and the collapse of social corporation.

SKIN AND PARCHMENT

Hoccleve, more than any other author of his period, gives his reflexive poetry a verisimilitude by referring to the things associated with writing: the pen, the parchment and the ink. Out of all the texts discussed in this book, Hoccleve's poetry is closest in date to the King's Lynn misericord, and it similarly and self-reflexively refers to the stuff of work: its tools and materials. Chaucer famously expressed his frustration at having to rely on inaccurate copyists to do some of his mundane writing work and is irritated at having to intervene to 'correcte and eke to rubbe and scrape'

('Chaucer's Words unto Adam, His Owne Scriveyn', 6); Hoccleve, in contrast, cuts out the middle man. Whilst Will's tools, in the C-text of *Piers Plowman*, are his paternoster and primer, Thomas's are much more evidently and indubitably also those of the writer and poet himself. They are also, of course, those of a professional writer, and Hoccleve, by self-consciously including them, evokes for his reader the mundane apparatus and day-to-day experience of his trade. The number of surviving autograph manuscripts of Hoccleve's work is unprecedented and suggests, just as his explicitly autobiographical verse does, that we have an immediate access to the figure of Thomas Hoccleve himself and his real-time world.[23] Hoccleve's narrator, in the prologue to *The Regiment of Princes* describes how, on leaving the old man he encounters on the road, he:

> ... sette I me adoun,
> And penne and ynke and parchemeyn I hente,
> And to parfourme his wil and his entente
> I took corage, and whyles it was hoot,
> Unto my lord the Prince thus I wroot:
>
> (*RP*, 2112–16)

The editor Charles Blyth has been encouraged to place a colon at the end of the final line here to capture the impression that the reader is privy to the moment and process of composition, that she watches the poet at work.[24] This is an intriguing writerly illusion, created by drawing attention not only to the literary resources and sources of the medieval poet, in the way that Chaucer and Gower do, but also to the mundane implements of writing as a trade, a trade which he contrasts in the prologue to *The Regiment of Princes* both with agricultural labour and the work of urban 'artificers'. Parchment was Hoccleve's bread and butter; he was responsible for purchasing parchment in the Privy Seal office, and includes bills for it in his *Formulary*.[25]

In making the contrast between different kinds of masculine labour, Thomas asserts that writing is a sufficient kind of employment but he does so in a way which incorporates, and attempts to forestall, the disruptive counter-opinion of 'many men' who 'weenen that wrytynge / No travaille is' (*RP*, 988–9). His retort centres on the question of bodily pain; Thomas defines work as suffering. This is just one of Hoccleve's varied and complex attitudes to work and labour in his writing. Hoccleve reifies his labour and his pain, producing it in relation to things: the paraphernalia of writing. In the passage below, for example, he refers to the parchment, through the synecdochic reference to its colour, to describe the stress that writing places on his eyes:

> Wrytyng also dooth grete annoyes thre,
> Of which ful fewe folkes taken heede
> Sauf we ourself, and thise, lo they be:
> Stomak is oon, whom stowpynge out of dreede
> Annoyeth sore; and to our bakkes neede
> Moot it be grevous; and the thridde oure yen
> Upon the whyte mochil sorwe dryen.
>
> What man that three and twenti yeer and more
> In wrytynge hath continued, as have I,
> I dar wel seyn, it smertith him ful sore
> In every veyne and place of his body;
> And yen moost it greeveth, treewely,
> Of any craft that man can ymagyne.
> Fadir, in feith, it spilt hat wel ny myne.
>
> (*RP*, 1016–29)

The syntax in these verses places emphases on the words 'Stomak', 'Annoyeth sore' and 'grevous', in the first stanza, and in the second on 'wrytynge', 'veyne', 'yen' and 'craft', binding up work with its effects: aching body parts and organs. Both stanzas end with the eyes: the first describes eye-strain in process; the second expresses the more drastic fact of permanent physical damage to the sight with the pivotal and devastating past participle 'spilt'.

Complaints about the painful labour of copying were a literary commonplace of some antiquity. Gregory Sadlek has found a similar motif in the Cistercian writings of Alan of Lille.[26] G. S. Ivy translates one from an eighth-century gospel manuscript that looks oddly familiar:

Ignorant people think the scribe's profession an easy one. Three fingers are engaged in writing, the two eyes in looking; your tongue pronounces the words and the whole body toils. But all labour comes to an end, though its reward shall have no end.[27]

Hoccleve styles his complaint, then, like those of the monastic scribes of the past who, as Ivy notes, 'often comment, in the text or in a colophon, on the labours of copying'. Indeed, the medieval philosophy and theology of work was inherited from the monastic *regulae* where different sorts of labour were compared and evaluated as worship. The definition of work as pain originated from another association between pain and worship;

painful labour and painful worship are particularly associated with the eremitical, as opposed to the cenobitic, monastic communities.[28] In the Antonine tradition, after all, work was solitary and to be endured as part of an immolation of the physical self, rather than a means of social cohesion as it was in the Benedictine monasteries – those great centres of community and culture, which were like cities in the way that labour was organized and stratified within them.[29] The benefits of copying, in the Benedictine monasteries, were considered to be not the subjugation of the body but rather the propagation of Christianity. Mary Carruthers has discussed the way in which medieval monasticism produced a 'civic being' which was 'brought into consciousness through learned practices that were both literary and rhetorical in their nature'; medieval monasticism relied on the equipment, craft and technology of thinking and writing in the construction of its communities.[30] Hoccleve writes of himself and his Privy Seal colleagues, his 'class of scribal labourers' in the communal spirit of monastic scriptoria.[31] However, whilst Hoccleve begins by writing in the spirit of community, his complaints become increasingly particular to himself as he switches from the plural 'we' and 'our' and the third person 'him' and 'his', to 'I' and, in the depressing final line cited here, 'myne' as he spins into increasing isolation. Thomas describes the tragedy of a fraternal community lost in the lonely ascetic relationship with his work, reiterating the problem that had vexed the writers of the monastic *regulae*: how can ascetics form communities?[32]

The tension in the eyes, that 'Upon the whyte mochil sorwe dryen', is also articulated in a line just before this passage in which the narrator describes how he and other writers 'stowpe and stare upon the sheepes skyn' (*RP*, 1014). Burrow has described this as a moment of alienation: the intensity of the writer's gaze makes him lose sight of the parchment and he sees only the stuff of which it is made.[33] The word 'whyte' produces a similar effect: the writer is so close to the page that he can see nothing but its colour, an experience that Knapp has captured well in his phrase 'the dizzying blankness of the page'.[34] The word 'dryen' is idiosyncratic and Blyth glosses it as 'endure'. Of course, 'dryen' also means to dry or cure and, as such, is a telling lexical choice when produced so close to the mention of the parchment. Indeed, it is a word that necessarily comes up in recipes 'Forto make Parchemyne gode and ffyne':

Take þe a schepis skynne & caste hit inne lyme & water & late hit ligge ix dayes þer inne þanne take hit vp & stryne hit a brode on a harowe made for þe nonys þanne take suche a fleyssyng knyf as þis parchemyners vse & chaufe a wey þe flesshe on þe flesshe side & euermore loke þat þov have pouder of chalk inne þi handys forto casten on þe skyn so þat hit mowe alle wey renne a dovne be forne þe knyfe þan **set houte þyn skynne on þe harowe forto drye þanne whanne hit is drye** scave hit efte sonys on þe flesche syde vntil hit be al smothe & þanne take þyn knyfe & kit hit of & rolle hit to geders.[35]

'Drye' is used as a pun (meaning both to suffer torment and to dry out) in the descriptions of the crucifixion in the commonplace 'Charter (or Testament) of Christ' tradition. In these extraordinary and macabre poems, Christ finds that he has no parchment on which to write a charter, granting mankind various rights and freedoms. His own skin, stretched and dried, serves the purpose:

> To a pilour y was py3t
> I tugged and towed al a ny3t
> And waschen on myn owne blode
> And strey3t y streyned on þe rode
> Streyned to drye on a tre
> As parchemyn ou3t for to be
> (LCC, A-text, 75–80)[36]

In this passage the processes of stretching, washing and drying Christ's body reproduce the steps set out in the recipe above, and make the original copy of the charter. The wounds of Christ are black letters against his pale flesh, chalked like parchment. The charter is sealed with liquid wax from his melted heart and witnessed by the two thieves crucified on his either hand. An indenture – a duplicate copy of the agreement for mankind to keep – is made at the last supper and repeatedly reproduced in the sacrament of the Eucharist.[37]

Whilst it is no longer thought that the translation of the charter poem from Guillaume Deguileville's *Pèlerinage de l'âme* is Hoccleve's, he may well have known it for its proximity to another that he rendered as 'Conpleynte Paramont' in one of the autograph manuscripts.[38] Hoccleve also uses the charter motif at several moments in *The Regiment of Princes*. The old man, for example, believes his painful poverty to have been 'feffid' to him by Christ (*RP*, 670), using language that resembles the legal diction of the 'Charter' poems. And a much more explicit reference to the 'chartre of mercy' comes up later in *The Regiment*:

> Him lothid nat His precious body sprede
> Upon the Crois, this lord benigne and good;
> He wroot our chartre of mercy with His blood.
> (*RP*, 3337–9)

The term 'sprede' is another technical parchment-making word, used to describe the stretching of skin on a frame and, in using it, Hoccleve reveals his sensitivity to this metaphorical tradition – a monastic commonplace – that made parchment of divine skin, turning both page and poem into tangible evidence of the passion.[39] Thomas warns 'Whoso shal wryte' (*RP*, 1002) that the silence and stillness that he will have to maintain means that 'His labour to him is the elengere' (*RP*, 1008). He articulates in 'elengere' the tediousness – as Blyth's gloss has it – of the job, but 'elengere' is also a word to do with drawing out and stretching, with its etymology in the Old Teutonic 'langjo' (long), via the Old English 'ælenge', and as such supplies a sense, again, of the physical tension and strain of the written on and writing body.[40] Hoccleve's autobiography appropriates the self-conscious first-person conventions of this kind of affective and popular verse, and reproduces its interest in the materiality of parchment and ink, which stand for skin and blood. The 'Testament' poems attempt to efface intermediaries – the author, scribe and text – producing the illusion of the physical and emotional proximity of the reader to Christ himself. Hoccleve's autobiographical verse, even more emphatically, relies on the equipment of writing both to efface its textuality (as James Simpson has argued) and to make his narrator tangible and plausible to a reader as a representative of the author himself.[41]

However, the 'Charter' poems, written as they were in the diplomatic of the royal charter or charters of pardon, nevertheless incorporated evidence of their clerical makers with their special responsibility for legal writing.[42] Hoccleve's autograph manuscripts are, of course, in a court or business hand as opposed to a book hand and so consistently speak his bureaucratic identity.[43] Hoccleve and his Privy Seal colleagues would have been responsible for the drafting of so-called charters of pardon, amongst their other letters-patent business. Although the royal charters were more the stuff of the Great Seal, this is a period in which writs ordering the production of such documents were being processed in the Privy Seal office.[44] The terms and forms of these sorts of document would also have been a staple part of a young clerk's training in the 'business colleges' where Brown locates Hoccleve's education.[45] But the 'Testament' poems also gave the bureaucratic writer the opportunity to write in the persona of Christ and to transform the familiar charter into the body and blood of Christ as surely as the priest at Mass translates the bread and wine of the Eucharist; 'hoc facite in meam commemoracionem' (LCC, A, 63) Christ says as he delivers the Charter to mankind. Hoccleve's narrator's proximity to the 'whyte' 'sheepes skyn' in *The Regiment* makes explicit the implicit claims of devotional poetry like the 'Testament of Christ' tradition, enunciating the special role of the clerical writer in mediating both spiritual truth and legal claim.

The suffering eyes of Thomas and his fellow writers, which 'Upon the whyte mochil sorwe dryen', are reminiscent of the pains of the crucified Christ and are metaphorically made into manuscript. Writing, indeed the same piece of writing we read, is made out of the narrator's distressed body, formed in every painful 'veyne and place of his body' and represents the site where the narrator's eyesight was 'spilt'. The word 'whyte', the *Middle English Dictionary* tells us, is a metonym for skin but also suggests the whites of the eyes themselves, producing an uncomfortable association between the eye and the page.[46] The concentration of studying, says the friend in 'The Dialogue', might well cause a fusion between the body and the book, and he worries that Thomas might be partially eaten by his own library:

> So farest thow / ioie hastow for to muse
> Vpon thy book / and there in stare & poure
> Til þat it thy wit / consume and deuoure.
> (Dialogue, 404–6)

The word 'stare' comes up again in this passage; the eyes are the place where text and body meet and merge. In Hoccleve's verse his references to the page and his other writing materials purport to express the real self of an embodied narrator. Whilst Hoccleve's writing instruments may appear more naturalistic than the 'scourges'/'penne', 'Iewes spotol'/'ynke' (LCC, A, 83–6) of 'Christ's Charter', they are, in fact, used in the same way, to articulate the somatic suffering of the writer-narrator. Hoccleve's account of work constructs his narrator as a clerical *imitatio christi*, physically marked by the penitential asceticism of writing.

However, the 'Charter' poems also draw attention to a necessarily uneasy relationship between the stuff of which they are made and their makers. Whilst the owners of such poems saw their manuscripts transformed into flesh, their authors and scribes found their work-a-day belongings and routines similarly and grotesquely affected. The poems implicate their makers in the crucifixion, horribly realized on the page they inscribe. In Hoccleve's defensive tone can also be detected the feelings of guilt that demand his laborious sacrifice; like the old man, Thomas is punished until he himself resembles the Christ. In the 'Testament' tradition, the poem itself as a material object becomes the body of Christ and the reader's attention is drawn to the stuff, the (sheep)skin of Christ (*agnus dei*) on which it is written. In recalling the idea of God as sacrificial lamb, the

'Testament' poems also remind their readers of the human sinfulness, of their own sinfulness, which so requires their redemption by Christ. I shall say more about guilt in the next section of this chapter but the invocation of work as pain makes the narrator's body a site both of redemption and punishment; it is at that site that the divergent voices – the homiletic and the homosocial – of Hoccleve's poetry meet.

The humility topoi that Hoccleve deploys in *The Regiment* recall the humility of the suffering Christ and, as such, are very different from those used by the other authors considered in this book, or indeed the 'petitionary poses' that Hoccleve strikes elsewhere:

> For thogh I to the steppes clergial
> Of thise clerkes thre nat may atteyne,[47]
> Yit for to putte in prees my conceit smal,
> Good wil me artith take on me the peyne.
> But sore in me ther qwappith every veyne,
> So dreedful am I of myn ignorance;
> The Crois of Cryst my werk speede and avance.
>
> (*RP*, 2150–6)

The standard rhetorical pose of unlearned humility is expressed here in relation to the narrator's viscera. Thomas's throbbing veins remind him to invoke, and so they simulate, Christ's crucifixion experience. The combination of a first-person address and a catalogue of suffering was part of a new affective emphasis in late-medieval devotional poetry, and Hoccleve appropriates it here.[48] In his account of the torment of writing, Thomas regularly singles out particular parts of the body for special mention – here, of course, it is 'every veyne' – and emulates the way in which medieval artists were inclined to provide inventories of, say, the instruments of the passion and the stations of the cross.[49] In these ways Hoccleve appropriates for his narrator the affective compassion reserved for the dying and afflicted Christ.

The damage that writing has done to his back, says Thomas, makes him physically unsuitable for work in arable agriculture: 'My bak unbuxum hath swich thyng forsworn' (*RP*, 985). It is a phrase which recalls Long Will's excuse for resisting agricultural employment – that he is too tall and weak to work – but Thomas gives a more convincing reason for his incapacity – his work-related injury – and goes on, unlike Will, to stress the manual rather than the intellectual aspect of his work.[50] In his preface to the *Pachomian Rule*, St Jerome (a man who pursued his Biblical studies in the Syrian desert with the assistance of several scribal copyists) included copying with other manual activities, valued not in social terms but as a means of regulating and subjugating the body.[51] In particular, Hoccleve describes the difficulty of holding the parts of his body in unison:

A wryter moot thre thynges to him knytte,
And in tho may be no disseverance:
Mynde, ye, and hand – noon may from othir flitte,
But in hem moot be joynt continuance;
The mynde al hool, withouten variance,
On ye and hand awayte moot alway,
And they two eek on him it is no nay.

Whoso shal wryte, may nat holde a tale
With him and him, ne synge this ne that;
But al his wittes hoole, grete and smale,
Ther muste appeere and holden hem therat;
And syn he speke may ne synge nat,
And bothe two he needes moot forbere,
His labour to him is the elengere.

Thise artificers see I day by day,
In the hotteste of al hir bysynesse,
Talken and synge and make game and play,
And foorth hir labour passith with gladnesse;
But we laboure in travaillous stilnesse;
We stowpe and stare upon the sheepes skyn,
And keepe moot our song and wordes yn.

(*RP*, 995–1015)

In the final couplet can again be seen the relationship between the narrator's skin and his page; his struggle to keep himself contained within his own skin is connected to his strained attention to the sheep*skin* on which he writes. The first stanza here places centrifugal and centripetal forces in competition. Words associated with either combination or division collect at the end of the first five lines. The narrator's struggle for coordination is also a fear of fragmentation. In the narrator's singling out of his various body parts – his mind, his eye, his hand and, in the quotations I cited earlier, his stomach, back, eyes and veins – he effects his own dismemberment in his verse. He advises the would-be writer in the second stanza here that he must create and maintain an illusion of bodily unity by repressing his conversation and song. In the word 'appeare' is an admission of the impossibility of the writer's finding internal coherence. Self-surveillance is described through the personification of the narrator's various parts and most explicitly his 'mynde': in giving pieces of himself separate identities he dislocates rather than collates them. His poetry does not keep the narrator 'hoole' but rather parcels him into pieces.

Indeed, in this respect it imitates the kind of self-expression that is available to the artificers who are able to talk, sing and sport while at work. The artificers can communicate and fool around because they are not similarly compelled to keep their 'wittes hoole'. They find a safe way of letting loose their interior selves. Thomas cannot replicate the ludic, social quality of their self-expression; his poetry is a release of the self but also an account of his mental and bodily disintegration. Here Hoccleve contrasts communal and solitary work; whilst he uses the word 'we' of himself and his colleagues there is no movement or sound to associate them as a community. Hoccleve describes two different sorts of urban labour: the one that integrates you into a fraternal community and another in which you are always alone even in a great crowd, and these, I suggest, are reminiscent of the alternative understandings of labour recalled from monastic heritage and transposed into the new circumstances of fifteenth-century London.[52] Contrast the way in which Langland considers labour only in social and secular, although perhaps not ludic, terms and, although Piers becomes a version of Christ humanized in Passus XIX of the B-text, Langland is less interested in the physical immolation of the workman than he is in the unity of the working Christian community, constructed as an agrarian idyll. Indeed, whilst the economic circumstances of post-Black Death England had resulted in a systematic amplification of the positive aspects of labour, recommending and glamourizing a social need, Hoccleve, on the other hand, recalls an older association between work and pain that he found in the self-immolating labour practices of the ascetic monastic traditions.[53] I locate the difference between Langland's and Hoccleve's understandings of pious labour in those two authors' very different attitudes to marriage and appropriate male sexuality. For Langland, marriage is a labour bond; for Hoccleve, marriage – the source of his shame – can only detract from work, disrupting its homosocial communities.

THE 'BODYES GILT'

If the materiality of the text takes on the impression of the narrator's body, he endeavours too to keep it clean through the process of translation:

> And þat haue I / purposid to translate,
> If God his grace / list therto me lene,

> Syn he of helthe / hath opned me the yate;
> For wher my soule is / of vertu al lene
> And thurgh my bodyes gilt / foul and vnclene,
> To clense it / sumwhat by translacioun
> Of it shal be myn occupacioun.
>
> ('Dialogue', 211–17)

The translation of edifying, homiletic texts washes and rinses the narrator's soul so sullied by his filthy body.[54] Vernacular translations of moral tales, such as those that are translated in *The Series*, remove a surface tarnish to expose a newly sanitary self. In this way, and as D. C. Greetham has observed, the didactic Englishing of material from the *Gesta Romanorum* and of *Horologium sapientiae* are as subjective as 'The Dialogue and Complaint'; in the same way *The Regiment* proper (a translation of three sources about which Hoccleve is explicit) is intimately bound up with its first-person Prologue.[55] The act of translation is a purification ritual rather like the process of Christian confession and absolution and it is written in a reflexive spirit. Hasler has shown how Hoccleve's *Regiment of Princes*, which constructs the body of the ideal prince, is in complex specular dialogue with the unregimented body of the subject in the prologue.[56] *The Regiment of Princes*, after all, asserts a syllabus for the holistic man, just as Book VII of the *Confessio* does, and attempts to countervail the fears of fracture expressed by the narrator in the prologue that precedes it.

The lines that preface the translated texts in *The Series* contain a similarly extraordinary sentiment:

> Thogh I nat shapen be / to prike and praunce –
> Wole I translate / and þat shal pourge, I hope,
> My gilt / as cleene / as keuerchiefs dooth sope.
>
> ('Dialogue', 824–6)

The 'gilt' in this second quotation is somewhat different from the abstract 'bodyes gilt' in the one above. The 'gilt' in this passage is, we learn from the surrounding lines, the one that Hoccleve feels at the offence he has caused women in his earlier Englishing of Christine de Pizan's 'Epistre au dieu d'amours' as the 'Epistle of Cupid'. However, that earlier translation – or rather 'shortened paraphrase' – appears to recapitulate the defence of women that he found in the French original; so the offence and the 'gilt' it engenders are spuriously and rhetorically fabricated.[57] Jill Mann sees in Hoccleve's apology an imitation of Chaucer's apologies to women, but one that slightly misses the point; however, I think we can see more in it than the bad management of Chaucerian influence.[58] The quotation above repeats the idea of translation as a cleansing act that we see in the previous passage; this reverberating imagery imports anxieties about the body into the narrator's 'gilt' about his writings on women. Thomas is positioned in relation to the anti-feminist tradition in a way that may recall the equivocation and irony of Chaucer's *Legend of Good Women*, for example, and yet the prim attitudes to women and sex (and in particular his preference for chastity over marriage) that pervade Hoccleve's verse make this poet's engagement with anti-feminist discourses distinctly different; Thomas claims a writerly and clerical identity that is related to and no doubt inspired by, but not the same as, Chaucer's.

Whether or not Hoccleve is anti-feminist is not a question, for all his posturing, that he seems much to care about. The apparent anxiety at the close of the 'Dialogue' is surely effaced by the misogynist poison of 'The Tale of Jonathas', the last item in *The Series*, in whose inappropriate dedication to 'my lady westmerland' Lee Patterson has found evidence of a 'mind at odds with itself, filled with a mixture of ambition and resentment'.[59] The discussions that hedge the two *Gesta* – 'Jereslaus's Wife' and 'The Tale of Jonathas' – round are reminiscent of the equivocation of Chaucer's Clerk, unsure of how far an *exemplum* relates to, or should serve as a model for, women more generally.[60] 'Of course the *Regement* isn't without some chaff on the Woman question', Furnivall noted, reflecting the perfunctory way in which Hoccleve mapped out the proper patriarchal hierarchy in that poem, using the example of Adam and Eve.[61] Hoccleve's discussion of the 'woman question' is palpably not very interested in women *per se*; although the friend in *The Series* refers to Chaucer's Wife of Bath, he does not make an impression of feminine subjectivity out of the inherited arguments of the anti-feminists and their pro-feminist critics, in the way that *her* creator does. Rather, the antagonism between misogynist clerics and writers like Christine de Pizan generates a crux around which Hoccleve can construct his narrator as a clerical figure who, however unconvincingly, is made at least naïve about, if not at odds with, the Wife and all her 'sect', to appropriate the words of that other Clerk from *The Canterbury Tales*.[62] We might identify a similar feature in the gynophobic hysteria of the 'Ballad to Sir John Oldcastle', a poem that demonstrates, as Richard Firth Green has noted, Hoccleve's hyper-orthodox clericalism.[63] Further, in the first line of the quotation from 'The Dialogue' above, Hoccleve defines himself against what he is not: the jousting knight, a model more suitable for his patron, Humphrey duke of Gloucester. Throughout the discussion about

Thomas's dedication of the book to the duke, Thomas is made the *orator* to Humphrey of Gloucester's *bellator*. Whilst Thomas is portrayed as an innocent where women are concerned, the earl is shown to have an interest in courtship that is fitting for his secular estate and is recruited to improve the narrator's reputation amongst the 'ladyes' ('Dialogue', 701–7).

In the middle of Thomas's discussion with his friend about this reputation, he is asked about his own marriage:

> '. . .
> Thomas / how is it twixt thee & thy feere?'
> 'Wel, wel', quod I / 'What list yow thereof heere?
> My wyf mighte haue hokir & greet desdeyn
> If I sholde in swich cas / pleye a soleyn.'
> ('Dialogue', 739–42)

Two lines sum up this uncommunicative and dreary marriage and they are prefaced by the bored inquiry at line 740. Thomas does not understand nor converse with women well, not his own wife nor women as a group: he has no idea what pleases or offends them. Hoccleve describes himself, most notably in *The Regiment* and *The Series*, as a representative of the first estate, and can certainly assimilate himself on the basis of the work he does; his marital status, however, is something of an obstruction, and in order to manoeuvre around it he credits his narrators, his representatives in the text, with a sexual disinterest: a natural inclination to chastity. It is notable that none of Hoccleve's narrators, even at their most confessional, and in places where it might conventionally be expected, admit to excessive lechery.[64] Only when Hoccleve writes in the persona of another can he write a sexual confession; the old man in *The Regiment* regrets his previous womanizing (*RP*, 648–58). This admission from the contrite bedesman – 'whose own biography bears a suspicious resemblance to Hoccleve's' – is, indeed, the only thing that prevents him merging with the narrator indistinguishably.[65] Hoccleve represents himself in his poetry as a translator of moral texts, as a man without sexual feelings, with a body cleansed of its sexual foulness.

Singularly amongst the authors investigated in this volume, Hoccleve regards women only as distractions, impediments and embarrassments. 'Now wole I torne ageyn to my sentence' (*LaMR*, 160) says the narrator of 'La male regle', relegating the previous three stanzas on the attractions of the women who frequent the St Paul's Head Tavern to the status of an aside. In the same poem, looking for a metaphor to portray avaricious flatterers, Hoccleve plumps for the familiar misogynist nightmare of the voracious and distracting siren:

> Who-so þat list in 'the book of nature
> Of besstes' rede / ther-in he may see
> (If he take heede vn-to the scripture,)
> Where it spekth of meermaides in the See,
> How þat so inly mirie syngith shee,
> Þat the shipman ther-with fallith a sleepe,
> And by hir aftir deuoured is he:
> From al which song, is good, men hem to keepe.
>
> (LaMR, 233–40)

Women in Hoccleve's poetry, like these fantastical mermaids, are so often hindrances and digressions from a main masculine project or occupation. Even the discussions of the narrator's wife, or 'Mrs Hoccleve' as she is styled by Furnivall,[66] are somewhat parenthetical; she is a burden and an embarrassment, little more than a brake on an otherwise promising, clerical career. Furnivall was keen to discover an affective conjugality in Hoccleve's poetry, and finds only two hints, of which he makes much: one where Thomas, in the prologue to *The Regiment*, insists that he married for love, and one in the translation of 'Jereslaus's Wife' from the *Gesta Romanorum*, which insists that there is no love like that of a wife and mother (394–9).[67] In truth, though, these are out-weighed by other, less positive statements on the subject of women and marriage and, in particular, by the narrator of *The Regiment*'s regrets about his career-impeding marriage.

In the prologue to *The Regiment of Princes* there is evidently an intimate association between Thomas's economic concerns and his domestic situation. On first meeting the narrator in *The Regiment of Princes*, the old man suggests three possible reasons for Thomas's depression: the worries of making money, keeping wealth and unrequited love (*RP*, 234–8). This imagines the narrator as the kind of lover-narrator familiar from sources such as the troubadour ballads and, more latterly, the *Confessio Amantis*. However, the financial issues take up much of the verse and the idea of the narrator as a rejected lover is never addressed. Over a thousand lines since the old bedesman's question, the narrator does come to describe his domestic life during a discussion of his poverty:

> . . . It were a greet penance
> For me – God sheelde me fro that streit chance.
> Six marc yeerly to scars is to susteene

> The charges that I have, as that I weene.
> Tow on my distaf have I for to spynne
> More, my fadir, than yee woot of yit
> (*RP*, 1222–7)

The word 'charges' identifies Thomas's family as an onerous burden. Later in the poem, Thomas, again using the word 'charge', is explicit about his wife's being this 'tow on his distaff' and the reason for his being unable to become a priest and take a benefice (*RP*, 1447–58). Six marks would indeed have been a poor wage for a married man at the time, being slightly less than was common for a chantry priest.[68] The *Middle English Dictionary* groups Hoccleve's use of the phrase 'tow on my distaf' – which it glosses as 'having something to attend to' – with Chaucer's in *The Miller's Tale*, in which Absolon is looking for a weapon at the forge – a place alive with industry – to avenge himself in love.[69] The phrase metaphorically figures a burdensome or unresolved situation as an unfinished production process, as raw flax still to be spun. In *The Miller's Tale*, the expression describes Absolon's idle exploits as important matters of 'business' (*MilT*, 3772–5) and contrasts them ironically with the blacksmith's 'pley' – his teasing of Absolon. In Chaucer's use, then, the idiom draws attention to the ironic substitution that can be made between work and sexual play. In Hoccleve's poem, work and domesticity/sexuality are more fatally intersected; the lament about the scarcity of wages is made more desperate by the onerous 'tow on his distaf'. Absolon has been sexually humiliated and there is a similar sense of disgrace in Hoccleve's use of the phrase. John Carpenter's *Liber Albus* records that scolds and brawlers should be punished by being made to hold a distaff with flax on it and process with minstrels as a shaming spectacle.[70] The distaff was also, of course, a female tool; the apparatus of small-scale textile production was exclusively associated with women.[71] Emblematic of women's work, the distaff was an especially demeaning symbol to apply to men.[72]

In *The Regiment*, the question of Thomas's marriage – his reasons for marriage and its implications for his ambitions to the priesthood – surfaces periodically during the discussion of his financial worries. The conversation lurches unnaturally when Thomas's marriage becomes its subject. After a lengthy complaint about fraudulent practices at the office of the Privy Seal, Thomas is anxious for a response from his interlocutor:

> 'Now, fadir myn, how thynkith yow heerby?
> Suppose yee nat that this sit us sore?'

'Yis, certes, sone; that ful wel woot I.
Hastow seid, sone? Wilt thow aght seye more?'
'Nay, sire, as now, but ay upon your lore
I herkene as bisyly as I best can.'
'Sone, than lat us speke as we bygan.

Seye on the soothe, I preye thee hertily,
What was thy cause why thow took a wyf?
  . . .'

(RP, 1548–56)

The old man is abrupt, clearing away the previous topic of conversation mechanically to get on to the evidently separate and 'magnificently unmotivated' subject of the narrator's marriage.[73] Similarly, when the old man sums up, he switches, in a rather ungainly way, back to the subject of Thomas's 'annuitee' (*RP*, 1780): 'And forthy, sone, wole I make a leep' (*RP*, 1767). This staggering between subjects is indicative of the problematic relationship between money and marriage: the dilemma at the heart of a bureaucratic identity.

Whilst Albrecht Classen has seen in the narrator's account of his love-match marriage evidence of a new conjugal affectivity that ran counter to social praxis, this, however, is rather the anomaly in Hoccleve's accounts of marriage, the only place where the erotic or emotional potential of wedlock is mentioned.[74] What is more, the narrator is shown to be wrong-headed in his assumption that 'Shee is my wyf – who may therof me lette?' (*RP*, 1570); he is unapprised, as the old man makes clear, of the canon-law position on marriage. Memorably, January, in Chaucer's *Merchant's Tale*, expresses a similar complacency about committing sexual sin within marriage (*MerT*, 1841). In response to the narrator's error, the old man rehearses the three legitimate reasons for sex within marriage: procreation, the prevention of fornication and the payment of the marital debt.[75] The old man insists that love is the only proper spur to marriage – Thomas claims that this was his own motive – condemning those who marry for lust or money instead. Crucially, of course, this admission doesn't cancel out the possibility that the narrator is chaste. This is an excursus that is evidently inspired by contemporary marriage sermons which are similarly structured, but it also has much in common with the statements on marriage to be found in William Langland's *Piers Plowman*.[76] In particular, the old man repeats the Langlandian anxieties about 'lordes mariages' (*RP*, 1667): that is arranged marriages and child marriages. Whilst some of those prematurely married come in adulthood to love their spouses, the old man says, others find that:

> Thanne is to hem an helle hir mariage;
> Than they desyren for to been unknyt,
> And to that ende studie in al hir wit.
>
> *(RP*, 1657–9)

The miserably married recruit Studie and Wit, those married advocates of marriage in *Piers Plowman* (B, IX–X), to seek a divorce and to intensify the tragedy of their being mismatched.

This detour into the contemporary ethics of marriage, though, is less integrated into Hoccleve's text than in *Piers Plowman*. When Thomas asks for financial advice he is given, unaccountably, advice on marriage as if there were a connection between them that were too obvious to state. Medieval marriage sermons usually took the wedding at Cana for their text – Chaucer's Parson uses this in his discussion of marriage, for example (*ParsT*, 918) – whilst Langland uses the story of Adam and Eve to describe the divinely instituted principles of marriage. None of the exempla in *The Regiment*, however, support the arguments on the legit-imate reason for, and the purpose of, sex within marriage. Instead they are all on the subject of adultery; what is more, to illustrate the injunction against adultery, the old man begins with the story of Abraham and Sarah in Egypt (1695–745), a story not about a man tempted into adultery, but rather of a man who encourages adultery in those around him by denying his wife and claiming her only as his sister. The exemplum, indeed, does not seem to fit the central theme of the sermon. The Abraham story, though, *is* an apt story to relate to the narrator whose marriage is explicitly described as a shame and a burden, who would rather, in fact, that he were his wife's brother.

In another place, the old man assures Thomas that God has given him his wife for the best: to prevent his becoming a wayward and wanton priest (*RP*, 1471–6). This notion of marriage as a method of damage limitation is, of course, an unremarkable medieval attitude; however, in other places, like *Piers Plowman* for example, more positive under-standings of the joys and 'goods' of marriage countervail this negative account of wedlock. Whilst Will in *Piers Plowman* is a little sheepish about his being anomalous, a *clericus uxoratus*, and while Thomas in *The Regiment* is occasionally represented as similarly and comically callow, he is also a resentful figure who cannot participate, or be paid in the way he would like, by taking a benefice. Whilst, in *Piers Plowman*, Will's work is inappropriate given his marriage (C, V), Thomas's marriage, in *The Regiment of Princes*, is wrongly conceived given his calling. The Church still actively legislated against married men taking up any ecclesiastical jurisdiction, reiterating and extending the exclusion it had always preferred.[77] Furthermore, Malcolm Richardson has noted the discomfort that married officials were made to feel by the moves being made in the early fifteenth century to keep them out of government office; in particular, restrictions were being placed on married clerks working in chancery, as recorded in the *Ordinaciones cancellarie*.[78]

Hoccleve's poetry is an interiorization of this cultural disapproval of men in his middling position. An unenthusiastic account of marriage suffuses Hoccleve's work as he regularly asserts his proximity to a clerical rather than a secular identity. *The Regiment of Princes*, true to its Aristotelian source and citing St Paul (Ephesians 6.16), recommends chastity over marriage: 'That fyry sparcle algate he muste qwenche / And lustes leve of lady and of wenche' (*RP*, 3667–8).[79] Although this is directed at men, the injunction to remain chaste is unisex. The exempla of the 'De castitate' section of *The Regiment* feature both men and women who disfigure themselves in order to evade the sexual advances of others: a seemly young man 'with his nayles cracchid he his face, / And scocchid it with knyves and torente,' (*RP*, 3726–7), while two sisters tie putrid chicken flesh under their breasts to discourage any potential suitors (*RP*, 3774–80); these ingenious virgins are thus spared anything 'unclene' (*RP*, 3725, 3780). The stories of souls made hygienic through the dirtying and mutilation of the body, thus rendered in English, articulate the moral cleanliness of their translator who disdains the body and its contaminating influence. As Diane Bornstein despairingly notes '[w]hen Hoccleve praises women, it is as saints and martyrs rather than as human beings in natural relationships with men'; I just add that, palpably, Hoccleve would rather that *men* became saints and martyrs rather than be in any 'natural' relationship with women.[80] Although, of course, such aggressive anti-somatic attitudes are suggested, in part, by the stance of the source material, it is instructive to compare the chastity section in Book VII of John Gower's *Confessio Amantis*, which also styles itself as an 'advice to princes' manual. Gower fails to recommend chastity so unequivocally, and chooses a bizarre illustrative example in the polygamous David, concluding that such promiscuity can be excused if it is matched by a great martial reputation (*CA*, VII, 4344–60). The corresponding section of *The Regiment* introduces no such doubt or confusion, maintaining the integrity of the body as an indispensable attribute of the perfect prince; Hoccleve never shows the kind of commitment that Gower does to conjugality and never wavers in his confidence about the pious superiority of virginity.[81]

Even where Hoccleve translates the story of Jereslaus's wife – a good woman who endures a panoply of torments in order to remain faithful to her husband – he cannot bring himself to recommend marriage to either men or women. In the 'moralization', the story is allegorized into a dispute between the body and the soul:

> and the flessh apparceyuynge þat / solicitith and bysyeth hire / stirynge the ful noble soule, which is Crystes spowse / vn- to synne / but nathelees the soule þat is wel beloued of god, and vn-to Cryst weddid & oned, wole nat forsake god and consente to synne / wherfore the wrecchid flessh despoillith often and robbith the soule of hir clothes / þat is to seyn, goode vertues
>
> (J'sW *Moralizacio*, p. 176)

Although Thomas claims that the tale of Jereslaus's virtuous wife will improve his relations with women, in the moralization he makes her and the abuse she suffers into a more general struggle between the virile and rapacious flesh and the vulnerable soul. It has been suggested too that this move to the universal, in the moralization above, is designed to resist making any incautious comment upon the romantic fortunes of the duke of Gloucester;[82] the moralization makes the text politic, polite and pure. Here marriage is used as an image to describe the relationship between the divine and the human soul; this is a common metaphor that Hoccleve uses a lot (see, for example, *RP*, 1349). It comes from exegesis on the Song of Songs, by Bernard of Clairvaux and others, a tradition in which medieval clerical commentators both sanitized erotic writing through allegorical interpretation and infused religious worship with erotic energy.[83] However, it could also work the other way: the relationship between Christ and the soul, or Christ and the Church, could be used as a metaphor to legitimate secular marriage, to sanctify it as a divine institution and to describe the appropriate hierarchy of husband and wife – as indeed Chaucer's Parson does, for example (*ParsT*, 921). So, whilst this metaphor was potentially reversible, Hoccleve is not interested in finding accommodation for secular married people within his understandings of piety, and Jereslaus's wife is left as a disembodied abstraction.

CONCLUSION: CLOTHING THE BODY POLITIC

Medieval sermons on dress were often directed against women and their dressing to seduce.[84] The old man's invective against contemporary clothing in *The Regiment of Princes*, though, conspicuously focuses on the male body in both a microcosmic and a macrocosmic sense; clothing is clearly another important regulating 'skin' with the power to right a 'land' in confusion. The old man's objections to contemporary styles of clothing are about the failures of masculine industry and their damaging effect on economy and society; these are the same anxieties, about labour and gender, that reach to the heart of Hoccleve's representation of the troubled *autos*. The denunciation of extravagant clothing in *The Regiment* has much in common with a similar diatribe in Chaucer's *Parson's Tale*; they share a homiletic tone appropriated from contemporary sermon culture. Chaucer's Parson launches a two-pronged attack both on long, draped styles, which are quickly dirtied and ruined, and on skimpy, revealing clothing, which exposes the contours of the 'swollen membres' and 'buttokes' (*ParsT*, 422). The anxiety here is first about the waste of good cloth which could have been dispersed amongst the poor, and secondly about the sexual body. Hoccleve's old man is not concerned about short and tight clothes, only about long and flowing garments; further, his concern about them is different from Chaucer's pilgrim: he worries about the confusion of the estates and the divestment of the body politic. He worries, indeed, about the impoverishment of great households, rather than the exigencies of the poor (*RP*, 491–7).

In particular, the concern is about the propriety of men's working clothes:

> Let every lord his owne men deffende
> Swich greet array, and thanne, on my peril,
> This land withynne a whyle shal amende.
> In goddes name, putte it in exyl;
> It is a synne outrageous and vyl;
> Lordes, if yee your estat and honour
> Loven, fleemeth this vicious errour.
>
> What is a lord withouten his meynee?
> I putte cas that his foos him assaille
> Sodeynly in the street: what help shal he
> Whos sleeves encombrous so syde traille
> Do his lord? He may him nat availle;
> In swich a cas he nis but a womman;
> He may nat stande him in stide of a man.
>
> His armes two han right ynow to doone,
> And sumwhat more, his sleeves up to holde.
> (*RP*, 456–69)

There is nothing unisex here; Hoccleve is explicitly interested in the way in which dress articulates – or at least ought to – masculinity and status differences between men. In particular, the old man expresses his concern about the disruption of traditional masculine roles and occupations, as ludicrously elongated sleeves frustrate the duties of the retainers that make up the lord's 'meynee'. Hoccleve's beggar is not, like Chaucer's Parson, interested in the lack of charity for the poor but instead in the intelligibility, or otherwise of cultural signs. The old man's concerns are, unlike the Parson's, about the dissolution rather than the enunciation of sexuality. Clear distinctions between men and women and between the estates, signalled through the wearing of distinct uniforms, produces an ordered body politic. The imperative to 'exyl' 'greet array' personifies ostentatious chic as an agent of sedition. These anxieties are similar to the concerns of the petitioners who were requesting, in the early fifteenth century, a new sumptuary statute that would replace the repealed 1363 Statute of diet and apparel.[85] This piece of legislation was similarly concerned with designating particular fabrics and styles according to masculine occupations and status groups; it is evidently understood in that text that the health of the body politic is determined by the way in which it is clothed. The statute allocates particular forms of dress on the basis of masculine occupation, each being qualified by the formula 'and that their Wives, Daughters, and Children, be of the same Condition in their Vesture and Apparel'.[86] Indeed, with its complaints about rising prices and wages, it replicates many of the anxieties of the 1351 Statute of Labourers. Hoccleve too makes clothing all about masculine labour, and, tellingly, the old man wears a simple garment made of 'bare old russet', the fabric recommended for ploughmen – those iconic estates models – in the sumptuary statute.[87]

Whilst Chaucer's Parson and the 1363 statute writers, like Hoccleve's old man, are concerned with the various effects of wearing showy clothing, Hoccleve's old man is also worried about their impact upon the textile and clothing manufacturing industries. Just as the sleeves of the lord's retainer thwart his military service, so those same sleeves disrupt the workshops in which they should be cut and sewn:

> The taillours, trowe I, moot heeraftir soone
> Shape in the feeld; they shul nat sprede and folde
> On hir bord, thogh they nevere so fayn wolde,
> The clooth that shal been in a gowne wroght;
> Take an hool clooth is best, for lesse is noght.

> The skynner unto the feeld moot also
> His house in Londoun is to streit and scars

To doon his craft; sumtyme it was nat so.
O lordes, geve unto your men hir pars
That so doon, and aqweynte hem bet with Mars,
God of bataille; he loveth noon array
That hurtith manhode at preef or assay.

Who now moost may bere on his bak at ones
Of clooth and furrour hath a fressh renoun;
He is a lusty man clept, for the nones.
But drapers and eek skynners in the toun
For swich folk han a special orisoun,
That droppid is with curses heer and there,
And ay shal til they paied be for hir gere.
                                    (*RP*, 472–90)

The word 'manhode', of course, is a word that implies both nobility and virility; in discouraging these extraordinary costumes, through an emphasis upon military training, the old man says that the lord will protect the authority of men, and especially those in a position of privilege. Chaucer's Parson has a good understanding of the technical vocabulary of tailoring, condemning 'embrowdynge, the degise endentynge or barrynge, owndyge, palynge, wyndynge or bendynge' (*ParsT*, 416) and mentions the tools that cut and perforate the cloth in elaborate ways (*ParsT*, 417) and yet he doesn't, in the intricate way that Hoccleve does, imagine the workshops and workbenches where these flamboyant fashions are cut. Hoccleve is unusual, and quite unlike Chaucer, for example, in setting his character's sermon on modish attire much more clearly in 'Londoun' and in the workshops of the urban tailors, skinners and drapers. The limited space on the tailor's bench and in the skinner's London workshop forces these two workmen to leave the town boundaries and conduct their work in the 'feeld'.[88] There is currently no workshop large enough within which to cut the cloth – the skin – that might contain the sprawling body politic of present times. The surplus quantities of fabric spill beyond the confines of the London workshops, beyond the limits of the city itself. The removal to the suburbs suggests a transition into the morally dubious areas of socially excluded trades.[89] The final stanza here frets about the insubordination fostered in these craftsmen by the foolishness of their clients.

The cloth workers' disaffected muttering, as a response to the lack of payment, is not a reaction that usually accompanies the legion complaints in Hoccleve's verse about the breakdown of systems of remuneration. Hoccleve's petitionary verse is, of course, too politic to display such naked mutiny, even though the skinners and drapers in *The Regiment* are neither blamed nor censured for their defiance. Yet part of the old man's polemic maintains, on the narrator's behalf, that excessive lengths of cloth soak up the cash that would otherwise be liberally dispersed in the community to which the narrator belongs:

> Than mighte silver walke more thikke
> Among the peple than that it dooth now.
> Ther wolde I fayn that were yset the prikke –
> Nat for myself, I shal do wel ynow –
> But, sone, for that swiche men as thow,
> That with the world wrastlen, mighte han plentee
> Of coyn, whereas yee han now scarsetee.
>
> (*RP*, 526–32)

This is the 'trickle-down' of corrupted masculinity; flashy liveries sponsor social unrest and insurrection in the workshops of the household crafts rather than effecting the proper circulation of capital. In this passage is seen the distinction which is maintained throughout the prologue between the old man and the narrator. The old man observes this, as is his wont, as a distinction of dress: 'poore be my clothing and array / And nat so wyde a gowne have as is thyn – / So smal ypynchid ne so fressh and gay' (*RP*, 408–10). The narrator is characterized as a man compelled to live in, 'wrastlen' with the world, a world that is also inhabited by silver (one of Hoccleve's many little personifications) who walks about in it as if he were a person that the narrator might bump into now and again. In a deft rhetorical shift, any grouch about the 'scarsetee' of 'coyn' comes out not as a 'special orisoun', like that of the skinners and drapers, but rather as an expression of the beggar's simple, generous and self-effacing concern for the narrator.[90] The old man becomes an advocate for the narrator, asking for benefits that the narrator cannot request for himself.

The subject of *The Regiment* is schizoid, to borrow the word that Tambling uses of the subject in the 'Complaint', but manages, in this way, to claim for itself the authority of both personae.[91] Standing respectively for plain piety and writerly craft, the two interlocutors embody two contradictory aspects of the clerical *habitus*. Here, for example, *The Regiment of Princes* proper, with its earnest advice, is personified and approaches Prince Henry, the dedicatee of the poem, as modestly clad as the beggar and as a near-naked supplicant:

> O litel book, who gaf thee hardynesse
> Thy wordes to pronounce in the presence
> Of kynges ympe and princes worthynesse,

Syn thow al nakid art of eloquence?
And why approchist thow his excellence
Unclothid sauf thy kirtil bare also?
(*RP*, 5440–5)

Here the narrator is an embarrassed spectator, in brotherhood with the prince, who understands the contemporary dress conventions that keep princes and beggars apart. In contrast, the advice manual itself becomes the type of Christ, and, although it is richly endowed with moral virtue, is plainly dressed in the vernacular. This passage is clearly deeply rhetorical and disingenuous, demonstrating literary panache whilst all the time insisting that truth (the counselling text) is unmediated, free of authorial interference. This passage describes translations as naked texts, stripped of their occluding Latin coverings.

However, the narrator is not censured for his finely pleated and 'wyde' 'gowne'; he is not expected to realize the old man's abstinent renunciations. And in his being well dressed we might see too – because ornate clothing is a metaphor for rhetorical art in Hoccleve's verse – Hoccleve's claims for his literary artfulness. His humility topoi – which purport to expose the denuded truth – are, like the King's Lynn misericord with which this book began, concerned to craft an artificially conceived, mimetic and quotidian scene. The apparent banality of the medium – English – and the representations of the stuff – the tools of the bureaucrat's trade – are supposed to guarantee the text's authenticity and yet they simultaneously draw attention to the writer's superlative art, command of rhetoric and the dignity of his masculine labours. Hoccleve writes his narrators as large and as toiling as the carver, whose imposing form takes up the central space on the misericord. Hoccleve and the maker of the King's Lynn misericord are exact contemporaries, and evidently occupy the same rhetorical space in which the masculine self is most naturalistically depicted within the homosocial community, in relation to occupational accoutrements, spaces and ideologies.

Notes

INTRODUCTION

1 Augustine, *Confessions*, O'Donnell (ed.), I, 128. 'Certainly, O Lord, I am working hard on it, and my work is being done on myself; I have become unto myself a soil of difficulty, and of too much sweat.' Augustine, *Confessions*, Bourke (trans.), p. 284.

2 The cover of Anderson, *Misericords* uses the image to depict 'medieval life' in this way. Swanson, 'The Illusion of Economic Structure', esp. p. 29.

3 This misericord is dated *c.* 1419. See the catalogue of the Victoria and Albert Museum, where the piece is now displayed: Tracy, *English Medieval Furniture*, p. 62, plate 30.

4 The average number of apprentices was one or two; see Hovland, 'Apprenticeship in the Records of the Goldsmiths' Company', p. 97, n. 34.

5 On the provenance of this carving, see Tracy, *English Medieval Furniture*, p. 62.

6 For the processes of English stained glass production see Marks, *Stained Glass*, p. 30.

7 Anderson, 'The Iconography of British Misericords', p. xxiii.

8 Anderson, *Misericords*, p. 6. Every literary critic, familiar with the way that the Chaucerian canon has been distinguished from work by Chaucer's contemporaries, will remember similar comments. For example, this is F. J. Furnivall on Hoccleve's 'Mother of God' (which 'some of us at one time attributed to Chaucer'): 'The Virgin's *teats* too, [...] didn't look like Chaucer's good taste.' Hoccleve, *Hoccleve's Works*, Furnivall and Gollancz (eds.), p. xxxix, n. 3.

9 See, for example, Olney, *Memory and Narrative*, p. xv; Amelang, *The Flight of Icarus*, pp. 15–16; de Looze, *Pseudo-Autobiography in the Fourteenth Century*, pp. 1–2, and Zumthor, 'Autobiography in the Middle Ages?', *passim*.

10 Olney, *Memory and Narrative*, p. xv. 'Life writing' was originally used to group autobiography, biography, memoirs and so on into one genre; now it is also used to refer to writing about or around the self. See, for example, the definition offered by Kadar, *Essays on Life Writing*, p. 10.

11 de Looze, *Pseudo-Autobiography*, pp. 1–2.
12 This discussion is very much indebted to Tambling, *Confession*, esp. pp. 2–3 and 35–65.
13 Cited in Olney, *Memory and Narrative*, p. xv.
14 Amelang, *Flight of Icarus*, p. 16
15 See the discussion of Burkhardt and his legacy for scholars of medieval autobiography in Ferguson, 'Autobiography as Therapy', esp. p. 189. For an example of Burkhardt at work in modern autobiographical theory see Smith, *Subjectivity, Identity and the Body*, p. 5.
16 Tambling, *Confession*, p. 58.
17 See, for example, the discussion of anxiety and the use of Burkhardt in Breitenberg, *Anxious Masculinity*, pp. 1–2 and 7. On Weber and masculinity see Hearn and Collinson, 'Theorizing Unities and Differences Between Men', p. 99.
18 See, for an example of this strategy being deployed in relation to Marx and Engels, Tocqueville, Weber and Freud, Kimmel, 'Masculinity as Homophobia', pp. 121–2.
19 The quotation comes from Connell, *Masculinities*, pp. 186–9.
20 Peters, *Patterns of Piety*, pp. 1–7, esp. p. 2.
21 Heale, *Autobiography and Authorship*, pp. 5–8.
22 See, for example, the way that faith is used to contrast Augustine the 'model servant of God' with Montaigne the 'irreproducible individual' in Gunzenhauser, 'Autobiography: General Survey', pp. 75–6.
23 The term 'self-fashioning' comes from Greenblatt's seminal *Renaissance Self-Fashioning*, p. 9, who finds the Renaissance individual not free, as Burkhardt implies, but subject to, and invested in, systems of authority. Evidently I am arguing that this is not exclusive to the Renaissance period.
24 Throughout this book I maintain the distinction between authors and their narrators who share their name by using the first name for the narrator (e.g. Thomas) and the second for the author (e.g. Usk). In this respect I follow Staley, *Dissenting Fictions*, p. 3.
25 See Patterson, 'Perpetual Motion', p. 30, and chapter four below.
26 See Middleton, 'Acts of Vagrancy', p. 244, and chapter one below.
27 Weintraub, *The Value of the Individual*, p. xvi.
28 On the idea of the autobiographical impulse or motive see Ferguson, 'Autobiography', pp. 191–2.
29 For a discussion of these two predicaments in psychoanalytic terms see Rank, *Will Therapy*, pp. 134–6.
30 Rees Jones, 'Household, Work and the Problem of Mobile Labour', p. 139.
31 The discussion of migration, service and young people is indebted to P. J. P. Goldberg, and especially his *Women, Work and Life Cycle*, pp. 212–16.

32 Many discuss this bureaucratic circle and the links within it. See, for example, Kerby-Fulton and Justice, 'Langlandian Reading Circles', pp. 59–83.

33 For a discussion of Chaucer's involvement, see Robertson, 'Laboring in the God of Love's Garden', esp. pp. 117–26.

34 On the liminal gendered status of the lay clergy and bureaucrats, see Cullum, 'Clergy, Masculinity and Transgression', p. 180; Burger, *Chaucer's Queer Nation*, pp. 48–9.

35 Davis, 'John Gower's Fear of Flying', pp. 131–52.

36 See, for example, Aristotle, *De partibus animalium I and De generatione animalium I*, Balme (trans.), pp. 40–2, and Cadden, *Meanings of Sex Difference*, pp. 77 and 176.

37 Sadlek, *Idleness Working*, esp. pp. 102–3.

38 McIntosh, *Controlling Misbehaviour in England*, pp. 129–30; Rees Jones, 'Household, Work and the Problem of Mobile Labour', p. 145 (the following discussion is indebted to this article).

39 The phrase 'cognitive purification' is borrowed from Connell, *Gender and Power*, p. 246.

CHAPTER I

1 Peter Dronke has memorably described the poem's interest in horticultural figures as a 'seemingly unpremeditated interplay of vegetal notions', '*Arbor caritas*', p. 210.

2 In this chapter, unless otherwise stated, I shall be referring to the B-text version of *Piers Plowman*. I use the following editions: for the B-text, Langland, *The Vision of Piers Plowman*, Schmidt (ed.); Langland, *Piers Plowman: The C-text*, Pearsall (ed.), and Langland, *Piers the Plowman: The A Version*, Kane (ed.).

3 See, for example, *The Life of Adam and Eve*, in Blake (ed.), *Middle English Religious Prose*, esp. p. 109, and Cohen, '*Be Fertile and Increase . . .*', *passim*.

4 Several critics have analysed the poem in relation to the labour statutes; see especially Aers, *Community, Gender, and Individual Identity*, esp. pp. 26–30; Middleton, 'Acts of Vagrancy', pp. 208–317.

5 *Wynnere and Wastoure* is certainly written in a similar cultural space to *Piers Plowman* and is also related closely to the labour legislation of the period. For a survey of the literature on, and discussion of, these relationships see the introduction in Trigg (ed.), *Wynnere and Wastoure*, esp. pp. xxvi–xxvii and xlii–xliv. On the household register of *Wynnere and Wastoure* and *Piers Plowman* see Smith, *Arts of Possession*, pp. 72–107 and 111.

6 See, for example, Goldberg, *Women, Work and Life Cycle*, esp. pp. 289 and 297, Mate, *Women in Medieval English Society*, pp. 28–9, 40–1 and 47–8, and Dyer, 'Work Ethics', pp. 31, 33 and 38.

7 Shahar, *The Fourth Estate*, p. 2.

8 See especially Lees, 'Gender and Exchange in *Piers Plowman*', pp. 112–30. See also Trigg, 'The Traffic in Medieval Women', pp. 5–29 and Fowler, 'Civil Death and the Maiden', pp. 760–92.

9 See, for example, Connell, *Masculinities*, p. 93, and Tosh, *A Man's Place*, p. 2.

10 On the usefulness of the poem to historians see, for example, Barron, 'William Langland: A London Poet', p. 91, and Hatcher, 'England in the Aftermath of the Black Death', pp. 3–35. For a discussion of marriage and family, see Tavormina, *Kindly Similitude*. The one exception that considers both masculinity and work is: Ralph Hanna III, 'Will's Work'. My differences with Hanna and Tavormina will become clear in the course of the chapter.

11 See chapter four for a longer discussion. On the regulation of labour and the household see Rees Jones, 'Household, Work and the Problem of Mobile Labour', pp. 133–53.

12 The phrase is borrowed from Connell, *Gender and Power*, p. 246.

13 Wendy Scase has also argued for a 'new' discourse, in her case a 'new anticlericalism', emergent in *Piers Plowman*. She has also noted the '[r]hetorical unease' that this generates around the figure of the dreamer-poet himself, who is the type of the 'gyrovague': '*Piers Plowman*' and the New Anticlericalism, esp. pp. 168–9.

14 Cullum, 'Clergy, Masculinity and Transgression', esp. p. 180.

15 Burrow, *Langland's Fictions*, pp. 82–108.

16 The fullest analysis of the poem's multivocal subjectivity can be found in: Lawton, 'The Subject of *Piers Plowman*', *passim*.

17 See, for example, Paxson, 'Inventing the Subject and the Personification of Will in *Piers Plowman*', pp. 226–9, Hanna, 'School and Scorn', p. 215, and Bowers, *The Crisis of Will in 'Piers Plowman'*, p. 2.

18 Salter, *Fourteenth-Century English Poetry*, p. 102, and Kasten, *In Search of 'Kynde Knowynge'*, p. 57.

19 [Let every man abide in the same calling in which he was called.]

20 Oddly, Jerome equates virginity rather than marriage with the state of circumcision: His argument is that marriage makes you bound, as too does a foreskin, whereas virginity is a state of freedom from such binding. *Adversus Jovinianum*, PL 23, VI, i, 12, col. 0229B.

21 Yeager, 'The Body Politic and the Politics of Bodies in the Poetry of John Gower', pp. 146–50.

22 23 Edwardi III, and 25 Edwardi III, 2 in *Statutes of the Realm*, I, 307–13.

23 See the conclusion to the Ordinance, p. 309.

24 See the Statute preamble, p. 311, and Ordinance, c. iii, p. 307.

25 Compare Heather Swanson's argument about the records of urban economic regulation in 'The Illusion of Economic Structure', pp. 29–48.

26 Middleton, 'Acts of Vagrancy', p. 244. Unlike Middleton ('Acts of Vagrancy', p. 214) I am not so convinced that the *Apologia* necessarily post-dates the 1388 vagrancy statute, nor that vagrancy legislation was a direct corollary of the 1381 rising; as Christopher Given-Wilson has shown, in particular through his

analysis of a 1376 *grante bille*, mobile labour was a long-standing concern which was crystallized in the 1388 Statute. Given-Wilson, 'Labour in the Context of English Government', pp. 88–9. Furthermore, I think it entirely possible that a popular poem, like *Piers Plowman*, which we know from the work of Steven Justice and Kathryn Kerby-Fulton was produced in physical proximity to the labour legislation of the period, might have influenced law makers and enforcers (helping both to shape as well as resist the culture of surveillance that Middleton describes), just as much as their legislative productions fed back into Langland's on-going poetic project. Justice and Kerby-Fulton, 'Langlandian Reading Circles', pp. 59–83. Indeed, *Piers Plowman* often anticipates phrases and ideas in the labour statutes, which suggests at least a discursive connection, if not the direct influence of the poem on the makers of legislation. Compare, for example, the indexes of outrage in B, VI, 315–16 and 5 Richard II, 1 *Statutes of the Realm*, II, c. v, 20.

27 'But I say to the unmarried, and to the widows: It is good for them if they so continue, even as I.'
28 Middleton, 'Acts of Vagrancy', pp. 252–3.
29 Hanna, 'Will's Work', esp. pp. 30–1, has considered the gender implications of Will's vocational status. I don't agree, though, that Will is represented as feminized by his disconnection from any particular monastic rule.
30 Hanna, 'School for Scorn', p. 215.
31 Donaldson, *The C-Text and its Poet*, pp. 202–5; see the extensions and qualifications made to his case by, for example, Hanna, 'William Langland', p. 154, and Hanna, 'Will's Work', pp. 23–5.
32 Middleton, 'Acts of Vagrancy', *passim*, and Scase, *'Piers Plowman' and the New Anticlericalism*, pp. 168–9.
33 'men who are barbers, from uppelande unto the said city, who are not instructed in their craft, and do take houses and intermeddle with barbery, surgery and the cure of other maladies no stranger from uppelande, or any other place shall keep house or shop for barbery within the city,' cited in Riley, *Memorials of London*, pp. 393–4.
34 Poos, 'The Heavy-Handed Marriage Counsellor', p. 295.
35 See, for example, the confidence that Langland has in the sexual morality of static hermits and anchorites (B, Prologue, 28–30).
36 See Swanson, 'The Illusion of Economic Order', p. 29, and Rees Jones, 'Household, Work and the Problem of Mobile Labour', p. 135.
37 McSheffrey, 'Men and Masculinity', pp. 243–78; Goldberg, 'Masters and Men', p. 59.
38 On the way in which Langland juxtaposes an agrarian idyll with a depraved city existence, see Derek Pearsall, 'Langland's London', pp. 187–8.
39 Middleton, 'Acts of Vagrancy', e.g. p. 257.
40 Kean, 'Justice, Kingship and the Good Life', pp. 76–110.
41 See Schmidt's notes to Passus VIII of the B-text, p. 327. There is also a related and sometimes conflated suggestion that the Dos represent the Active, Contemplative and Mixed Lives. For discussions of these matters see, for

example, Hussey, 'Langland, Hilton and the Three Lives', e.g. p. 132, and Kean, 'Justice, Kingship and the Good Life', *passim*.

42 On the Passus markers in the B and C versions and the way in which they signal transitions between the Dos, see Clopper, 'Langland's Markings for the Structure of *Piers Plowman*', pp. 245–55.

43 Du Boulay, *The England of 'Piers Plowman'*, p. 26 (the quote is from him). See also, Keller, 'For Better and Worse', p. 68.

44 Tavormina, *Kindly Similitude*, p. xiii.

45 See, for example, the commentary added to the Douay-Rheims version in the middle of the eighteenth century by Bishop Richard Challoner. http://www.drbo.org

46 *Adversus Jovinianum*, PL 23, I, XIII, col. 0232B. [The difference, then, between marriage and virginity is as great as between not sinning and doing well; nay rather, to speak less harshly, as great as between good and better.] Translation: Jerome, *Letters and Select Works*, trans. and ed. Wace and Schaff.

47 Aers, *'Piers Plowman' and Christian Allegory*, pp. 85–8.

48 See, for example, Lees, 'Gender and Exchange', *passim*.

49 'dixit quoque Dominus Deus non est bonum esse hominem solum faciamus ei adiutorium similem sui.' [And the Lord God said: It is not good for man to be alone: let us make him a help like unto himself.]

50 Smith, 'Body Doubles', pp. 3–19, has elaborated on these ideas, describing them as prevalent in the Middle Ages, but he does not discuss Langland. He has, however, discussed Langland elsewhere, although doesn't consider the issue of gender. See, for example, Smith, *The Book of the Incipit* and *Arts of Possession*, chapter 4.

51 Schmidt, in Langland, *Piers Plowman: B-text*, p. 98, glosses 'Wreke' as 'vent'.

52 *OED*: wreak: '4.a. To punish or chastise (a person); to visit with retributive punishment. b. To injure, hurt, or harm (a person). 5.a. To avenge (a person).'

53 Sheehan, 'Sexuality, Marriage, Celibacy, and the Family', p. 299.

54 Hanawalt, '"The Childe of Bristowe" and the Making of Middle-Class Adolescence', p. 165, notes the way that the wilderness of adolescence was often compared to the civility of the household in late medieval texts.

55 For an account of the medieval marriage sermon, see D'Avray and Tausche, 'Marriage Sermons in *Ad status* Collections', *passim*.

56 Indeed, in *Wynnere and Wastour*, Wastour is given some fairly compelling arguments. See, for example, line 253 onwards. Wastour, in *Wynnere and Wastoure*, is also evidently of a very different social status to Langland's character, and this may explain why the moral case against Wastour is made less equivocally in *Piers Plowman*. It may also, though, testify to the different audiences that these poems expect. See the discussion in Burrow, 'The Audience of *Piers Plowman*', pp. 379–83.

57 On the question of Meed's legitimacy, see Tavormina, *Kindely Similitude*, p. 7, and Fowler, 'Civil Death and the Maiden', p. 778.

58 For the objection in *Wynnere and Wastoure* about 'boyes of blode' marrying above themselves, see Fitt I, 14–15.

59 Hanawalt, 'Remarriage as an Option for Urban and Rural Widows', p. 151, suggests that the rates of remarriage may have been higher in the urban centres.

60 See Du Boulay, *The England of 'Piers Plowman'*, p. 95.

61 Goldberg, *Women, Work and Life Cycle*, p. 210, and Razi, *Life and Death in a Medieval Parish*, p. 138.

62 Owst, *Literature and Pulpit in Medieval England*, pp. 379–81. Scott Waugh has argued that regular moral complaints about incestuous and inappropriate marriages amongst the survivors of the Black Death say 'more about social order than about actual practice': Waugh, *England in the Reign of Edward III*, pp. 86–7.

63 For a discussion of the political implications for the differences between the B and C-texts, see Kerby-Fulton, 'Langland and the Bibliographic Ego', pp. 69 and 74–6, and Simpson, 'The Constraints of Satire in *Piers Plowman* and *Mum and the Sothsegger*', pp. 11–30. For the political implications of the C revisions of the Tree of Charity scene, see Cole, 'Trifunctionality and the Tree of Charity', pp. 16–17.

64 Hanna, 'William Langland', p. 148.

65 See, for example, Adams, 'Langland's Theology', pp. 95–8, and Shenman, 'Grace Abounding', *passim*.

66 Here I disagree with Andrew Galloway's understanding of the way that Langland makes this into an affirmation of femininity, in his otherwise excellent study of the Tree of Charity, 'Intellectual Pregnancy', p. 143.

67 See, for example, Tavormina, 'Kindly Similitude: Langland's Matrimonial Trinity', pp. 126–7.

68 The quotation is from Pearsall's notes to the C-text, XVIII, 215; this is how Pearsall accounts for Abraham's use of the man, wife, child model as a figure for the Trinity, a metaphor which Augustine explicitly rejected.

69 See, for example, Jerome, *Adversus Jovinianum*, PL 23, II, iv, col. 0288B.

70 See, for example, *De nuptiis et concupiscentia*, PL 44, I, ca. IX, x, col. 0419; II, ca. X, xxiii, col. 0449; II, ca. XIX, xxxiv, col. 0456.

71 Augustinus, *De bono conjugali*, PL 40, ca. XXII, xxvii, col. 0392.

72 *Ibid.*, ca. XIX, cols. 0388–9; 'Sed illi homines istum naturae mortalis affectum, cujus in suo genere castitas accedente Dei cultu' [But those men, with mind far holier, surpassed this affection of mortal nature, the chastity whereof in its own kind, there being added therto the worship of God] Translation: 'On the Good of Marriage', in: St Augustine, *On the Holy Trinity*, Schaff (ed. and trans.), p. 22.

73 Bloomfield, '*Piers Plowman* and the Three Grades of Chastity', esp. pp. 247–8 and plates I and II.

74 On the fourteenth- and fifteenth-century manuscripts of Joachim's *Liber figurarum*, and Langland's distance from them, see Reeves and Hirsch-Reich, *The Figurae of Joachim of Fiore*, pp. 314. If Langland knew them it may have

been through his reading of Bonaventure or other Franciscan writings. On the Franciscan history of Joachim's work, see West and Zimdars-Swartz, *Joachim of Fiore*, pp. 103–4. On the Franciscan influence on Langland, see Clopper *'Songes of Rechelesnesse'*, esp. pp. 117–21.

75 Aers, *Chaucer, Langland and the Creative Imagination*, pp. 62–3 and p. 209, n. 4.
76 Aers, *'Piers Plowman' and Christian Allegory*, pp. 92–3.
77 See, for example, Goldsmith, *The Figure of Piers Plowman*, pp. 58–71 and Dronke, *'Arbor caritas'*, *passim*.
78 Galloway, 'Intellectual Pregnancy', p. 143.
79 Tavormina, '"Gendre of a Generation": *Piers Plowman* B.16.222', p. 5.
80 Tavormina, 'Langland's Matrimonial Trinity', pp. 126–7 and *Kindly Similitude*, p. 220.
81 For Abraham's special relationship to questions of fertility, see Augustinus, *De nuptiis et concupiscentia*, PL 44, ca XIII, xxvi, col. 0451.
82 Tavormina has also written that this phrase gave marriage a parity with virginity, '"Bothe Two Ben Gode"', pp. 320–30.
83 See Pearsall's note to C, XVIII, 8.
84 See the arguments put by Tavormina against Pearsall in '"Bothe Two Ben Gode"', pp. 327–8.
85 On the alternative readings of this verse and its implications for Christian debates on virginity, marriage and procreation, see Cohen, *'Be Fertile and Increase[. . .]'*, esp. pp. 12, 230–8 and 243–6.
86 See, for example, Wittig, *'Piers Plowman* B, Passus IX-X', pp. 241–2, who considers the passage in relation to William of St Thierry's *De natura corporis et animae*, and Alford 'The Idea of Reason', pp. 210–11, who posits a passage from Ulpian as an antecedent.
87 Augustinus, *De nuptiis et concupiscentia*, PL 44, I, IV, v, cols. 0415–16. Translation: 'On Marriage and Concupiscence', in *Anti-Pelagian Writings*, Holmes and Wallis (trans. and eds.), V, V, iv.
88 Augustinus, *De bono conjugali*, PL 40, ca. XIX, col. 0388.
89 Zeeman, 'Studying in the Middle Ages', esp. pp. 200–1.
90 Kruger, 'Mirrors and the Trajectory of Vision', p. 74, has also discussed the narcissistic and reflexive dynamics of this section of the poem.
91 Burger, *Chaucer's Queer Nation*, p. 46.
92 I have discussed this sadness elsewhere: Davis, 'On the Sadness of Not Being a Bird'.

CHAPTER 2

1 Usk, *The Testament of Love*, Shawver (ed.); all quotations will be from this edition.
2 The *Appellum* is published as an Appendix in Usk, *The Testament of Love*, Shoaf (ed.), pp. 423–9.
3 Shawver, 'Introduction' to Usk, *The Testament of Love*, Shawver (ed.), pp. 14 and 23.

4 Strohm, 'Politics and Poetics', p. 100.

5 Hanrahan, 'The Seduction of *The Testament of Love*', pp. 1–15, and Turner, 'Thomas Usk and *Troilus and Criseyde*', pp. 26–39; Turner twice describes Usk's language as a 'shroud' (pp. 31 and 34).

6 I shall adopt Lynn Staley's practice in making a distinction between the author and persona by calling the author Usk and his narrator Thomas; Staley, *Dissenting Fictions*, p. 3.

7 Middleton, 'Usk's "Perdurable letters"', p. 68.

8 Middleton, 'The Idea of Public Poetry', pp. 94–114. She writes for example, that writers like Usk, Gower and Langland developed a notion of 'common love' which 'was an emotion as fully natural and universal as *eros*, but it defined man as a social being, and, unlike its private counterpart, was turned outward to public expression' (p. 96); she also argues that in *The Testament* and Gower's *Confessio Amantis* 'love as communal and historical bond, not as transcendental force or as erotic servitude, is the impetus to literary creation' (p. 97).

9 Middleton, 'The Idea of Public Poetry', p. 97.

10 See, for example, Strohm's observation that the royal party was rewarding its supporters with both property and office – 'diversz Manoirs, Terres, Tenementz, Rentes, Offices, & Ballifs' – and the concern of the Westminster chronicler to note that Usk agreed to collaborate with Brembre after lodging in his own house – 'in domo majoris manebat'; Strohm, 'Politics and Poetics', pp. 83 and 87.

11 Middleton, 'Usk's "Perdurable letters"', p. 68, and Storey, 'Gentlemen Bureaucrats', *passim*.

12 For an exposition of this ethos see Riddy, 'Mother Knows Best', esp. pp. 67–8.

13 On the association between social class and affective capacity see, for example, Aers, *Community, Gender and Individual Identity*, p. 123.

14 See, for example, Waugh, *England in the Reign of Edward III*, pp. 127–8.

15 On the medieval ideal of the master-craftsman in his workshop with his one or more apprentices, see Swanson, *Medieval British Towns*, p. 53.

16 Strohm, 'Politics and Poetics', *passim*, and chapter 7 of *Hochon's Arrow*, pp. 145–60. He contextualizes Usk's work in relation to the documentary record. A similar approach is taken in the early innovatory readings of Bressie, 'The Date of Thomas Usk's *Testament of Love*', pp. 17–29.

17 Bird, *The Turbulent London of Richard II*.

18 Usk's *Appellum*, in Usk, *The Testament of Love*, Shoaf (ed.), p. 424, 25–9.

19 Sharpe (ed.), *Calendar of Letter-books*, H, VIII, xxxiv.

20 Nightingale, 'Capitalists, Crafts and Constitutional Change'. Medcalf has structured his work on Usk around this new reading, and suggests that Nightingale might be more accurate in describing Northampton's rise to power and Bird's might be a good reading of the two years of Northampton's mayoral term; 'The World and the Heart', pp. 223–4.

21 Nightingale, 'Capitalists', p. 33.

22 Strohm, 'Politics and Poetics', p. 99, n. 2.

23 Usk's part in these events is taken from his own account in the *Appellum*, pp. 423–9. Others give more thorough accounts of Usk's life; see, for example, Strohm, 'Politics and Poetics', esp. pp. 85–90 and, for a different and somewhat literal reading, *The Testament of Love*, Shawver (ed.), pp. 7–23.

24 Ramsay, 'Scriveners and Notaries', p. 119.

25 Bird, *Turbulent London*, pp. 82–3, and Nightingale, 'Capitalists', p. 29.

26 Bird, *Turbulent London*, pp. 83–4 and 86.

27 Bressie, 'The Date of Thomas Usk's *Testament of Love*', *passim*, is convinced by, and finds further evidence to support, the view put by Henry Bradley that there must have been a second and unrecorded period of imprisonment during which time Usk wrote *The Testament of Love*. On this basis she dates the text between December 1384 and June 1385. Strohm, 'Politics and Poetics', pp. 97–8, n. 18, has established the date of *The Testament of Love* as 1385–6, arguing that the work does not have to have been written in prison. However, this is contested by Medcalf, 'World and Heart', p. 231, who argues that the book could have been written during the second period of imprisonment – Bressie considered this to be a third term and one which was too short to represent the period of composition – from November 1387 to Usk's execution in March 1388, or in two distinct periods of composition.

28 Bird, *Turbulent London*, p. 87, and Strohm. 'Politics and Poetics', p. 88.

29 Strohm, 'Politics and Poetics', pp. 89–90.

30 Strohm, *Hochon's Arrow*, p. 160.

31 See, for example, the way in which John Hirsch separates out the spiritual and the quotidian material in *The Book of Margery Kempe*, ascribing the former to the male amanuensis and the latter to Margery Kempe; Hirsch, 'Author and Scribe in *The Book of Margery Kempe*', p. 149. Contrast it with Lynn Staley's more recent approach in which the scribe is considered as a fiction of the author, Kempe (who is again distinct from the unlettered but pious persona, Margery); Staley, *Dissenting Fictions*, e.g. p. 11.

32 Both Strohm 'Politics and Poetics', p. 101, and Turner, 'Thomas Usk and *Troilus and Criseyde*', p. 27, stress the word 'worldly'. *The Book of Margery Kempe* was also, of course, worldly, interested in the social environment as much as spiritual revelation; see, for example, Staley's introduction to her edition of *The Book of Margery Kempe*, p. 1.

33 Augustine, *Confessions*, O'Donnell (ed.), Book X, iii. On the problem of motive in the *Confessions*, see Olney, *Memory and Narrative*, p. 1.

34 On the idea of the autobiographical impulse see Ferguson, 'Autobiography as Therapy', pp. 191–2.

35 Strohm ('Politics and Poetics', p. 97) has argued that the intended readers of *The Testament* are the royal Brembre faction and that Usk petitions for preferment and exoneration. In contrast, Middleton ('Usk's "Perdurable letters"', pp. 67–9) has argued for an audience of bureaucrats a little like the readership identified by Justice and Kerby-Fulton, 'Langlandian Reading Circles', pp. 59–83. This, Middleton argues, is similar to the audience of legal

practitioners identified by Newman Hallmundsson, 'The Community of Law and Letters', esp. p. 360.

36 These are epithets that are given to Usk by the Appellants and recorded in the *Rolls of Parliament*; Strohm, 'Politics and Poetics', p. 87.

37 *Complete Works of Chaucer*, Skeat (ed.), VII, xxv, and Hanrahan, 'The Seduction of *The Testament of Love*', p. 3.

38 Turner, 'Thomas Usk and *Troilus and Criseyde*', p. 36, and Hanrahan, 'The Seduction of *The Testament of Love*', p. 2.

39 As Leigh Gilmore has noted, the 'rhetoric of spiritual confessions is filled with such deference; the humility *topos* is common to the point of being pro forma'; 'Policing Truth', p. 63; see, for example, Julian of Norwich, *A Revelation of Love*, Glasscoe (ed.), c. 2, p. 2 and her claim that 'These revelations were shewed to a simple creature that cowde no letter.'

40 Middleton, 'Usk's "Perdurable letters"', pp. 94–5, also argues for this explicit assertion of sophistication.

41 Turner, 'Thomas Usk and *Troilus and Criseyde*', p. 26, describes Usk's writing himself into Chaucerian literary and political communities.

42 Hanrahan, 'The Seduction of *The Testament of Love*', p. 2–4. For discussion of the practical problems faced by translators of the *Consolatio* see Copeland, *Rhetoric, Hermeneutics, and Translation*, p. 128. The term 'degraded' is supplied by Samuel Johnson; see Ralph Hanna and Traugot Lawlor's introduction to the *Boece*, in Chaucer, *The Riverside Chaucer*, Benson *et al.* (eds.), pp. 396–7. Usk clearly used Chaucer's translation of Boethius extensively; for an extended discussion of this use see Carlson, 'Chaucer's Boethius and Thomas Usk's *Testament of Love*', *passim*.

43 Sanderlin, 'Usk's *Testament of Love* and St Anselm', p. 72.

44 Medcalf, 'Transposition', p. 182. Middleton, 'Usk's "Perdurable letters"', pp. 64–5, has also described Usk's work positively as 'a synthetic enterprise of some intellectual ambition and originality, of a kind as yet mostly "unattempted yet in prose or rhyme" in English'.

45 For a discussion of the use of rhetoric in *The Franklin's Prologue* and *Tale* see Knight, 'Rhetoric and Poetry', esp. pp. 17–19.

46 Turner, 'Thomas Usk and *Troilus and Criseyde*', pp. 35–6 has a different and more cynical reading. See Middleton, 'Usk's "Perdurable letters"', p. 95, who describes Usk as a 'connoisseur and designer, if not a direct practitioner, of every level of the textmaker's art'.

47 For a discussion of these themes in *The Franklin's Tale*, see Burger, *Chaucer's Queer Nation*, pp. 113–18.

48 See, for example, Bertolet, 'The Rise of London Literature', pp. 14, 17 and 53–4.

49 Eco, *Travels in Hyperreality*, p. 83.

50 Niranjana, *Siting Translation*, pp. 58–9.

51 See, for example, *Complete Works of Chaucer*, Skeat (ed.), VII, xxv, and Turner, 'Thomas Usk and *Troilus and Criseyde*', p. 27.

52 *Ibid.*, p. 26.

53 *Ibid.*, esp. pp. 30 and 36.

54 de Certeau, *The Practice of Everyday Life*, Rendall (trans.), p. xiv.

55 Strohm, 'Politics and Poetics', p. 101; Copeland, *Rhetoric, Hermeneutics, and Translation*, p. 129.

56 Strohm, 'Politics and Poetics', p. 90.

57 Gilmore, 'Policing Truth', pp. 75–7.

58 See Hanrahan, 'The Seduction of *The Testament of Love*', esp. p. 5, on the erotic charge of many of Usk's metaphors.

59 The following discussion about the changing shape of the household is indebted to Rees Jones, 'Women's Influence on the Design of Urban Homes', esp. pp. 191 and 201–4.

60 *Ibid.*, pp. 201–3.

61 *MED*, meanings 1.c. and 1.e.

62 See, for example, the anxieties about vagrancy and mobile labour in 12 Richard II, *Statutes of the Realm*, II, 56–8.

63 *MED*, kitthe: '1.a. Familiar country, homeland; country, kingdom, region, place', and '2.a. People, race, kinsmen, family'.

64 Summers, 'Gower's *Vox clamantis* and Usk's *Testament of Love*', p. 57.

65 See, for a longer discussion of travelling in winter, Scattergood and Stokes, 'Travelling in November', pp. 79 and 82.

66 *The Testament of Love*, Shawver (ed.), p. 20, suggests that this might be a reference to a literal exile.

67 *Le très riches heures du Duc de Berry*, Longnon (ed.), f. 10ᵛ and f. 11ᵛ. See also Pearsall and Salter, *Landscapes and Seasons*, p. 130.

68 Strohm, 'Politics and Poetics', p. 102.

69 The following discussion is indebted to the research of P. J. P. Goldberg on life-cycle servants and apprentices living in the household: *Women, Work and Life Cycle*, esp. pp. 212, 227 and 231; 'Masters and Men', esp. pp. 59–62; 'Household and the Organisation of Labour in Late Medieval Towns', pp. 59–70.

70 Shannon McSheffrey describes household heads, with responsibility for brokering and preventing marriage matches, as 'fathers of the community'; 'Men and Masculinity', p. 245.

71 In the following examples, masters are leaving tools and workshops to their apprentices: Raine (ed.), *Testamenta Eboracensia*, vol. 3, CCXLIX, and Raine (ed.), *Testamenta Eboracensia*, vol. 4, XXVI.

72 Heather Swanson has written about the ideal in the guild records for a 'hierarchical and above all male-orientated order'; 'The Illusion of Economic Structure', p. 29. Sarah Rees Jones has noted that local institutions like the Ward courts preferred to staff their hearings with male householders; 'Household, Work and the Problem of Mobile Labour', p. 135.

73 Goldberg, 'What Was a Servant?', esp. pp. 2–3.

74 Usk's indebtedness to Higden's *Polychronicon* was first noted by Bressie, 'The Date of Thomas Usk's *Testament of Love*', pp. 19–21; the commentary of *The Testament of Love*, Shawver (ed.), notes that Usk is using Trevisa's translation

of Higden (which is cited pp. 212–13). The italics in the quotation I have cited from Usk are Shawver's and show the debt to Trevisa's translation of Bartholomæus Anglicus' *De proprietatibus rerum*.

75 Middleton, 'Usk's "Perdurable letters"', pp. 69–70.

76 Copeland, *Rhetoric, Hermeneutics, and Translation*, pp. 11 and 35–6.

77 See *Complete Works of Chaucer*, Skeat (ed.), VII, 452, n. 89.

78 On the male householder as an instrument of urban government see Rees Jones, 'Household, Work and the Problem of Mobile Labour', p. 152.

79 Turner, 'Thomas Usk and *Troilus and Criseyde*', e.g. pp. 26–7, notes Usk's emulation of the service vocabulary in *Troilus and Criseyde*.

80 Galloway, 'Private Selves and the Intellectual Marketplace', p. 296.

81 Contrast, for example, *Troilus and Criseyde* I, 425–34 and *Il filostrato* I, 38–9 placed side by side in Chaucer, *Troilus and Criseyde*, Windeatt (ed.); see also Sadlek, 'Love, Labor and Sloth in Chaucer's *Troilus and Criseyde*', esp. p. 354.

82 Windeatt, '"Love that oughte ben secree"', p. 116.

83 For a discussion of the mutual obligations of masters and servants see Hovland, 'Apprenticeship in the Records of the Goldsmiths' Company', p. 90.

84 Middleton, 'Usk's "Perdurable letters"', p. 98.

85 Bracton, *De legibus et consuetudinibus Angliæ*, Woodbine (ed.), Thorne (trans.), p. 428. 'Has quidem claves habere debet uxor sub custodia et cura sua, claves videicet despensæ suæ. arcæ suæ, et scrinii sui.'

86 Cullum and Goldberg, 'How Margaret Blackburn Taught her Daughters', p. 225.

87 *Book of Margery Kempe*, Staley (ed.), p. 23.

88 Goldberg, 'Orphans and Servants', pp. 231–46, and McSheffrey (ed. and trans.), *Love and Marriage*, p. 18.

89 Walker Bynum, *Holy Feast and Holy Fast*, e.g. pp. 94, 103 and 171.

90 Usk clearly has Augustine's relationship with his mother in mind, as his discussion of good and bad mothers culminates in a consideration of true and false belief and the great confrontation between Augustine and the Manichean Faustus (II, 14, 22–4).

91 It is curious that critics have not been surprised by the imagery in this passage. See, for example, the way in which Bressie, 'The Date of Thomas Usk's *Testament of Love*', p. 25, and Carlson, 'Chaucer's Boethius and Thomas Usk's *Testament of Love*', p. 54, read the 'strumpet' as a straightforward representation of John of Northampton.

92 [I have woven my bed with cords, I have covered it with painted tapestry, brought from Egypt. I have perfumed my bed with myrrh, aloes, and cinnamon. Come, let us be inebriated with the breasts, and let us enjoy the desired embraces, till the day appear.]

93 *MED* '7.a. Our, my: often used with a singular referent, indicating familiarity, endearment, or domestic intimacy; – sometimes with pejorative connotations'.

94 Central panel, 'Garden of Earthly delights', triptych, Museo del Prado, Madrid. A discussion of this image and a reproduction of the painting can be found in Gibson, *Hieronymus Bosch*, p. 81 and fig. 65.
95 For the association between Marian devotion and French love lyrics see, Saupe (ed.), *Middle English Marian Lyrics*, p. 28.
96 See Clark (ed.), *St. Augustine on Marriage and Sexuality*, pp. 5–7.
97 Gold, 'The Marriage of Mary and Joseph', p. 102.
98 For a discussion of the development of the doctrine of consent see, for example, Murray, 'Individualism and Consensual Marriage', pp. 125–7, and Gold, 'The Marriage of Mary and Joseph', *passim*.
99 Helmholz, *Marriage Litigation*, p. 35.
100 McSheffrey (ed.), *Love and Marriage*, p. 5.
101 Augustine, *De nuptis et concupiscentia*, I, c. 13. On the inclusion of the three goods of marriage into marriage sermons see D'Avray and Tauche, 'Marriage Sermons in *Ad status* Collections', pp. 92–4.
102 Gold, 'The Marriage of Mary and Joseph', pp. 103–4.
103 Helmholz, *Marriage Litigation*, p. 87.
104 See, for a full analysis of medieval marriage and its formation, *ibid.*, *passim*, and Brundage, *Medieval Canon Law*, pp. 73–4.
105 For a discussion of the consent of the heart as it is expressed, for example, in Thomas of Chobham's *Summa confessorum*, see Murray, 'Individualism and Consensual Marriage', p. 133.
106 The knot was often used as a metaphor to describe an agreement between two people and the knot of wedlock was the most common of these figurative knots. *MED*, knotte: '3.c. a bond between persons; an agreement; ~ of wedlok (mariage)'.
107 Gold, 'The Marriage of Mary and Joseph', pp. 116–17.
108 Jefferies Collins (ed.), *Manual ad usum percelebris ecclesiae Sarisburiensis*, pp. 47–8.
109 On Usk's knowledge of *Troilus and Criseyde* see, for example, Bressie, 'The Date of Thomas Usk's *Testament of Love*', pp. 28–9, Strohm, 'Politics and Poetics', p. 106, and Turner, 'Thomas Usk and *Troilus and Criseyde*', *passim*.
110 On the subject of humoral theory, see Siraisi, *Medieval and Early Renaissance Medicine*, pp. 104–6.
111 See, for example, Westerdorf, 'Some Observations on the Concept of Clandestine Marriage', pp. 101–26, Maguire, 'The Clandestine Marriage of Troilus and Criseyde', pp. 262–78, and Kelly, 'Marriage in the Middle Ages, 2: Clandestine Marriage and Chaucer's *Troilus*', pp. 435–57. For details of the care with which consent had to be phrased to validate a union, see Helmholz, *Marriage Litigation*, p. 36.
112 Turner, 'Thomas Usk and *Troilus and Criseyde*', pp. 28–9.
113 Sheehan, *Marriage, Family and Law*, p. 102.
114 See, for example, the description of the knight errant in de Charny, *The Book of Chivalry*, Kaeuper (ed.) and Kennedy (trans.), esp. pp. 166–70.

115 On the lay clergy see Cullum, 'Clergy, Masculinity and Transgression', esp.
    p. 180; on the laicization of the central bureaucracy see Knapp, 'Bureaucratic
    Identity and the Construction of Self', p. 360.
116 Middleton, 'Usk's "Perdurable letters"', pp. 67–9.
117 The question of Usk's borrowing from Langland is discussed by Lewis,
    'Langland's Tree of Charity and Usk's "Wexing Tree"', pp. 429–33.
118 [propter hoc relinquet homo patrem et matrem suam et adherebit uxori suae
    et erunt duo in carne una].
119 Margery Kempe, *The Book of Margery Kempe*, Meech and Allen (eds.)., Bk I,
    c. 35, 86–7. I have discussed the episode and its strategic representation of the
    narrator in 'Men and Margery', pp. 40–2.

CHAPTER 3

1 All quotations are from John Gower, *The English Works of John Gower*,
   Macaulay (ed.). The translations of Gower's Latin verses are my own but I
   have also found useful those of Andrew Galloway in Gower, *The Confessio
   Amantis*, Peck (ed.).
2 de Certeau, *The Practice of Everyday Life*, esp. pp. 106, 115 and 118–22. The
   other references in this paragraph are to the same sections.
3 For Gower's use of Geoffrey of Monmouth, see Wogan-Browne *et al.* (eds.),
   The Idea of the Vernacular, p. 179.
4 See, for example, Strohm, 'A Note on Gower's Persona', p. 294. Strohm
   writes that Gower's 'strong push toward universality may be one of the
   reasons why modern readers find Gower's persona less various and less
   exciting than Chaucer's'.
5 As noted by Manzalaoui, 'Gower's English Mirror for Princes', p. 161.
6 Federico, *New Troy*, esp. p. 1.
7 Olsson, 'Love, Intimacy, and Gower', pp. 88–9, and Olsson, 'John Gower's
   Vox clamantis and the Medieval Idea of Place', p. 144.
8 Davis, 'John Gower's Fear of Flying', pp. 131–52.
9 See, for example, Middleton, 'The Idea of Public Poetry', pp. 95 and 102.
10 Features identified and discussed in Minnis, *'De vulgari auctoritate'*, p. 52.
11 Simpson, *Sciences and the Self*, p. 185.
12 Hanning, 'Toward a Lapsarian Poetics for *The Canterbury Tales*', esp.
   pp. 49–52 and 56.
13 See Strohm, 'Note on Gower's Persona', *passim*.
14 Hanning, 'Toward a Lapsarian Poetics', p. 56.
15 Simpson, *Sciences and the Self*, esp. pp. 7 and 138.
16 Wogan-Browne *et al.* (eds.), *Idea of the Vernacular*, p. 179.
17 Derek Pearsall has found similar ironies in this verse, 'Gower's Latin in the
   Confessio Amantis', pp. 16–17.
18 McDonald, '"Lusti tresor"', p. 144.
19 Amans asks Genius outright in Book III whether crusading is lawful; Genius
   answers that Christ's example teaches us to suffer, rather than kill in order to

spread the faith (III, 2485–515). He seems to have changed his mind by Book IV.

20 See Gower, *The Complete Works of John Gower: The French Works*, Macaulay (ed.), I, 5125–6180.

21 For a discussion of sexuality as the 'true discourse' of confession, see Foucault, *The History of Sexuality*, I, 63.

22 For the influence of penitential handbooks see, for example, Kinneavy, 'Gower's *Confessio Amantis* and the Penitentials', *passim*.

23 Sadlek, 'John Gower's *Confessio Amantis*, Ideology, and the "Labor" of "Love's Labour"', esp. pp. 156–7.

24 For a discussion of the date of the text and its various revisions and dedications, see Macaulay's introduction to Gower, *The English Works*, I, xxi–xxviii (p. xxi), Nicholson, 'Gower's Revisions in the *Confessio Amantis*', *passim*, and Nicholson, 'The Dedications of Gower's *Confessio Amantis*', pp. 159–80. For a discussion of the truce years in the Hundred Years' War, see Curry, *The Hundred Years' War*, p. 74.

25 See, for example, Keen, 'Chaucer's Knight', esp. p. 60.

26 For a discussion of the increasing elitism of English knighthood, see Ormrod, 'The Domestic Response to the Hundred Years' War', p. 86, and, on the expenses of war, Ayton, 'English Armies in the Fourteenth Century', p. 23.

27 Wetherbee, 'John Gower', p. 589.

28 See the debate between Jones, *Chaucer's Knight*, *passim* and Keen, 'Chaucer's Knight', *passim*.

29 Barber, *The Knight and Chivalry*, pp. 141–4.

30 For fol. 202^v of the Luttrell Psalter, the image of Geoffrey Luttrell's arming, see Backhouse, *The Luttrell Psalter*, p. 6, plate 1. See also Emmerson and Goldberg, 'Lordship and Labour in the Luttrell Psalter', *passim*, and Camille, *Mirror in Parchment*, e.g. p. 46.

31 Fol. 82; Backhouse, *Luttrell Psalter*, p. 59, plate 70.

32 This problem is productively interrogated in Ashley and Clark, 'Medieval Conduct: Texts, Theories and Practices', pp. x–xi.

33 See, for example, Coss, *The Knight in Medieval England*, pp. 64–5.

34 de Charny, *The Book of Chivalry*, pp. 66–70.

35 de Charny, *The Book of Chivalry*, p. 90.

36 I use this as a comparative text because of its importance as a statement of chivalric ideology and as a 'portrait' of French chivalric culture, which was so 'decisive in finalising the shape of chivalrous modes and ideology'; as noted by Keen, *Chivalry*, pp. 12–15 and 31. It is also one of the rare chivalric manuals written by a military figure rather than a cleric like Raimon Lull. For a discussion of the differences between de Charny's *Livre* and Lull's *Libre del orde de cavalleria*, see Barber, *Knight and Chivalry*, pp. 134–7.

37 Manzalaoui, 'Gower's English Mirror for Princes', p. 160.

38 James Simpson has also dealt comprehensively with the Aristotelian syllabus and Gower's hierarchy of the sciences in his excellent *Sciences and the Self*; see esp. pp. 205–6. See also the influential article on Book VII and the medieval idea of the microcosm, Elizabeth Porter, 'Gower's Ethical Microcosm', *passim*.

39 Keen, 'Chaucer's Knight', p. 46, has noted how unusually comprehensive is Chaucer's Knight's military career.

40 The quotation is from Delano-Smith and Kain, *English Maps*, p. 142. See, for an example of this kind of map, Edson, *Mapping Time and Space*, plate VI; it demonstrates what has been described as the '*omphalos* syndrome' as adumbrated by Harley, 'Maps, Knowledge, and Power', p. 290.

41 The quotation is *ibid.*, p. 281.

42 This is particularly true of the knight's depiction in manuals of chivalry written by the clergy, as it is in Lull's *Libre*. See Barber, *Knight and Chivalry*, p. 134.

43 For an account of the medieval hierarchies of the senses, see for example, Biernoff, *Sight and Embodiment*, p. 103.

44 de Charny, *The Book of Chivalry*, pp. 90–2 and 120–2.

45 Curry, 'Sex and the Soldier in Lancastrian Normandy', pp. 23–4.

46 See, for a discussion of military masculinity as 'required masculinity', Jamieson, 'The Man of Hobbes', esp. 20.

47 de Certeau, *Practice of Everyday Life*, p. 174.

48 These issues are also discussed in Kiefer, 'My Family First', *passim*.

49 These inconsistencies are also discussed by Yeager, 'Pax poetica', esp. 99. I shall show, though, that I come to quite different conclusions. The translations from the *Mirour* are from John Gower, *Mirour de l'omme (The Mirror of Mankind)*, Wilson (trans.).

50 Keen, *Chivalry*, pp. 227–30.

51 See, for example, the way in which Gower's narrators' pacifist views have been admired as humane and understood as the author's own in Yeager, 'Pax poetica', esp. p. 121, and Barnie, *War in Medieval English Society*, pp. 75 and 122–3. On the comedy of the Amans *persona* see, for example, Pearsall, 'Gower's Narrative Art', pp. 65–6.

52 Siberry, 'Criticism of Crusading', esp. p. 130.

53 See, for example, Middleton, 'Public Poetry', pp. 107 and 112–13.

54 See, for example, the debate between Terry Jones and Maurice Keen, described in Keen, 'Chaucer's Knight', esp. p. 60.

55 Yeager attributes this inconsistency between the *Mirour* and the *Confessio* to the changing estimation of the French war in English public opinion between the composition dates of the two poems: Yeager, 'Pax poetica', p. 99.

56 See, for an example of a discussion of Amans' effeminacy, McCarthy, 'Love and Marriage in the *Confessio Amantis*', p. 493.

57 For the idea of 'masculine plots', see Sussman, *Victorian Masculinity*, p. 13.

58 Powicke, *Military Obligation*, pp. 178–9. Barnie, *War in Medieval English Society*, p. 26, discusses this in relation to Gower's earlier poem *Vox clamantis*.

59 Ayton, 'English Armies', p. 29–30, and Keen, *Chivalry*, p. 144.

60 Powicke, *Military Obligation*, p. 180.

61 The biographical material discussed here is all derived from Fisher, *John Gower*, especially pp. 39, 43, 46, 54, 58 and 66.

62 A particularly nice example, telling in its homosocial interest in credit networks, is Gower's use of the word 'morgage' in a discussion of faithfulness in love (*CA*, VII, 4228). Gower's is the first use of the word in English and the first figurative use.

63 Burger, *Chaucer's Queer Nation*, p. 49.

64 Fisher, *John Gower*, p. 65.

65 Carlin, *Medieval Southwark*, p. 210.

66 Middleton, 'Public Poetry', pp. 95 and 102.

67 Mohl, *The Three Estates*, pp. 140–2.

68 Sadlek, 'John Gower's *Confessio Amantis*', p. 148.

69 Sadlek, 'Love, Labour and Sloth in Chaucer's *Troilus and Criseyde*', p. 354.

70 Ronan Crampton, 'Action and Passion in Chaucer's *Troilus*', p. 24.

71 Contrast, for example, the approaches of McInerney, '"Is this a mannes herte?"', *passim*, with Lewis, 'What Chaucer Really did to *Il filostrato*', pp. 27–44, and Mann, 'Troilus' Swoon', *passim*.

72 Langland, *The Vision of Piers Plowman*, Schmidt (ed.), XX, 10.

73 For other comparisons, see Lewis, 'Gower', p. 34, and Levin, 'The Passive Poet', p. 125.

74 Diamond, '*Troilus and Criseyde*: The Politics of Love', pp. 93–4.

75 See, Chaucer, *Troilus and Criseyde*, IV, 397–9. On Pandarus's work and social status see, for example, Windeatt's notes to Chaucer, *Troilus and Criseyde*, Windeatt (ed.), p. 291.

76 Stanbury, 'The Voyeur and the Private Life', esp. pp. 146–7.

77 For a discussion of the various conflicting forms of love in Gower's poem, see Simpson, 'Ironic Incongruence', p. 618.

78 Minnis, '*De vulgari auctoritate*', pp. 56–7.

79 Of course there is much critical discussion of the ending of *Troilus and Criseyde*. See, for example, Ratazzi Papka, 'Transgression, the End of Troilus, and the Ending of Chaucer's *Troilus and Criseyde*', pp. 267–81, and Donaldson, 'The Ending of *Troilus*', pp. 115–30.

80 Manzalaoui, 'Gower's English Mirror for Princes', pp. 166–7. A similar comparison of the endings of the *Confessio* and *Troilus* is made by Peck, 'The Phenomenology of Make Believe', pp. 267–8, although I would want to maintain an agnosticism on his statement that: 'Gower lacks the brilliance of Chaucer in incorporating philosophical matter into fictive comedies.'

81 *OED*, sub verbo.

82 T. S. Eliot, 'The Lovesong of J. Alfred Prufrock' (1917), in *Complete Poems and Plays*, p. 14. Gower's influence on Eliot's work has been noted before. See, for example, Roberts, 'A Source for T. S. Eliot's Use of "Elsewhere" in "East Coker"', pp. 24–5, and Schmitz, 'Rhetoric and Fiction', pp. 117 and 142.

83 Aers, *Community, Gender and Individual Identity*, pp. 128–9. See also Jill Mann's careful anatomy of the power dynamics within Troilus and Criseyde's relationship in 'Troilus' Swoon', *passim*.
84 On Pandarus' spatial abuses, see Stanbury, 'Voyeur and the Private Life', pp. 152 and 154–5, and Brody, 'Making a Play for Criseyde', *passim*.
85 Federico, 'Fourteenth-Century Erotics of Politics', pp. 131–2.

CHAPTER 4

1 See, for example, Patterson, 'Perpetual Motion', p. 25, n. 1.
2 See, for example, Dinshaw, *Getting Medieval*, pp. 126–36, where they are treated together.
3 Burger, *Chaucer's Queer Nation*, pp. 79–100.
4 Patterson, 'Perpetual Motion', p. 30, n. 14.
5 Beattie, 'Meanings of Singleness', pp. 170–7 and 180–9.
6 Many critics have discussed this curious structure; see, for example, Hartung, '"Pars Secunda"', p. 112.
7 McCraken, 'The Confessional Prologue', esp. p. 289.
8 See, for a bibliography on this crux, John Reidy's notes to *The Canon's Yeoman's Prologue* in *The Riverside Chaucer*, p. 946.
9 Grennen, 'The Canon's Yeoman's Alchemical "Mass"', pp. 548–9.
10 Howard, *The Idea of 'The Canterbury Tales'*, p. 294.
11 See, for example, Bruhn, 'Art, Anxiety, and Alchemy', e.g. pp. 302–5, and Patterson, 'Perpetual Motion', p. 55.
12 *Ibid.*, p. 54–7.
13 Grennen, 'Chaucer's Characterization of the Canon and his Yeoman', esp. p. 281.
14 Zeeman, 'Studying in the Middle Ages', *passim*, esp. p. 193.
15 See, for example, the two opposing views set out in Carlton, 'Complicity and Responsibility in Pandarus's Bed and Chaucer's Art', esp. p. 56, and S. A. Barney's notes to *Troilus and Criseyde* in *The Riverside Chaucer*, p. 1043, n. 1555–82.
16 Several critics discuss the question of 'pryvetee' in the *Tale*; see, for example, Knapp, 'The Work of Alchemy', p. 583.
17 On the Pardoner's inconstant attitude to his pardons see Dinshaw, *Getting Medieval*, p. 135.
18 For discussions of the theory of alchemy, see Patterson, 'Perpetual Motion', *passim*, and Grennen, (e.g.) 'The Canon's Yeoman's Cosmic Furnace', pp. 225–40; for other discussions of the ethics of labour and the workshop economy, see Harwood 'Chaucer and the Silence of History', pp. 338–50, and Knapp, 'The Work of Alchemy', *passim*.
19 Landman, 'Laws of Community', esp. p. 401.
20 E.g. Patterson, 'Perpetual Motion', p. 30.

21 Rosser, 'London and Westminster', p. 51. See also, for a discussion on the suburbs in this tale: Scattergood, 'Chaucer in the Suburbs', pp. 155–6, and Harwood, 'Chaucer and the Silence of History', p. 344.

22 Grennen's work has shown the important connections between these *Tales*; see 'Saint Cecilia's Chemical Wedding', pp. 466–81.

23 Bruhn, 'Art, Anxiety and Alchemy', p. 289.

24 On the gender demographics of late medieval migration, see Goldberg, *Women, Work and Life Cycle*, p. 216.

25 Karma Lochrie has written extensively about the multiple meanings of the word 'pryvetee': Lochrie, '"Women's Pryvetees"', *passim*. Several critics have discussed homosocial competition and erotic triangles in *The Canterbury Tales*. See, for example, Laskaya, *Chaucer's Approach to Gender in 'The Canterbury Tales'*, p. 78.

26 Patterson, 'Perpetual Motion', pp. 34–5.

27 Rosser, 'London and Westminster', p. 53.

28 For a discussion of immigration and 'stranger servants', see Hovland, 'Apprenticeship in the Records of the Goldsmiths' Company', pp. 93–4.

29 The discussion over the following two paragraphs is indebted to Rees Jones, 'Household, Work and the Problem of Mobile Labour', pp. 133–53. See also Given-Wilson, 'Service, Serfdom and English Labour Legislation', pp. 21–37.

30 Hamilton, 'The Clerical Status of Chaucer's Alchemist', p. 107, has identified them as Black Augustinian canons, arguing that the canons are 'guilty of that *instabilitas loci* forbidden to monastics'.

31 Hovland, 'Apprenticeship', pp. 90–1. On the possible relationship between the guilds and the municipal authorities, see Swanson, 'The Illusion of Economic Structure', *passim*, and Swanson, *Medieval British Towns*, pp. 98–9.

32 McIntosh, *Controlling Misbehaviour in England*, pp. 129–30.

33 Goldberg, *Women, Work and Life Cycle*, pp. 212, 227 and 231, and Ben-Amos, *Adolescence and Youth*, p. 5.

34 Swanson, 'The Illusion of Economic Structure', p. 29. For an alternative view see Miller and Hatcher, *Medieval England: Towns, Commerce and Crafts*, pp. 369–79.

35 For an extraordinary exploration of the romantic notions and harsh realities of migrant manhood see Berger and Mohr, with Blombert, *A Seventh Man*, esp. p. 186.

36 Cobban, *The Medieval Universities*, pp. 133–4; Leff, *Paris and Oxford Universities*, p. 107, notes that the founding of halls at Oxford was a response to the need to supervise a youthful and disorderly population who were boarding in private houses. For a discussion of student masculinities see Mazzo Karas, 'Sharing Wine, Women, and Song', pp. 187–202.

37 On life-cycle service and the combination of intimacy/care and hostility/rivalry that characterized master–servant relationships, see Goldberg, 'What Was a Servant?', p. 18.

38 In particular, the puns of *The Shipman's Tale* have been much discussed. See for example Hahn, 'Money, Sexuality, Wordplay', pp. 235–49.

39 The following discussion is indebted to Goldberg, 'Masters and Men', esp.
    p. 58.
40 Hovland, 'Apprenticeship', pp. 90–1.
41 The following discussion engages with Patterson, 'Perpetual Motion', p. 30.
42 Percy (ed.), *York Memorandum Book*, p. 5. All quotations from this indenture
    are from the same page.
43 Riley (ed.), *Memorials of London*, pp. 245, 258 and 322.
44 *Ibid.*, p. 278.
45 See, for example, Sellers (ed.), *York Memorandum Book, Part I*, p. 185, *York
    Memorandum Book, Part II*, p. 285, and Riley (ed.), *Memorials of London*,
    p. 180.
46 The quotation comes from Percy (ed.), *York Memorandum Book*, p. 5.
47 See, Henebry, 'Apprentice Janekyn/Clerk Jankyn', p. 155.
48 On Perkyn and the stereotype of apprentices, see for example Scattergood,
    'Perkyn Revellour and *The Cook's Tale*', p. 16, and Strohm, '"Lad with revel
    to Newegate"', p. 166.
49 Phillips, *An Introduction to 'The Canterbury Tales'*, p. 204.
50 Smith, 'Body Doubles', p. 7.
51 On the *Tale* as a digression, see Grenberg, '*The Canon's Yeoman's Tale*:
    Boethian Wisdom and the Alchemists', p. 37.
52 See, for example, Riley (ed.), *Memorials of London*, pp. 232–3 and 626, and
    Goldberg, 'What Was a Servant?', p. 18.
53 Phillips, *An Introduction to 'The Canterbury Tales'*, p. 72.
54 See Bowers (ed.), *'The Canterbury Tales': Fifteenth-Century Continuations and
    Additions*, pp. 1–2.
55 Riley (ed.), *Memorials of London*, pp. 610–11.
56 Bertolet, '"Wel bet is rotten appul out of hoord"', p. 239.
57 Patterson, 'Perpetual Motion', pp. 54–7, and Cook, 'The Canon's Yeoman
    and his *Tale*', p. 32.
58 See, for example, the extract from Thomas Brinton in Horrox (trans. and
    ed.), *The Black Death*, p. 147, and Lerner, 'The Black Death and Western
    European Eschatological Mentalities', pp. 78 and 86.
59 See, for example, Goldberg, 'Introduction', in *The Black Death in England*,
    pp. 1–2.
60 For a discussion of the nature of the disease and its patterns of infection, see
    for example, Twigg, *The Black Death*, pp. 200–22, and Gottfried, *The Black
    Death*, p. 3.
61 However, for a contemporary account of Christians as the victims of
    iniquitous Muslim carriers, see Alfonso of Cardova, cited in Campbell, *The
    Black Death and Men of Learning*, pp. 52–3.
62 Grennen, 'Chaucer's Characterization', p. 281.
63 On service as the dominant ideology of the period see Horrox, 'Service', p. 61.
64 See, for example, Hatcher, *Plague, Population, and the English Economy*, esp.
    the Introduction, and Bridbury, 'The Black Death', pp. 577–92. See, for the
    contemporary connection, 23 Edward III, *Statutes of the Realm*, I, 307.

65 This is an alternative view to that set out by David Aers and Karma Lochrie, using the evidence from the Tuscan Catasto, that the *senex amans Tales* – like *The Miller's* and *The Merchant's* – offer an effective critique of actual medieval marriage practice. Aers, *Chaucer*, p. 71, and Lochrie, '"Women's Pryvetees"', p. 288. For the English evidence on age at marriage, see, for example, Smith, 'Geographical Diversity in the Resort to Marriage in Late Medieval Europe', *passim*, esp. pp. 18 and 22–4.

CHAPTER 5

1 Brown, 'The Privy Seal Clerks in the Early Fifteenth Century', p. 272, my emphasis.
2 Smith, 'Identity's Body', p. 267; the title for this section also comes from Smith's article.
3 I use the following editions of the poems: 'La male regle' and *The Series* (apart from 'The Complaint and Dialogue') in Hoccleve, *Hoccleve's Works: The Minor Poems*, Furnivall and Gollancz (eds.); Hoccleve, *The Regiment of Princes*, Blyth (ed.); Hoccleve, *The Complaint and Dialogue*, Burrow (ed.).
4 Smith, 'Identity's Body', p. 267; her quotation is from Biddy Martin and Chandra Talpade Mohanty, 'Feminist Politics: What's Home Got to Do with It?', in *Feminist Studies/Critical Studies*, ed. Teresa de Lauretis (Bloomington, IA, 1986), pp. 191–212.
5 Burrow, 'Autobiographical Poetry in the Middle Ages', esp. 394.
6 Thornley, 'The Middle English Penitential Lyric and Hoccleve's Autobiographical Poetry', *passim*; I think that Thornley's argument has been misapprehended in some quarters; her interest in Hoccleve's penitential conventions does not stand opposed to the notion that his verse is autobiographical. See, for example, Kohl, 'More than Virtues and Vices', p. 115.
7 Hasler, 'Hoccleve's Unregimented Body', pp. 164–83.
8 See, for example, Knapp, 'Bureaucratic Identity and the Construction of the Self', pp. 357–76, Knapp, 'Bureaucratic Identity and Literary Practice', pp. 64–72, and Knapp, *The Bureaucratic Muse*, p. 72.
9 See, for example, Goldie, 'Psychosomatic Illness and Identity in London', esp. p. 41, Simpson, 'Madness and Texts', pp. 15–26, and Patterson, '"What is Me?"', pp. 437–70.
10 Tambling, 'Allegory and the Madness of the Text', p. 230.
11 For an account of Hoccleve's part in the making of Cambridge, Trinity College MS R. 3.2 (581) (a manuscript of the *Confessio Amantis*), see Parkes and Doyle, 'The Production of Copies of *The Canterbury Tales* and the *Confessio Amantis*', esp. p. 220. Hoccleve translated part of Henry Suso's *Horologium sapientiae* as the text he called 'Lerne to Dye', one of the items in *The Series*. Suso's dualist influence is suggested by Goldie, 'Psychosomatic Illness', p. 41.
12 Furnivall, 'Introduction' to *The Minor Poems*, p. xxxvi, n. 2.

13 Burrow, 'Autobiographical Poetry', pp. 404–5, Burrow also notes the conflation of home and work in *Authors of the Middle Ages*, pp. 7–8.

14 See Furnivall's Introduction to *The Minor Poems*, p. xix.

15 Others have also expressed scepticism about this institution. See, for example, Thompson, 'A Poet's Contacts with the Great and the Good', pp. 90–1, n. 37.

16 Burrow, 'The Poet as Petitioner', pp. 61–75. Ferster, *Fictions of Advice*, p. 155.

17 Scanlon, *Narrative, Authority and Power*, pp. 300–1.

18 Burrow, *Thomas Hoccleve*, pp. 7–8.

19 See, for example, Knapp, 'Bureaucratic Identity and the Construction of the Self', pp. 359–62, and Ferster, *Fictions of Advice*, pp. 142–7.

20 Knapp, *Bureaucratic Muse*, p. 72.

21 Burrow, 'Hoccleve's *Series*: Experience and Books', p. 263–4, Burrow, 'Autobiographical poetry', p. 403, Scanlon, *Narrative, Authority and Power*, p. 304.

22 Hasler, 'Hoccleve's Unregimented Body', p. 173.

23 For a facsimile and description of the Hoccleve's holographs see Hoccleve, *A Facsimile of the Autograph Verse Manuscripts*, Burrow and Doyle (eds.).

24 Several others have commented on this effect, primarily in *The Series*: Burrow, 'Hoccleve's *Series*', pp. 263 and 265, Simpson, 'Madness and Texts', e.g. pp. 19–20, Goldie, 'Psychosomatic Illness', p. 45.

25 Brown, 'Privy Seal Clerks', p. 270, n. 1; the bill for parchment can be seen in Burrow, *Thomas Hoccleve*, p. 4.

26 Sadlek, *Idleness Working*, p. 108.

27 Ivy, 'The Bibliography of the Manuscript-Book', p. 37.

28 Ovitt, *The Restoration of Perfection*, pp. 88–105, and de Vogüé, *The Rule of Saint Benedict*, p. 241.

29 Mumford, *The Culture of Cities*, p. 17.

30 Carruthers, *The Craft of Thought*, p. 2.

31 The quotation comes from, Knapp, 'Bureaucratic Identity and Literary Practice', p. 66.

32 For a discussion of this problem, see Leyser, *Authority and Asceticism*, p. 101.

33 Burrow, 'Autobiographical Poetry', p. 406.

34 Knapp, *Bureaucratic Muse*, p. 91. My analysis of this passage is similar to Knapp's, who has seen it as pertinent to ideas about community and labour, but, by showing that the passage is in dialogue with older monastic discourses on labour and the 'Testament of Christ' tradition, I aim to sharpen the definition of what Knapp describes as 'a broadly penitential set of categories' (pp. 91–2).

35 Cited in Ivy, 'Bibliography of the Manuscript-Book', p. 35 (the emphasis is mine).

36 Spalding (ed.), *The Middle English Charters of Christ*, pp. 26–7.

37 Readings of this kind of imagery are provided in Woolf, *The English Religious Lyric*, pp. 210–13, and Gray, *Themes and Images*, p. 130 and plate 5.

38 At the instigation of Gollancz, Furnivall printed fourteen poems in his edition of *The Regiment*, which were translations of Deguileville's *Pèlerinage*.

While he was initially sceptical of their provenance, Furnivall became convinced that Hoccleve had been responsible for them. More recently, however, both Burrow and Roger Ellis have argued that they are probably not Hoccleve's. Hoccleve, *Hoccleve's Works: The Regement of Princes and Fourteen Minor Poems*, Furnivall (ed.), p. vii; Burrow, *Thomas Hoccleve*, p. 24, and Ellis's 'Introduction', in Hoccleve, *My Compleinte and Other Poems*, p. 18. For a discussion of the popularity of Deguileville's *Pèlerinages* and the Charter of Christ tradition in late medieval England, see Steiner, *Documentary Culture*, pp. 29–31.

39 Carruthers discusses the use of parchment as a metaphor and the 'Charter of Christ' tradition as part of monastic meditative practice. See *The Craft of Thought*, pp. 102–3.

40 *OED, sub verbo.*

41 Simpson, 'Madness and Texts', *passim.*

42 The royal charter and the charter of pardon are different kinds of document but were evidently often confused in this penitential use. See, Woolf, 'The Tearing of the Pardon', p. 56.

43 Schulz, 'Thomas Hoccleve, Scribe', p. 72.

44 Richardson, 'Hoccleve in his Social Context', p. 315.

45 Brown, 'The Privy Seal Clerks', p. 263. For a more detailed discussion of training, see Christianson, 'A Community of Book Artisans in Chaucer's London', p. 208.

46 *MED*, definitions 3 and 4.

47 'thise clerkes thre' refer to Hoccleve's sources. Hoccleve tells us that he compiles his text from the pseudo-Aristotelian *Secreta secretorum*, Giles of Rome's *De regimine principum*, and Jacob de Cessolis' *Chessbook* (*RP*, 2038–9, 2052–3 and 2109–11).

48 Woolf, *English Religious Lyric*, p. 29.

49 See, for example, Gray, *Themes and Images*, plates 5 and 6.

50 Langland, *Piers Plowman: The C-text*, Pearsall (ed.), V, 43a–58.

51 Ovitt, *The Restoration of Perfection*, pp. 96–7.

52 The urban context of Hoccleve's verse is considered by several critics: Richardson, 'Hoccleve in his Social Context', pp. 313–4, Goldie, 'Psychosomatic Illness', *passim*, and Patterson, '"What is Me?"', pp. 466–70.

53 Often, studies of medieval labour will over-emphasize the relationship between pain and labour. See, for example, Frantzen and Moffat, *The Work of Work*, esp. p. 2.

54 Again, Carruthers finds some similar preoccupations – with cleaning and clothing as metaphors for rhetorical acts – in her study of monastic intellectual work, *The Craft of Thought*, p. 128.

55 Greetham, 'Self-Referential Artefacts', pp. 245 and 247.

56 Hasler, 'Hoccleve's Unregimented Body', pp. 164 and 167.

57 I use the word 'appears' advisedly. Whilst the critical orthodoxy is that there is little to offend women in 'The Epistle', Diane Bornstein, from whom the quotation is taken, has plausibly argued that the subtle rearrangements and

omissions water down and parody de Pizan's project. Bornstein, 'Anti-feminism in Thomas Hoccleve's Translation of Christine de Pizan's *Epistre au dieu d'amours*', pp. 7–14. Contrast the earlier, ingenious argument of John Fleming that Hoccleve's poem preserves both the 'tone and thrust of her poem' but critiques de Pizan's inability to grasp the concept of a persona and its difference from an author. Fleming, 'Hoccleve's "Letter of Cupid"', pp. 22 and 35.

58 Mann, 'Apologies to Women', pp. 21–2.

59 Patterson, '"What is Me?"', p. 450. Another moment of hysterical gynophobia in Hoccleve's writing must be stanza nineteen of the 'Ballade to Sir John Oldcastle', with its rather nasty *double entendre* in the final line: Hoccleve, *The Minor Poems*, pp. 8–24.

60 Chaucer, *The Clerk's Tale*, 1142–76.

61 Furnivall, Introduction, *The Regement of Princes*, p. xviii. Hoccleve produces a similarly plain and unquestioning account of patriarchal structures in the 'Ballade to Sir John Oldcastle', which I have discussed elsewhere: Davis, 'Men and Margery', pp. 35–54. See also, Nissé, '"Oure Fadres Olde and Modres"', pp. 275–99.

62 Knapp has come to an intriguing but rather different conclusion about how Hoccleve positions himself in relation to clerical authority: *Bureaucratic Muse*, pp. 72–3.

63 Green, *Poets and Princepleasers*, pp. 183–6. Also, we might see a similar hyper-orthodoxy in the way that Hoccleve uses the 'Charter of Christ' tradition, demonstrating Emily Steiner's thesis about the way in which the fifteenth-century revisers of the *Long Charter of Christ* sought to 're-affiliate the poem with an unambiguously orthodox polemic', *Documentary Culture*, p. 195.

64 Burrow has tried to account for this curiosity in 'La male regle', for example: 'Autobiographical Poetry', p. 411.

65 The quotation comes from Patterson, '"What is Me?"', pp. 442.

66 Furnivall, Introduction to *The Minor Poems*, p. xxxvii.

67 *Ibid.*, p. xxiii.

68 Personal communication with P. J. P. Goldberg.

69 *MED, sub verbo.*

70 Riley (ed. and trans.), *Liber Albus*, pp. 395–6. For a discussion of the *Liber Albus* in relation to Hoccleve, see Knapp, *Bureaucratic Muse*, pp. 83–6. See also Revard, 'The Tow on Absalom's Distaff', pp. 168–70.

71 Grössinger, *Picturing Women in Medieval and Renaissance Art*, pp. 115–17 and plates 19, 47 and 48.

72 The implied sexual humiliation in this phrase has also been stressed by Batt, 'The Idioms of Women's Work', pp. 29–35.

73 Hasler, 'Hoccleve's Unregimented Body', p. 172.

74 Classen, 'Love and Marriage in Late Medieval Verse', p. 171.

75 Sheehan, 'Marriage Theory and Practice', pp. 415 and 452.

76 For an account of the standard and little varying form of medieval marriage sermons, see D'Avray and Tausche, 'Marriage Sermons in *Ad status* Collections', *passim*.

77 Sheehan, 'Marriage Theory and Practice', p. 455.

78 Richardson, 'Hoccleve in his Social Context', p. 320.

79 'in omnibus sumentes scutum fidei, in quo possitis omnia tela nequissimi ignea extinguere' [In all things taking the shield of faith, wherewith you may be able to extinguish all the fiery darts of the most wicked one.] Ephesians 6.16.

80 Bornstein, 'Anti-feminism', p. 14.

81 On Gower's commitment to conjugality see Bennett, 'Gower's "Honeste love"', pp. 49–61.

82 Patterson, '"What is Me?"', p. 449.

83 On the provenance of this metaphor, see Woolf, *English Religious Lyric*, p. 188.

84 Owst, *Literature and Pulpit*, pp. 399–403.

85 On the petitions in 1378, 1402 and 1406 see Hunt, *Governance of the Consuming Passions*, p. 305. See, for a discussion of dress and medieval hierarchy, Baldwin, *Sumptuary Legislation*, p. 53. And, for a similar association between this passage in *The Regiment* and sumptuary anxieties, Scanlon, *Narrative, Authority and Power*, p. 304.

86 37 Edward III, *Statutes of the Realm*, I, e.g. c. ix.

87 37 Edward III, c. xiv.

88 The word 'feeld' can of course just mean 'field' but can also have the meaning of pasture or arable land next to a town, which in the context sounds plausible. *MED*: feld: '2. Land adjoining the town appropriated to pasture or tillage'.

89 See Scattergood, 'Chaucer in the Suburbs', p. 151.

90 James Simpson has looked at the justified 'grucchinge' in *The Regiment* and found a veiled threat applied to the poem's dedicatee about the need for financial reform. Simpson, 'Nobody's Man', pp. 171–4, esp. p. 172, n. 29.

91 Tambling, 'Authority and Madness of the Text', p. 230.

Bibliography

PRIMARY SOURCES

Aristotle, *De partibus animalium I and De generatione animalium I*, D. M. Balme (trans.) (Oxford: Clarendon Press, 1972).

Augustine, St, Bishop of Hippo (Augustinus Hipponensis), *Confessions*, J. J. O'Donnell (ed.), 3 vols. (Oxford: Clarendon Press, 1992).

> *Confessions*, Vernon J. Bourke (trans.), Fathers of the Church 21, Writings of Saint Augustine 5 (Washington, DC: Catholic University of America Press, 1953).

> *De bono conjugali*, PL 40.

> *De nuptiis et concupiscentia*, PL 44.

> 'On Marriage and Concupiscence', in *Anti-Pelagian Writings*, Peter Holmes and Robert Ernest Wallis (trans. and ed.), Benjamin B. Warfield (rev.), Nicene and Post-Nicene Fathers of the Christian Church, ser. I, 14 vols. (Edinburgh: T & T Clark, 1887), V.

> *On the Holy Trinity, Doctrinal Treatises, Moral Treatises*, Philip Schaff (ed. and trans.), Nicene and Post-Nicene Fathers, ser. I, 14 vols. (Edinburgh: T & T Clark, 1887), III.

Backhouse, Janet, *The Luttrell Psalter* (London: British Library, 1989).

Berger, J., and Mohr, J., with Blombert, S., *A Seventh Man: A Book of Images and Words about the Experience of Migrant Workers in Europe* (Harmondsworth: Penguin, 1975).

Blake, N. F. (ed.), *Middle English Religious Prose* (London: Edward Arnold, 1972).

Bowers, J. M. (ed.), *'The Canterbury Tales': Fifteenth-Century Continuations and Additions* (Kalamazoo, MI: Western Michigan University Press, 1992).

Bracton, Henry, *De legibus et consuetudinibus Angliæ*, G. Woodbine (ed.), S. E. Thorne (trans.) (Cambridge, MA: Belknap Press, 1968), http://bracton.law.cornell.edu/bracton/Common/index.html.

Chaucer, Geoffrey, *The Riverside Chaucer*, L. Benson *et al.* (eds.), 3rd edn (Oxford: Oxford University Press, 1989).

Chaucer, Geoffrey, *Troilus and Criseyde*, B. A. Windeatt (ed.) (Harlow: Longman, 1990).

Clark, E. A. (ed.), *St Augustine on Marriage and Sexuality* (Washington, DC: Catholic University of America Press, 1996).

de Charny, Geoffroi, *The Book of Chivalry of Geoffroi de Charny: Text, Context, and Translation*, R. W. Kaeuper (ed.) and E. Kennedy (trans.) (Philadelphia, PA: University of Pennsylvania Press, 1996).

Eliot, T. S., 'The Lovesong of J. Alfred Prufrock', in *The Complete Poems and Plays of T. S. Eliot* (London: Faber and Faber, 1969), pp. 13–15.

Gower, John *Mirour de l'Omme (The Mirror of Mankind)*, William Burton Wilson (trans.) (East Lansing: Colleagues Press, 1992).

The Complete Works of John Gower: The French Works, G. C. Macaulay (ed.), 4 vols. (Oxford: Clarendon Press, 1899), I.

The Confessio Amantis, Russell A. Peck (ed.), 3 vols. (Kalamazoo, MI: Western Michigan University Press, 2000).

The English Works of John Gower, G. C. Macaulay (ed.), 2 vols., EETS, ES 81 and 82 (Oxford, 1900).

Hoccleve, Thomas, *A Facsimile of the Autograph Verse Manuscripts*, J. A. Burrow and A. I. Doyle (eds.), EETS, SS 19 (Oxford, 2002).

Hoccleve's Works: The Minor Poems, F. J. Furnivall and I. Gollancz (eds.), J. Mitchell and A. I. Doyle (rev.), EETS, ES 61 and 73 (Oxford, 1970).

Hoccleve's Works: The Regement of Princes and Fourteen Minor Poems, F. J. Furnivall (ed.), EETS, ES 72 (Oxford, 1897).

My Compleinte and Other Poems, R. Ellis (ed.) (Exeter: University of Exeter Press, 2001).

The Complaint and Dialogue, J. A. Burrow (ed.), EETS, OS 313 (Oxford, 1999).

The Regiment of Princes, C. R. Blyth (ed.) (Kalamazoo, MI: Western Michigan University Press, 1999).

Horrox, Rosemary (trans. and ed.), *The Black Death* (Manchester: Manchester University Press, 1994).

Jefferies Collins, A. (ed.), *Manual ad usum percelebris ecclesiae Sarisburiensis*, Henry Bradshaw Society 91 (London, 1960).

Jerome, St (Hieronymus Stridonensis) *Adversus Jovinianum*, *PL* 23.

Letters and Select Works, Henry Wace and Philip Schaff (trans. and ed.), A Select Library of Nicene and Post-Nicene Fathers of the Christian Church, ser. II, 14 vols. (Oxford: Parker, 1893).

Kempe, Margery, *The Book of Margery Kempe*, Sanford Brown Meech and Hope Emily Allen (eds.), EETS, OS 212 (Oxford, 1940).

The Book of Margery Kempe, Lynn Staley (ed.) (Kalamazoo, MI: Medieval Institute, Western Michigan University Press, 1996).

Langland, William, *Piers Plowman: The C-text*, D. Pearsall (ed.), 2nd edn (Exeter: Exeter University Press, 1994).

Piers the Plowman: The A Version, George Kane (ed.) (London: Athlone, 1960).

The Vision of Piers Plowman, A. V. C. Schmidt (ed.), 2nd edn (London: Everyman, 1987).

Longnon, J. (ed.), *Le très riches heures du Duc de Berry* (London: Thames & Hudson, 1969).

McSheffrey, Shannon (ed. and trans.), *Love and Marriage in Late Medieval London* (Kalamazoo, MI: Western Michigan University Press, 1995).

Norwich, Julian of, *A Revelation of Love*, M. Glasscoe (ed.) (Exeter: Exeter University Press, 1976).

Percy, J. W. (ed.), *York Memorandum Book*, Surtees Society 186 (Durham, 1973).

Raine, J. (ed.), *Testamenta Eboracensia: A Selection of Wills from the Registry at York*, vol. 3, Surtees Society 45 (Durham, 1864).

(ed.), *Testamenta Eboracensia: A Selection of Wills from the Registry at York*, vol. 4, Surtees Society 53 (Durham, 1869).

Riley, H. T. (ed. and trans.), *Liber Albus: The White Book of the City of London* (London: R. Griffin, 1861).

Riley, H. T. (ed.), *Memorials of London and London Life in the XIIIth, XIVth, and XVth Centuries* (London: Longman, 1868).

Saupe, K. (ed.), *Middle English Marian Lyrics* (Kalamazoo, MI: Western Michigan University Press, 1999).

Sellers, Maud (ed.), *York Memorandum Book*, Part I: *1376–1419*, Surtees Society 120 (Durham, 1912).

York Memorandum Book, Part II: *1419–93*, Surtees Society 125 (Durham, 1915).

Sharpe, R. (ed.), *Calendar of Letter-books Preserved among the Archives of the City of London at the Guildhall*, 11 vols. (London: J. E. Francis, 1899–1912), H (1907), VIII.

Skeat, W. W. (ed.), *Complete Works of Chaucer: Chaucerian and Other Pieces*, 7 vols. (Oxford: Clarendon Press, 1897), VII.

Spalding, Mary Caroline (ed.), *The Middle English Charters of Christ*, Bryn Mawr College Monographs Series 15 (Bryn Mawr, PA: Bryn Mawr College, 1914).

Statutes of the Realm, 10 vols. (London: Record Commission, 1816) I and II.

Trigg, Stephanie (ed.), *Wynnere and Wastoure*, EETS, OS 297 (Oxford, 1990).

Usk, Thomas, *The Testament of Love*, G. W. Shawver (ed.), based on John F. Leyerle (ed.), Toronto Medieval Texts and Translations 13 (Toronto: University of Toronto Press, 2002).

The Testament of Love, R. A. Shoaf (ed.) (Kalamazoo, MI: Western Michigan University Press, 1998).

Wogan-Browne, Jocelyn, *et al.* (eds.), *The Idea of the Vernacular: An Anthology of Middle English Literary Theory, 1280–1520* (Exeter: University of Exeter Press, 1999).

SECONDARY SOURCES

Adams, John, 'Langland's Theology', in *A Companion to 'Piers Plowman'*, J. A. Alford (ed.) (Berkeley, University of California Press, 1988), pp. 87–114.

Aers, David, *'Piers Plowman' and Christian Allegory* (London: Edward Arnold, 1975).

Chaucer, Langland and the Creative Imagination (London: Routledge and Kegan Paul, 1980).

Chaucer (Brighton: Harvester, 1986).

Community, Gender, and Individual Identity: English Writing 1360–1430 (London: Routledge, 1988).

Alford, John A. (ed.), *A Companion to 'Piers Plowman'* (Berkeley: University of California Press, 1988).

'The Idea of Reason in *Piers Plowman*', in *Medieval English Studies Presented to George Kane*, Edward Donald Kennedy, Ronald Waldron, and Joseph S. Wittig (eds.) (Cambridge: Brewer, 1988), pp. 199–215.

Amelang, James S., *The Flight of Icarus: Artisan Autobiography in Early Modern Europe* (Stanford: Stanford University Press, 1998).

Anderson, M. D., *Misericords: Medieval Life in English Woodcarving* (Harmondsworth: Penguin, 1954).

'The Iconography of British Misericords', in G. L. Remnant, *A Catalogue of Misericords in Great Britain* (Oxford: Clarendon Press, 1969), pp. xxii–xl.

Ashley, Kathleen and Clark, Robert L. A. (eds.), *Medieval Conduct*, Medieval Cultures 29 (Minneapolis, MN: University of Minnesota Press, 2001).

Ashley, Kathleen, and Clark, Robert L. A., 'Medieval Conduct: Texts, Theories and Practices', in *Medieval Conduct*, Kathleen Ashley and Robert L. A. Clark (eds.), Medieval Cultures 29 (Minneapolis, MN: University of Minnesota Press, 2001), pp. ix–xx.

Ashley, Kathleen, Gilmore, Leigh, and Peters, Gerald (eds.), *Autobiography and Postmodernism* (Amherst, MA: University of Massachusetts Press, 1995).

Ayton, Andrew, 'English Armies in the Fourteenth Century', in *Arms, Armies and Fortifications in the Hundred Years' War*, Anne Curry and Michael Hughes (eds.) (Woodbridge: Boydell, 1994), pp. 21–38.

Baldwin, F. E., *Sumptuary Legislation and Personal Regulation in England*, John Hopkins University Studies in Historical and Political Science 44:1 (Baltimore: Johns Hopkins Press, 1926).

Barber, Richard, *The Knight and Chivalry* (Woodbridge: Boydell, 1974).

Barney, S. A. (ed.), *Chaucer's Troilus: Essays in Criticism* (London: Scolar Press, 1980).

Barnie, John, *War in Medieval English Society: Social Values in the Hundred Years' War 1337–99* (London: Weidenfeld and Nicolson, 1974).

Barron, Caroline M., 'William Langland: A London Poet', in *Chaucer's England: Literature in Historical Context*, Barbara A. Hanawalt (ed.), Medieval Studies at Minnesota 4 (Minneapolis, MN: University of Minnesota Press, 1992), pp. 91–109.

Batt, Catherine, 'The Idioms of Women's Work and Thomas Hoccleve's Travails', in *The Middle Ages at Work: Practicing Labor in Late Medieval England*, Kellie Robertson and Michael Uebel (eds.) (New York: Palgrave, 2004), pp. 19–40.

Beattie, Cordelia, 'Meanings of Singleness: The Single Woman in Late Medieval England', unpublished PhD thesis, University of York (2001).

Beidler, Peter G. (ed.), *Masculinities in Chaucer: Approaches to Maleness in 'The Canterbury Tales' and 'Troilus and Criseyde'*, Chaucer Studies 25 (Cambridge: D. S. Brewer, 1998).

Ben-Amos, Ilana Krausman, *Adolescence and Youth in Early Modern England* (New Haven: Yale University Press, 1994).

Bennett, J. A. W., 'Gower's "Honeste love"', in *Gower's 'Confessio Amantis': A Critical Anthology*, Peter Nicholson (ed.), Publications of the John Gower Society 3 (Cambridge: D. S. Brewer, 1991), pp. 49–61, originally printed in *Patterns of Love and Courtesy: Essays in Memory of C. S. Lewis*, J. Lawlor (ed.) (London: Edward Arnold, 1966), pp. 107–21.

Bertolet, Craig E., 'The Rise of London Literature: Chaucer, Gower, Langland and the Poetics of the City in Late Medieval English Poetry', unpublished PhD thesis, Pennsylvania State University (1995).

'"Wel bet is rotten appul out of hoord": Chaucer's Cook, Commerce and Civic Order', *Studies in Philology* 99 (2002), 229–46.

Biernoff, Suzannah, *Sight and Embodiment in the Middle Ages* (Basingstoke: Palgrave, 2002).

Bird, R., *The Turbulent London of Richard II* (London: Longman, 1949).

Bloomfield, Morton W., '*Piers Plowman* and the Three Grades of Chastity', *Anglia* 76 (1958), 227–53.

Boffey, Julia, and Cowen, Janet (eds.), *Chaucer and Fifteenth-Century Poetry*, King's College London Medieval Studies 5 (London: King's College London, Centre for Late Antique and Medieval Studies, 1991).

Boffey, Julia, and King, Pamela (eds.), *London and Europe in the Later Middle Ages*, Westfield Publications in Medieval Studies 9 (London: Queen Mary and Westfield College, Centre for Medieval and Renaissance Studies, 1995).

Boitani, Piero, and Torti, Anna (eds.), *The Body and The Soul in Medieval Literature* (Cambridge: D. S. Brewer, 1999).

Bornstein, Diane, 'Anti-feminism in Thomas Hoccleve's Translation of Christine de Pizan's *Epistre au dieu d'amours*', *ELN* 19 (1981), 7–14.

Bothwell, James, Goldberg, P. J. P., and Ormrod, W. M. (eds.), *The Problem of Labour in Fourteenth-Century England* (York: York Medieval Press, 2000).

Bowers, John, *The Crisis of Will in 'Piers Plowman'* (Washington, DC: Catholic University of America Press, 1986).

Breitenberg, Mark, *Anxious Masculinity in Early Modern England*, Cambridge Studies in Renaissance Literature and Culture 10 (Cambridge: Cambridge University Press, 1996).

Bressie, Ramona, 'The Date of Thomas Usk's *Testament of Love*', *Modern Philology* 26 (1928), 17–29.

Bridbury, A. R., 'The Black Death', *Economic History Review*, 1st series 26 (1973), 577–92.

Brod, Harry, and Kauffman, M. (eds.), *Theorizing Masculinities* (Thousand Oaks, CA: Sage Publications, 1994).

Brody, Samuel N., 'Making a Play for Criseyde: The Staging of Pandarus's House in Chaucer's *Troilus and Criseyde*', *Speculum* 73 (1998), 115–40.

Brown, A. L., 'The Privy Seal Clerks in the Early Fifteenth Century', in *The Study of Medieval Records*, D. A. Bullough and R. L. Storey (eds.) (Oxford: Clarendon Press, 1971), pp. 260–81.

Bruhn, Mark J., 'Art, Anxiety, and Alchemy in *The Canon's Yeoman's Tale*', *Chaucer Review* 33 (1999) 288–315.

Brundage, J. A., *Medieval Canon Law* (London: Longman, 1995).

Bullough, D. A., and Storey, R. L. (eds.), *The Study of Medieval Records* (Oxford: Clarendon Press, 1971).

Bullough, V. L., and Brundage, J. (eds.), *Sexual Practices and the Medieval Church* (Buffalo, NY: Prometheus Books, 1982).

Burger, Glenn, *Chaucer's Queer Nation*, Medieval Cultures 34 (Minneapolis: University of Minnesota Press, 2003).

Burrow, J. A., 'The Audience of *Piers Plowman*', *Anglia* 75 (1957) 373–84.

'The Poet as Petitioner', *Studies in the Age of Chaucer* 3 (1981), 61–75.

'Autobiographical Poetry in the Middle Ages: The Case of Thomas Hoccleve', *Proceedings of the British Academy* 68 (1982) 389–412.

'Hoccleve's *Series*: Experience and Books', in *Fifteenth-Century Studies: Recent Essays*, R. F. Yeager (ed.) (Hamden, CT: Archon Books, 1984), pp. 259–73.

Langland's Fictions (Oxford: Clarendon Press, 1993).

Authors of the Middle Ages, 4: English Writers of the Late Middle Ages: Thomas Hoccleve (Aldershot: Variorum, 1994).

Bynum, Caroline Walker, *Holy Feast and Holy Fast: The Religious Significance of Food to Medieval Women* (Berkeley: University of California Press, 1987).

Cadden, Joan, *Meanings of Sex Difference in the Middle Ages: Medicine, Science and Culture* (Cambridge: Cambridge University Press, 1993).

Camille, Michael, *Mirror in Parchment: The Luttrell Psalter and the Making of Medieval England* (London: Reaktion Books, 1998).

Campbell, Anna Montgomery, *The Black Death and Men of Learning* (New York: AMS Press, 1931).

Carlier, M., and Soens, T. (eds.), *The Household in Late Medieval Cities: Italy and Northwestern Europe Compared. Proceedings of the International Conference Ghent, 21st–22nd January 2000*, Studies in Urban Social, Economic and Political History of the Medieval and Early Modern Low Countries 12 (Leuven: Garant, 2001).

Carlin, Martha, *Medieval Southwark* (London: Hambledon Press, 1992).

Carlson, David R., 'Chaucer's Boethius and Thomas Usk's *Testament of Love*: Politics and Love in the Chaucerian Tradition', in *The Centre and Its Compass: Studies in Medieval Literature in Honor of Professor Leyerle*, R. A. Taylor *et al.* (eds.), Studies in Medieval Culture 3 (Kalamazoo, MI: Western Michigan University Press, 1993), pp. 29–70.

Carlton, E., 'Complicity and Responsibility in Pandarus's Bed and Chaucer's Art', *PMLA* 94 (1979) 47–61.

Carruthers, Mary J., *The Craft of Thought: Meditation, Rhetoric, and the Making of Images, 400–1200*, Cambridge Studies in Medieval Literature 34 (Cambridge: Cambridge University Press, 1998).

Carruthers, Mary J., and Kirk, Elizabeth D. (eds.), *Acts of Interpretation: The Text in its Contexts 700–1600. Essays on Medieval and Renaissance Literature in Honour of E. Talbot Donaldson* (Norman, OK: Pilgrim Books, 1982).

Christianson, C. P., 'A Community of Book Artisans in Chaucer's London', *Viator* 20 (1989), 207–18.

Classen, Albrecht, 'Love and Marriage in Late Medieval Verse: Oswald Von Wolkenstein, Thomas Hoccleve and Michel Beheim', *Studia Neuphilologica* 62 (1990), 163–88.

Clopper, Lawrence M., 'Langland's Markings for the Structure of *Piers Plowman*', *Modern Philology* 2 (1988), 245–55.

'*Songes of Rechelesnesse*': Langland and the Franciscans* (Ann Arbor: University of Michigan Press, 1999).

Clough, Cecil H. (ed.), *Profession, Vocation, and Culture in Later Medieval England: Essays Dedicated to the Memory of A. R. Myers* (Liverpool: Liverpool University Press, 1982).

Cobban, A. B., *The Medieval Universities: Their Development and Organization* (London: Methuen, 1975).

Cohen, Jeffrey Jerome, and Wheeler, Bonnie (eds.), *Becoming Male in the Middle Ages*, The New Middle Ages 4 (New York: Garland, 1997).

Cohen, Jeremy, '*Be Fertile and Increase, Fill the Earth and Master It': The Ancient and Medieval Career of a Biblical Text* (Ithaca: Cornell University Press, 1989).

Cole, Andrew W., 'Trifunctionality and the Tree of Charity', *ELH* 62 (1995), 1–27.

Connell, R. W., *Gender and Power: Society, the Person and Sexual Politics* (Cambridge: Polity, 1987).

Masculinities (Cambridge: Polity, 1995).

Cook, Robert, 'The Canon's Yeoman and his *Tale*', *Chaucer Review* 22 (1987), 28–40.

Copeland, Rita, *Rhetoric, Hermeneutics, and Translation in the Middle Ages* (Cambridge: Cambridge University Press, 1991).

Corbier, M. (ed.), *Adoption et Fosterage* (Paris: De Boccard, 1999).

Cosgrove, Denis, and Daniels, Stephen (eds.), *The Iconography of Landscape: Essays on the Symbolic Representation, Design and Use of Past Environments* (Cambridge: Cambridge University Press, 1988).

Coss, Peter, *The Knight in Medieval England, 1000–1400* (Stroud: Allan Sutton, 1993).

Cullum, P. H., 'Clergy, Masculinity and Transgression in Late Medieval England', in *Masculinity in Medieval Europe*, D. M. Hadley (ed.) (London: Longman, 1999), pp. 178–96.

Cullum, P. J., and Goldberg, P. J. P., 'How Margaret Blackburn Taught her Daughters: Reading Devotional Instruction in a Book of Hours', in

Medieval Women: Texts and Contexts in Late Medieval Britain. Essays for Felicity Riddy, J. Wogan-Browne *et al.* (eds.), Medieval Women, Texts and Contexts 3 (Turnhout: Brepols, 2000), pp. 217–36.

Curry, Anne, 'Sex and the Soldier in Lancastrian Normandy, 1415–1450', *Reading Medieval Studies* 14 (1988) 17–45.

The Hundred Years' War (Basingstoke: Macmillan, 1993).

Curry, Anne, and Hughes, Michael (eds.), *Arms, Armies and Fortifications in the Hundred Years' War* (Woodbridge: Boydell, 1994).

Curry, Anne, and Matthews, Elizabeth (eds.), *Concepts and Patterns of Service in the Later Middle Ages*, The Fifteenth Century 1 (Woodbridge: Boydell, 2000).

Davis, Isabel, 'John Gower's Fear of Flying: Transitional Masculinities in the *Confessio Amantis*', *Rites of Passage: Cultures of Transition in the Fourteenth Century*, Nicola F. McDonald and W. M. Ormrod (eds.) (York: York Medieval Press, 2004), pp. 131–52.

'Men and Margery: Negotiating Medieval Patriarchy', in *A Companion to 'The Book of Margery Kempe'*, Katherine J. Lewis and John H. Arnold (eds.) (Cambridge: D. S. Brewer, 2004), pp. 35–54.

'On the Sadness of Not Being a Bird: Late-Medieval Marriage Ideologies and the Figure of Abraham in William Langland's *Piers Plowman*', in *Medieval Domesticity: Home, Housing, and Household*, P. J. P. Goldberg and Maryanne Kowaleski (eds.) (forthcoming).

D'Avray, D. L., and Tausche, M., 'Marriage Sermons in *Ad status* Collections of the Central Middle Ages', *Archives d'histoire doctrinale et litteraire du Moyen Age* 47 (1981) 71–119.

de Certeau, Michel, *The Practice of Everyday Life*, Steven Rendall (trans.) (Berkeley, CA: University of California Press, 1984).

de Looze, Laurence, *Pseudo-Autobiography in the Fourteenth Century: Juan Ruiz, Guillaume de Machaut, Jean Froissart, and Geoffrey Chaucer* (Gainsville: University Press of Florida, 1997).

de Vogüé, A., *The Rule of Saint Benedict: A Doctrinal and Spiritual Commentary*, J. B. Hasbrouck (trans.), Cistercian Studies Series 54 (Kalamazoo, MI: Cistercian Publications, 1983).

Delano-Smith, Catherine, and Kain, Roger J. P., *English Maps: A History*, The British Library Studies in Map History 2 (London: British Library, 1999).

Diamond, Arlyn, '*Troilus and Criseyde*: The Politics of Love', in *Chaucer in the Eighties*, Julian N. Wasserman and Robert J. Blanch (eds.) (Syracuse, NY: Syracuse University Press, 1986), pp. 93–103.

Dinshaw, Carolyn, *Getting Medieval: Sexualities and Communities, Pre- and Postmodern* (Durham, NC: Duke University Press, 1999).

Donaldson, E. Talbot, *The C-Text and its Poet*, Yale Studies in English 113 (New Haven: Yale University Press, 1949).

'The Ending of *Troilus*', in *Chaucer's Troilus: Essays in Criticism*, S. A. Barney (ed.) (London: Scolar Press, 1980), pp. 115–30, first published in *Early English and Norse Studies Presented to Hugh Smith*, A. Brown and P. Foote (eds.) (London: Methuen, 1963).

Dronke, Peter, '*Arbor caritas*', in *Medieval Studies for J. A. W. Bennett*, P. L. Heyworth (ed.) (Oxford: Clarendon Press, 1981), pp. 207–43.

Du Boulay, F. R. H., *The England of 'Piers Plowman': William Langland and his Vision of the Fourteenth Century* (Cambridge: D. S. Brewer, 1991).

Dyer, Christopher, 'Work Ethics in the Fourteenth Century', in *The Problem of Labour in Fourteenth-Century England*, James Bothwell, P. J. P. Goldberg and W. M. Ormrod (eds.) (York: York Medieval Press, 2000), pp. 21–41.

Eco, Umberto, *Travels in Hyperreality* (London: Picador, 1987).

Edbury, Peter E. (ed.), *Crusade and Settlement* (Cardiff: University College Cardiff Press, 1985).

Edson, Evelyn, *Mapping Time and Space: How Medieval Mapmakers Viewed their World*, The British Library Studies in Map History 1 (London: British Library, 1997).

Edwards, Robert R. (ed.), *Art and Context in Late Medieval English Narrative: Essays in Honor of Robert Worth Frank Jr* (Cambridge: D. S. Brewer, 1994).

Ellis, Roger (ed.), *The Medieval Translator: The Theory and Practice of Translation in the Middle Ages* (Cambridge: D. S. Brewer, 1989).

Emmerson, Richard K., and Goldberg, P. J. P., '"The Lord Geoffrey had me made": Lordship and Labour in the Luttrell Psalter', in *The Problem of Labour in Fourteenth-Century England*, James Bothwell, P. J. P. Goldberg and W. M. Ormrod (eds.) (York: York Medieval Press, 2000), pp. 43–63.

Erler, Mary C., and Kowaleski, Maryanne (eds.), *Gendering the Master Narrative: Women and Power in the Middle Ages* (Ithaca: Cornell University Press, 2003).

Federico, Sylvia, 'A Fourteenth-Century Erotics of Politics: London as a Feminine New Troy', *Studies in the Age of Chaucer* 19 (1997) 121–55.

New Troy: Fantasies of Empire in the Late Middle Ages, Medieval Cultures 36 (Minneapolis: University of Minnesota Press, 2003).

Ferguson, C. D., 'Autobiography as Therapy: Guibert de Nogent, Peter Abelard, and the Making of Medieval Autobiography', *The Journal of Medieval and Renaissance Studies* 13 (1983) 187–212.

Ferster, Judith, *Fictions of Advice: The Literature and Politics of Counsel in Late Medieval England* (Philadelphia: University of Pennsylvania Press, 1996).

Fisher, John, *John Gower: Moral Philosopher and Friend of Chaucer* (New York: New York University Press, 1964).

Fleming, John V., 'Hoccleve's "Letter of Cupid" and the "Quarrel" over the *Roman de la Rose*', *Medium Aevum* 40 (1971) 21–40.

Foucault, Michel, *The History of Sexuality: The Will to Knowledge*, Robert Hurley (trans.), 3 vols. (Harmondsworth: Penguin, 1990), I.

Fowler, Elizabeth, 'Civil Death and the Maiden: Agency and the Conditions of Contract in *Piers Plowman*', *Speculum* 70 (1995), 760–92.

Frantzen, Allen J., and Moffat, Douglas (eds.), *The Work of Work: Servitude, Slavery, and Labor in Medieval England* (Glasgow: Cruithne Press, 1994).

Galloway, Andrew, 'Private Selves and the Intellectual Marketplace in Late Fourteenth-Century England: The Case of the Two Usks', *Literary History* 28 (1997), 291–318.

'Intellectual Pregnancy, Metaphysical Femininity, and the Social Doctrine of the Trinity in *Piers Plowman*', *Yearbook of Langland Studies* 12 (1998), 117–52.

Gibson, W. S., *Hieronymus Bosch* (London: Thames and Hudson, 1973).

Gilmore, Leigh, 'Policing Truth: Confession, Gender, and Autobiographical Authority', in *Autobiography and Postmodernism*, Kathleen Ashley, Leigh Gilmore and Gerald Peters (eds.) (Amherst, MA: University of Massachusetts Press, 1995), pp. 54–78.

Given-Wilson, Christopher, 'Labour in the Context of English Government, c. 1350–1450', in *The Problem of Labour in Fourteenth-Century England*, James Bothwell, P. J. P. Goldberg and W. M. Ormrod (eds.) (York: York Medieval Press, 2000), pp. 85–100.

'Service, Serfdom and English Labour Legislation', in *Concepts and Patterns of Service in the Later Middle Ages*, Anne Curry and Elizabeth Matthews (eds.) (Woodbridge: Boydell, 2000), pp. 21–37.

Gold, P. S., 'The Marriage of Mary and Joseph in the Twelfth-Century Ideology of Marriage', in *Sexual Practices and the Medieval Church*, V. L. Bullough and J. Brundage (eds.) (Buffalo, NY: Prometheus Books, 1982), pp. 102–17.

Goldberg, P. J. P., *Women, Work and Life Cycle in a Medieval Economy: Women in York and Yorkshire, c. 1300–1520* (Oxford: Clarendon Press, 1992).

(ed.), *Woman is a Worthy Wight: Women in English Society, c. 1200–1500* (Stroud: Sutton, 1992).

'Introduction', in *The Black Death in England, 1348–1500*, W. M. Ormrod and Phillip G. Lindley (eds.), Paul Watkins Medieval Studies 15 (Stamford: Paul Watkins, 1996), pp. 1–15.

'Masters and Men in Later Medieval England' in *Masculinity in Medieval Europe*, D. M. Hadley (ed.) (London: Longman, 1999), pp. 56–70.

'Orphans and Servants: The Socialisation of Young People Living Away from Home in the English Later Middle Ages', in *Adoption et Fosterage*, M. Corbier (ed.) (Paris: De Boccard, 1999), pp. 231–46.

'What Was a Servant?', in *Concepts and Patterns of Service in the Later Middle Ages*, Anne Curry and Elizabeth Matthews (eds.) (Woodbridge: Boydell, 2000), pp. 1–20.

'Household and the Organisation of Labour in Late Medieval Towns: Some English Evidence', in *The Household in Late Medieval Cities: Italy and Northwestern Europe Compared. Proceedings of the International Conference Ghent, 21st–22nd January 2000*, M. Carlier and T. Soens (eds.), Studies in Urban Social, Economic and Political History of the Medieval and Early Modern Low Countries 12 (Leuven: Garant, 2001), pp. 59–70.

Goldberg, P. J. P., and Kowaleski, Maryanne (eds.), *Medieval Domesticity: Home, Housing, and Household* (forthcoming).

Goldie, Matthew Boyd, 'Psychosomatic Illness and Identity in London, 1416–1421: Hoccleve's *Complaint* and *Dialogue with a Friend*', *Exemplaria* 11 (1999) 23–52.

Goldsmith, Margaret E., *The Figure of Piers Plowman: The Image on the Coin*, Piers Plowman Studies 2 (Cambridge: D. S. Brewer, 1981).

Gottfried, Robert S., *The Black Death: Natural and Human Disaster in Medieval Europe* (New York: Free Press, 1983).

Gray, Douglas, *Themes and Images in the Medieval English Religious Lyric* (London: Routledge and Kegan Paul, 1972).

Green, Richard Firth, *Poets and Princepleasers: Literature and the English Court in the Late Middle Ages* (Toronto: University of Toronto Press, 1980).

Greenblatt, Stephen, *Renaissance Self-Fashioning: From More to Shakespeare* (Chicago: University of Chicago Press, 1980).

Greetham, D. C., 'Self-Referential Artefacts: Hoccleve's Persona as a Literary Device', *Modern Philology* 86 (1989), 242–51.

Grenberg, Bruce L., '*The Canon's Yeoman's Tale*: Boethian Wisdom and the Alchemists', *Chaucer Review* 1 (1966), 37–54.

Grennen, Joseph E., 'The Canon's Yeoman's Cosmic Furnace: Language and Meaning in *The Canon's Yeoman's Tale*', *Criticism* 4 (1962), 225–40.

'Chaucer's Characterization of the Canon and his Yeoman', *Journal of the History of Ideas* 25 (1964), 279–84.

'The Canon's Yeoman's Alchemical "Mass"', *Studies in Philology* 62 (1965) 546–60.

'Saint Cecilia's Chemical Wedding: The Unity of *The Canterbury Tales*, Fragment VIII', *Journal of English and German Philology* 65 (1966) 466–81.

Grössinger, Christa, *Picturing Women in Medieval and Renaissance Art* (Manchester: Manchester University Press, 1997).

Gunzenhauser, Bonnie J., 'Autobiography: General Survey', in *Encyclopedia of Life Writing: Autobiographical and Biographical Forms*, Margaretta Jolly (ed.), 2 vols. (London: Fitzroy Dearborn, 2001), I, 75–6.

Hadley, D. M. (ed.), *Masculinity in Medieval Europe* (London: Longman, 1999).

Hahn, T., 'Money, Sexuality, Wordplay, and the Context in *The Shipman's Tale*', in *Chaucer in the Eighties*, Julian N. Wasserman and Robert J. Blanch (eds.) (Syracuse, NY: Syracuse University Press, 1986), pp. 235–49.

Hamilton, Marie P., 'The Clerical Status of Chaucer's Alchemist', *Speculum* 16 (1941), 103–8.

Hanawalt, Barbara A. (ed.), *Chaucer's England: Literature in Historical Context*, Medieval Studies at Minnesota 4 (Minneapolis: University of Minnesota Press, 1992).

'Remarriage as an Option for Urban and Rural Widows in Late Medieval England', in *Wife and Widow in Medieval England*, Sue Sheridan Walker (ed.) (Ann Arbor: University of Michigan Press, 1993), pp. 141–64.

'"The Childe of Bristowe" and the Making of Middle-Class Adolescence', in *Bodies and Disciplines: Intersections of Literature and History in Fifteenth-Century England*, B. A. Hanawalt and David Wallace (eds.), Medieval Cultures 9 (Minneapolis: University of Minnesota, 1996), 155–78.

Hanawalt, Barbara A., and Wallace, David (eds.), *Bodies and Disciplines: Intersections of Literature and History in Fifteenth-Century England*, Medieval Cultures 9 (Minneapolis: University of Minnesota, 1996).

Hanna III, Ralph, 'William Langland', in *Authors of the Middle Ages: English Writers of the Late Middle Ages*, M. C. Seymour (ed.), 2 vols. (Aldershot: Variorum, 1994), II, no. 3.

'Will's Work', in *Written Work: Langland, Labor, and Authorship*, Steven Justice and Kathryn Kerby-Fulton (eds.) (Philadelphia: University of Pennsylvania Press, 1997), pp. 23–66.

'School and Scorn: Gender in *Piers Plowman*', *New Medieval Literatures* 3 (1999), 213–27.

Hanning, R. W., ' "And counterfete the speche of every man / He koude, whan he sholde telle a tale": Toward a Lapsarian Poetics for *The Canterbury Tales*', *Studies in the Age of Chaucer* 21 (1999), 29–58.

Hanrahan, M., 'The Seduction of *The Testament of Love*', *Literature and History* 7 (1998), 1–15.

Harley, J. B., 'Maps, Knowledge, and Power', in *The Iconography of Landscape: Essays on the Symbolic Representation, Design and Use of Past Environments*, Denis Cosgrove and Stephen Daniels (eds.) (Cambridge: Cambridge University Press, 1988), pp. 277–312.

Hartung, A. E., ' "Pars Secunda" and the Development of *The Canon's Yeoman's Tale*', *Chaucer Review* 12 (1977), 111–28.

Harwood, Britton J., 'Chaucer and the Silence of History: Situating *The Canon's Yeoman's Tale*', *PMLA* 102 (1987), 338–50.

Harwood, Britton J., and Overing, Gillian R. (eds.), *Class and Gender in Early English Literature: Intersections* (Bloomington: Indiana University Press, 1994).

Hasler, A. J., 'Hoccleve's Unregimented Body', *Paragraph* 130 (1990), 164–83.

Hatcher, John, *Plague, Population, and the English Economy, 1348–1530* (London: Macmillan, 1977).

'England in the Aftermath of the Black Death', *Past and Present* 144 (1994), 3–35.

Heale, Elizabeth, *Autobiography and Authorship in Renaissance Verse: Chronicles of the Self* (Basingstoke: Palgrave Macmillan, 2003).

Hearn, Jeff, and Collinson, David L., 'Theorizing Unities and Differences Between Men and Between Masculinities', in *Theorizing Masculinities*, Harry Brod and M. Kauffman (eds.) (Thousand Oaks, CA: Sage Publications, 1994), pp. 97–118.

Helmholz, R. H., *Marriage Litigation in Medieval England* (Cambridge: Cambridge University Press, 1974).

Henebry, Charles W. M., 'Apprentice Janekyn/Clerk Jankyn: Discrete Phases in Chaucer's Developing Conception of the Wife of Bath', *Chaucer Review* 32 (1997), 146–61.

Hewett-Smith, Kathleen M. (ed.), *William Langland's 'Piers Plowman': A Book of Essays* (New York: Routledge, 2001).

Heyworth, P. L. (ed.), *Medieval Studies for J. A. W. Bennett* (Oxford: Clarendon Press, 1981).

Hirsch, John, 'Author and Scribe in *The Book of Margery Kempe*', *Medium Aevum* 44 (1975), 145–50.

Horrox, Rosemary, 'Service', in *Fifteenth-Century Attitudes: Perceptions of Society in Late Medieval England*, Rosemary Horrox (ed.) (Cambridge: Cambridge University Press, 1994), pp. 61–78.

(ed.), *Fifteenth-Century Attitudes: Perceptions of Society in Late Medieval England* (Cambridge: Cambridge University Press, 1994).

Hovland, Stephanie R., 'Apprenticeship in the Records of the Goldsmiths' Company of London, 1444–1500', *Medieval Prosopography* 22 (2001), 89–114.

Howard, Donald R., *The Idea of 'The Canterbury Tales'* (Berkeley: University of California Press, 1976).

Hunt, Alan, *Governance of the Consuming Passions: A History of Sumptuary Law* (Basingstoke: Macmillan, 1996).

Hussey, S. S., 'Langland, Hilton and the Three Lives', *Review of English Studies* 7 (1956) 132–150.

(ed.), *'Piers Plowman': Critical Approaches* (London: Methuen, 1969).

Itnyre, Cathy Jorgensen (ed.), *Medieval Family Roles: A Book of Essays*, Garland Medieval Casebooks 15 (New York: Garland, 1996).

Ivy, G. S., 'The Bibliography of the Manuscript-Book', in *The English Library before 1700*, Francis Wormald and C. E. Wright (eds.) (London: Athlone, 1958), pp. 32–65.

Jamieson, Ruth, 'The Man of Hobbes: Masculinity and Wartime Necessity', *Journal of Historical Sociology* 9 (1996) 19–42.

Jolly, Margaretta, (ed.), *Encyclopedia of Life Writing: Autobiographical and Biographical Forms*, 2 vols. (London: Fitzroy Dearborn, 2001).

Jones, Terry, *Chaucer's Knight: The Portrait of a Medieval Mercenary* (London: Weidenfeld and Nicolson, 1980).

Justice, Steven, and Kerby-Fulton, Kathryn, 'Langlandian Reading Circles and the Civil Service in London and Dublin, 1380–1427', *New Medieval Literatures* 1 (1997) 59–83.

(eds.), *Written Work: Langland, Labor, and Authorship* (Philadelphia: University of Pennsylvania Press, 1997).

Kadar, Marlene, *Essays on Life Writing: From Genre to Critical Practice*, Theory/ Culture Series 11 (Toronto: University of Toronto Press, 1992).

Kasten, Madeline, *In Search of 'Kynde Knowynge': 'Piers Plowman' and the Origin of Allegorical Dynamics* (Amsterdam: ASCA Press, 2001).

Kean, P. M., 'Justice, Kingship and the Good Life in the Second Part of *Piers Plowman*', in *'Piers Plowman': Critical Approaches*, S. S.Hussey (ed.) (London: Methuen, 1969), pp. 76–110.

Keen, Maurice, 'Chaucer's Knight, the English Aristocracy and the Crusade', in *English Court Culture in the Later Middle Ages*, V. J. Scattergood and J. W. Sherborne (eds.) (London: Duckworth, 1983), pp. 45–61.

Chivalry (New Haven: Yale University Press, 1984).

Keller, K., 'For Better and Worse: Woman and Marriage in *Piers Plowman*', in *Medieval Family Roles: A Book of Essays*, Cathy Jorgensen Itnyre (ed.), Garland Medieval Casebooks 15 (New York: Garland, 1996), pp. 67–83.

Kelly, H. A., 'Marriage in the Middle Ages, 2: Clandestine Marriage and Chaucer's *Troilus*', *Viator* 4 (1973), 435–57.

Kennedy, Edward Donald, Waldron, Ronald, and Wittig, Joseph S. (eds.), *Medieval English Studies Presented to George Kane* (Woodbridge: Brewer, 1988).

Kerby-Fulton, Kathryn, 'Langland and the Bibliographic Ego', in *Written Work: Langland, Labor, and Authorship*, Steven Justice and Kathryn Kerby-Fulton (eds.) (Philadelphia: University of Pennsylvania Press, 1997), pp. 67–143.

Kermode, Jennifer (ed.), *Enterprise and Individuals in Fifteenth-Century England* (Stroud: Alan Sutton, 1991).

Kiefer, Laura, 'My Family First: Draft-Dodging Parents in the *Confessio Amantis*', *Essays in Medieval Studies* 12 (1996), 55–68.

Kimmel, M. S., 'Masculinity as Homophobia, Fear, Shame, and Silence in the Construction of Gender Identity', in *Theorizing Masculinities*, Harry Brod and M. Kauffman (eds.) (Thousand Oaks, CA: Sage Publications, 1994), pp. 119–41.

Kinneavy, Gerald, 'Gower's *Confessio Amantis* and the Penitentials', *Chaucer Review* 19 (1984), 144–61.

Knapp, Ethan, 'Bureaucratic Identity and Literary Practice in Lancastrian England', *Medieval Perspectives* 9 (1994), 64–72.

  'Bureaucratic Identity and the Construction of the Self in Hoccleve's *Formulary* and *La male regle*', *Speculum* 74 (1999), 357–76.

  The Bureaucratic Muse: Thomas Hoccleve and the Literature of Late Medieval England (University Park, PA: Pennsylvania State University Press, 2001).

Knapp, Peggy A., 'The Work of Alchemy', *Journal of Medieval and Early Modern Studies* 30 (2000), 575–99.

Knight, Stephen, 'Rhetoric and Poetry in *The Franklin's Tale*', *Chaucer Review* 4 (1970) 14–30.

Kohl, Stephan, 'More than Virtues and Vices: Self-Analysis in Hoccleve's "Autobiographies"', *Fifteenth-Century Studies* 14 (1988), 115–27.

Kruger, Steven F., 'Mirrors and the Trajectory of Vision in *Piers Plowman*', *Speculum* 66 (1991), 74–95.

Landman, James, 'Laws of Community, Margery Kempe and *The Canon's Yeoman's Tale*', *Journal of Medieval and Early Modern Studies* 28 (1998), 389–425.

Laskaya, Anne, *Chaucer's Approach to Gender in 'The Canterbury Tales'*, Chaucer Studies 23 (Cambridge: D. S. Brewer, 1995).

Lawton, David, 'The Subject of *Piers Plowman*', *The Yearbook of Langland Studies* 1 (1987) 1–30.

Lees, Claire. A., 'Gender and Exchange in *Piers Plowman*', in *Class and Gender in Early English Literature: Intersections*, Britton J. Harwood and Gillian R. Overing (eds.) (Bloomington: Indiana University Press, 1994), pp. 112–30.

Leff, Gordon A., *Paris and Oxford Universities in the Thirteenth and Fourteenth Centuries: An Institutional and Intellectual History* (New York: John Wiley and Sons, 1968).

Lerner, Robert E., 'The Black Death and Western European Eschatological Mentalities', in *The Black Death: The Impact of the Fourteenth-Century Plague*, Daniel Williman (ed.), Medieval and Renaissance Texts and Studies 13 (Binghampton, NY: Center for Medieval and Early Renaissance Studies, 1982), pp. 77–105.

Levin, Rozalyn, 'The Passive Poet: Amans as Narrator in Book 4 of the *Confessio Amantis*', *Essays in Medieval Studies* 3 (1986), 114–30.

Lewis, C. S., *Selected Literary Essays*, Walter Hooper (ed.) (Cambridge: Cambridge University Press, 1969).

  'What Chaucer Really did to *Il filostrato*', in *Selected Literary Essays by C. S. Lewis*, Walter Hooper (ed.) (Cambridge: Cambridge University Press, 1969), pp. 27–44, originally published in *Essays and Studies* 17 (1932), 56–75.

  'Gower', in *Gower's 'Confessio Amantis': A Critical Anthology*, Peter Nicholson (ed.), Publications of the John Gower Society 3 (Cambridge: D. S. Brewer, 1991), pp. 15–39, originally published in *The Allegory of Love: A Study in Medieval Tradition* (London: Oxford University Press, 1936), pp. 198–222.

Lewis, Katherine J., and Arnold, John H. (eds.), *A Companion to 'The Book of Margery Kempe'* (Cambridge: D. S. Brewer, 2004).

Lewis, Lucy, 'Langland's Tree of Charity and Usk's "Wexing Tree"', *N&Q* 42 (1995), 429–33.

Leyser, Conrad, *Authority and Asceticism from Augustine to Gregory the Great* (Oxford: Clarendon Press, 2000).

Lochrie, Karma, '"Women's Pryvetees" and Fabliau Politics in *The Miller's Tale*', *Exemplaria* 6 (1993), 287–304.

McCarthy, Conor, 'Love and Marriage in the *Confessio Amantis*', *Neuphilologus* 84 (2000), 485–99.

McCraken, S., 'The Confessional Prologue and the Topography of the Canon's Yeoman', *Modern Philology* 68 (1971), 281–91.

McDonald, Nicola F., '"Lusti tresor": Avarice and the Economics of the Erotic in Gower's *Confessio Amantis*', in *Treasure in the Medieval West*, Elizabeth M. Tyler (ed.) (York: York Medieval Press, 2000), pp. 135–56.

McDonald, Nicola F., and Ormrod, W. M. (eds.), *Rites of Passage: Cultures of Transition in the Fourteenth Century* (York: York Medieval Press, 2004).

McInerney, M. B., '"Is this a mannes herte?": Unmanning Troilus through Ovidian Allusion', in *Masculinities in Chaucer: Approaches to Maleness in 'The Canterbury Tales' and 'Troilus and Criseyde'*, Peter G. Beidler (ed.), Chaucer Studies 25 (Cambridge: D. S. Brewer, 1998), pp. 221–35.

McIntosh, Marjorie Keniston, *Controlling Misbehaviour in England, 1370–1600*, Cambridge Studies in Population, Economy, and Society in Past Time 34 (Cambridge: Cambridge University Press, 1998).

McSheffrey, Shannon, 'Men and Masculinity in Late Medieval London Civic Culture: Governance, Patriarchy and Reputation', in *Conflicted Identities and Multiple Masculinities: Men in the Medieval West*, Jacqueline Murray (ed.) (New York: Garland, 1999), pp. 243–78.

Maguire, J., 'The Clandestine Marriage of Troilus and Criseyde', *Chaucer Review* 8 (1974), 262–78.

Mann, Jill, 'Troilus' Swoon', *Chaucer Review* 14 (1980), 319–35.

'Apologies to Women', Inaugural Lecture (Cambridge, 1990).

Manzalaoui, M. A., '"Noght in the Registre of Venus": Gower's English Mirror for Princes', in *Medieval Studies for J. A. W. Bennett*, P. L. Heyworth (ed.) (Oxford: Clarendon Press, 1981), pp. 159–83.

Marks, Richard, *Stained Glass in England during the Middle Ages* (London: Routledge, 1993).

Mate, Mavis, *Women in Medieval English Society* (Cambridge: Cambridge University Press, 1999).

Mazzo Karas, Ruth, 'Sharing Wine, Women, and Song: Masculine Formation in the Medieval European Universities', in *Becoming Male in the Middle Ages*, Jeffrey Jerome Cohen and Bonnie Wheeler (eds.), The New Middle Ages 4 (New York: Garland, 1997), 187–202.

Medcalf, Stephen, 'Transposition: Thomas Usk's *Testament of Love*', in *The Medieval Translator: The Theory and Practice of Translation in the Middle Ages*, Roger Ellis (ed.) (Cambridge: D. S. Brewer, 1989), pp. 181–95.

'The World and the Heart of Thomas Usk', in *Essays on Ricardian Literature in Honour of J. A. Burrow*, A. J. Minnis, Charlotte C. Morse and Thorlac Turville-Petre (eds.) (Oxford: Clarendon Press, 1997), pp. 222–51.

Middleton, A., 'The Idea of Public Poetry in the Reign of Richard II', *Speculum* 53 (1978), 94–114.

'Acts of Vagrancy: The C Version "Autobiography" and the Statute of 1388', in *Written Work: Langland, Labor, and Authorship*, Steven Justice and Kathryn Kerby-Fulton (eds.) (Philadelphia: University of Pennsylvania Press, 1997), pp. 208–317.

'Usk's "Perdurable letters": *The Testament of Love* from Script to Print', *Studies in Bibliography* 51 (1998), 63–117.

Miller, Edward, and Hatcher, John, *Medieval England: Towns, Commerce and Crafts, 1086–1348* (London: Longman, 1995).

Minnis, A. J., (ed.), *Gower's 'Confessio Amantis': Responses and Reassessments* (Cambridge: D. S. Brewer, 1983).

(ed.), *Latin and Vernacular: Studies in Late-Medieval Texts and Manuscripts*, York Manuscripts Conferences, Proceedings Series 1 (Cambridge: D. S. Brewer, 1989).

'*De vulgari auctoritate*: Chaucer, Gower and the Men of Great Authority', in *Chaucer and Gower: Difference, Mutuality, Exchange*, R. F. Yeager (ed.), English Literary Studies 51 (Victoria, BC: University of Victoria, 1991), pp. 36–74.

Minnis, A. J., Morse, Charlotte C., and Turville-Petre, Thorlac (eds.), *Essays on Ricardian Literature in Honour of J. A. Burrow* (Oxford: Clarendon Press, 1997).

Mohl, Ruth, *The Three Estates in Medieval and Renaissance Literature* (New York: Columbia University Press, 1933).

Mumford, Lewis, *The Culture of Cities* (London: Secker and Warburg, 1938).

Murray, Jacqueline, 'Individualism and Consensual Marriage: Some Evidence From Medieval England', in *Women, Marriage and Family in Medieval Criticism: Essays in Memory of Michael M. Sheehan*, Constance M. Rousseau and Joel T. Rosenthal (eds.), Studies in Medieval Culture 37 (Kalamazoo, MI: Western Michigan University Press, 1998), pp. 121–51.

(ed.), *Conflicted Identities and Multiple Masculinities: Men in the Medieval West* (New York: Garland, 1999).

Newman Hallmundsson, M., 'The Community of Law and Letters: Some Notes on Thomas Usk's Audience', *Viator* 9 (1978), 357–65.

Nicholson, Peter, 'Gower's Revisions in the *Confessio Amantis*', *Chaucer Review* 19 (1984), 123–45.

'The Dedications of Gower's *Confessio Amantis*', *Mediaevalia* 10 (1984), 159–80.

(ed.), *Gower's 'Confessio Amantis': A Critical Anthology*, Publications of the John Gower Society 3 (Cambridge: D. S. Brewer, 1991).

Nightingale, Pamela, 'Capitalists, Crafts and Constitutional Change in Late Fourteenth-Century London', *Past and Present* 124 (1989), 3–35.

Niranjana, T., *Siting Translation: History, Post-Structuralism and the Colonist Context* (Berkeley: University of California Press, 1992).

Nissé, Ruth, '"Oure Fadres Olde and Modres": Gender, Heresy, and Hoccleve's Literary Politics', *Studies in the Age of Chaucer* 21 (1999), 275–99.

Olney, James, *Memory and Narrative: The Weave of Life Writing* (Chicago: University of Chicago Press, 1988).

Olsson, Kurt, 'John Gower's *Vox clamantis* and the Medieval Idea of Place', *Studies in Philology* 84 (1987), 134–58.

'Love, Intimacy, and Gower', *The Chaucer Review* 30 (1995), 71–100.

Ormrod, W. M., 'The Domestic Response to the Hundred Years' War', in *Arms, Armies and Fortifications in the Hundred Years' War*, Anne Curry and Michael Hughes (eds.) (Woodbridge: Boydell, 1994), pp. 83–101.

Ormrod, W. M., and Lindley, Phillip G. (eds.) *The Black Death in England, 1348–1500*, Paul Watkins Medieval Studies 15 (Stamford: Paul Watkins, 1996).

Ovitt Jr, G. R., *The Restoration of Perfection: Labor and Technology in Medieval Culture* (New Brunswick, NJ: Rutgers University Press, 1987).

Owst, G. R., *Literature and Pulpit in Medieval England: A Neglected Chapter in the History of English Letters and of the English People*, 2nd edn (Oxford: Blackwell, 1961).

Parkes, M. B. (ed.), *Scribes, Scripts and Readers: Studies in the Communication, Presentation and Dissemination of Medieval Texts* (London: Hambledon, 1991).

and Doyle, A. I., 'The Production of Copies of *The Canterbury Tales* and the *Confessio Amantis* in the Early Fifteenth Century', in M. B. Parkes (ed.), *Scribes, Scripts and Readers: Studies in the Communication, Presentation and Dissemination of Medieval Texts* (London: Hambledon, 1991), pp. 201–48.

Patterson, Lee, 'Perpetual Motion: Alchemy and the Technology of the Self', *Studies in the Age of Chaucer* 15 (1995), 25–57.

'"What is Me?": Self and Society in the Poetry of Thomas Hoccleve', *Studies in the Age of Chaucer* 23 (2001), 437–70.

(ed.), *Literary Practice and Social Change in Britain, 1380–1530* (Berkeley: University of California Press, 1990).

Paxson, J. J., 'Inventing the Subject and the Personification of Will in *Piers Plowman*: Rhetorical, Erotic, Ideological Origins and Limits in Langland's Allegorical Poetics', in *William Langland's 'Piers Plowman': A Book of Essays*, Kathleen M. Hewett-Smith (ed.) (New York: Routledge, 2001), pp. 195–231.

Pearsall, Derek, 'Gower's Narrative Art', in *Gower's 'Confessio Amantis': A Critical Anthology*, Peter Nicholson (ed.), Publications of the John Gower Society 3 (Cambridge: D. S. Brewer, 1991), pp. 62–80, first printed in *PMLA* 81 (1966), 475–84.

'Gower's Latin in the *Confessio Amantis*', in *Latin and Vernacular: Studies in Late-Medieval Texts and Manuscripts*, A. J. Minnis (ed.), York Manuscripts Conferences, Proceedings Series 1 (Cambridge: D. S. Brewer, 1989), pp. 13–25.

'Langland's London', in *Written Work: Langland, Labor, and Authorship*, Steven Justice and Kathryn Kerby-Fulton (eds.) (Philadelphia: University of Pennsylvania Press, 1997), pp. 185–207.

and Salter, Elizabeth, *Landscapes and Seasons of the Medieval World* (London: Elek, 1973).

Peck, Russell A., 'The Phenomenology of Make Believe in Gower's *Confessio Amantis*', *Studies in Philology* 91 (1994), 250–69.

Peters, Christine, *Patterns of Piety: Women, Gender and Religion in Late Medieval and Reformation England* (Cambridge: Cambridge University Press, 2003).

Phillips, Helen, *An Introduction to 'The Canterbury Tales': Reading, Fiction, Context* (New York: St Martin's Press, 2000).

(ed.), *Langland, the Mystics and the Medieval English Religious Tradition: Essays in Honour of S. S. Hussey* (Cambridge: D. S. Brewer, 1990).

Poos, Lawrence R., 'The Heavy-Handed Marriage Counsellor: Regulating Marriage in Some Later-Medieval English Local Ecclesiastical-Court Jurisdictions', *American Journal of Legal History* 39 (1995) 291–309.

Porter, Elizabeth, 'Gower's Ethical Microcosm and Political Macrocosm', in *Gower's 'Confessio Amantis': Responses and Reassessments*, A. J. Minnis (ed.) (Cambridge: D. S. Brewer, 1983), pp. 135–62.

Powicke, Michael, *Military Obligation in Medieval England: A Study in Liberty and Duty* (Oxford: Clarendon Press, 1962).

Ramsay, Nigel, 'Scriveners and Notaries as Legal Intermediaries in Later Medieval England', in *Enterprise and Individuals in Fifteenth-Century England*, Jennifer Kermode (ed.) (Stroud: Alan Sutton, 1991), pp. 118–131.

Rank, Otto, *Will Therapy and Truth and Reality* (New York: A. A. Knopf, 1950).

Ratazzi Papka, Claudia, 'Transgression, the End of Troilus, and the Ending of Chaucer's *Troilus and Criseyde*', *Chaucer Review* 32 (1998), 267–81.

Razi, Zvi, *Life and Death in a Medieval Parish: Economy, Society and Demography in Halesowen, 1270–1400* (Cambridge: Cambridge University Press, 1980).

Rees Jones, Sarah, 'Household, Work and the Problem of Mobile Labour: The Regulation of Labour in Medieval English Towns', in *The Problem of Labour in Fourteenth-Century England*, James Bothwell, P. J. P. Goldberg and W. M. Ormrod (eds.) (York: York Medieval Press, 2000), pp. 133–53.

'Women's Influence on the Design of Urban Homes', in *Gendering the Master Narrative: Women and Power in the Middle Ages*, Mary C. Erler and Maryanne Kowaleski (eds.) (Ithaca: Cornell University Press, 2003), pp. 190–211.

Reeves, Marjorie, and Hirsch-Reich, Beatrice, *The Figurae of Joachim of Fiore* (Oxford: Clarendon Press, 1972).

Remnant, G. L., *A Catalogue of Misericords in Great Britain* (Oxford: Clarendon Press, 1969).

Revard, Carter, 'The Tow on Absalom's Distaff and the Punishment of Lechers in Medieval London', *ELN* 17 (1980), 168–70.

Richardson, Malcolm, 'Hoccleve in his Social Context', *The Chaucer Review* 20 (1986), 313–22.

Riddy, Felicity, 'Mother Knows Best: Reading Social Change in a Courtesy Text', *Speculum* 71 (1996), 66–86.

(ed.), *Prestige, Authority and Power in Late Medieval Manuscripts and Texts* (York: York Medieval Press, 2000).

Roberts, F. X., 'A Source for T. S. Eliot's Use of "Elsewhere" in "East Coker"', *ANQ* 6 (1993), 24–5.

Robertson, Kellie, 'Laboring in the God of Love's Garden: Chaucer's Prologue to *The Legend of Good Women*', *Studies in the Age of Chaucer* 24 (2002), 115–47.

Robertson, Kellie, and Uebel, Michael (eds.) *The Middle Ages at Work: Practicing Labor in Late Medieval England* (New York: Palgrave, 2004).

Ronan Crampton, Georgia, 'Action and Passion in Chaucer's *Troilus*', *Medium Aevum* 43 (1974), 22–36.

Rosser, Gervase, 'London and Westminster; The Suburb in the Urban Economy in the Later Middle Ages', in *Towns and Townspeople in the Fifteenth Century*, John A. F. Thomson (ed.) (Gloucester: Sutton, 1988), pp. 45–61.

Rousseau, Constance M., and Rosenthal, Joel T. (eds.), *Women, Marriage and Family in Medieval Criticism: Essays in Memory of Michael M. Sheehan*, Studies in Medieval Culture 37 (Kalamazoo, MI: Western Michigan University Press, 1998).

Sadlek, Gregory M., 'Love, Labor and Sloth in Chaucer's *Troilus and Criseyde*', *Chaucer Review* 26 (1992), 350–68.

'John Gower's *Confessio Amantis*, Ideology, and the "Labor" of "Love's Labour"', in *Re-visioning Gower*, R. F. Yeager (ed.) (Asheville, NC: Pegasus Press, 1998), pp. 147–58.

Idleness Working: The Discourse of Love's Labor from Ovid through Chaucer and Gower (Washington: The Catholic University of America Press, 2004).

Salter, Elizabeth, *Fourteenth-Century English Poetry: Context and Reading* (Oxford: Oxford University Press, 1983).

Sanderlin, G., 'Usk's *Testament of Love* and St Anselm', *Speculum* 17 (1942), 69–73.

Scanlon, Larry, *Narrative, Authority and Power: The Medieval Exemplum and the Chaucerian Tradition*, Cambridge Studies in Medieval Literature 20 (Cambridge: Cambridge University Press, 1994).

Scase, Wendy, *'Piers Plowman' and the New Anticlericalism*, Cambridge Studies in Medieval Literature 4 (Cambridge: Cambridge University Press, 1989).

Scattergood, John, and Stokes, Myra, 'Travelling in November: Sir Gawain, Thomas Usk, Charles of Orleans and the *De re militari*', *Medium Aevum* 53 (1984), 78–82.

Scattergood, V. J., 'Perkyn Revellour and *The Cook's Tale*', *Chaucer Review* 19 (1984), 14–23.

'Chaucer in the Suburbs', in *Medieval Literature and Antiquities: Studies in Honour of Basil Cottle*, Myra Stokes and T. L. Burton (eds.) (Woodbridge: Brewer, 1987), pp. 145–62.

and Sherborne, J. W. (eds.), *English Court Culture in the Later Middle Ages* (London: Duckworth, 1983).

Schmitz, G., 'Rhetoric and Fiction: Gower's Comments on Eloquence and Courtly Poetry', in *Gower's 'Confessio Amantis': A Critical Anthology*, Peter Nicholson (ed.), Publications of the John Gower Society 3 (Cambridge: D. S. Brewer, 1991), pp. 117–42.

Schulz, H. C., 'Thomas Hoccleve, Scribe', *Speculum* 12 (1937), 71–81.

Shahar, Shulamith, *The Fourth Estate: A History of Women in the Middle Ages*, C. Galai (trans.) (London: Methuen, 1983).

Sheehan, Michael M., 'Marriage Theory and Practice in the Conciliar Legislation and Diocesan Statutes of Medieval England', *Medieval Studies* 40 (1978), 408–60.

Marriage, Family, and Law in Medieval Europe: Collected Studies, J. K. Farge (ed.) (Toronto: University of Toronto Press, 1996).

Shenman, Paul, 'Grace Abounding: Justification in Passus 16 of *Piers Plowman*', *Papers on Language and Literature* 34 (1998), 162–78.

Siberry, Elizabeth, 'Criticism of Crusading in Fourteenth-Century England', in *Crusade and Settlement*, Peter E. Edbury (ed.) (Cardiff: University College Cardiff Press, 1985), pp. 127–34.

Simpson, James, 'Ironic Incongruence in the Prologue and Book I of Gower's *Confessio Amantis*', *Neuphilologus* 72 (1988), 617–32.

'The Constraints of Satire in *Piers Plowman* and *Mum and the Sothsegger*', in *Langland, the Mystics and the Medieval English Religious Tradition: Essays in Honour of S. S. Hussey*, Helen Phillips (ed.) (Cambridge: Brewer, 1990), pp. 11–30.

'Madness and Texts: Hoccleve's Series', in *Chaucer and Fifteenth-Century Poetry*, Julia Boffey and Janet Cowen (eds.), King's College London Medieval Studies 5 (London: King's College, Centre for Late Antique and Medieval Studies, 1991), 15–26.

'Nobody's Man: Thomas Hoccleve's *Regiment of Princes*', in *London and Europe in the Later Middle Ages*, Julia Boffey and Pamela King (eds.), Westfield Publications in Medieval Studies 9 (London: Queen Mary and Westfield College, Centre for Medieval and Renaissance Studies, 1995), pp. 149–80.

Sciences and the Self in Medieval Poetry: Alan of Lille's 'Anticlaudianus' and John Gower's 'Confessio Amantis', Cambridge Studies in Medieval Literature 25 (Cambridge: Cambridge University Press, 1995).

Siraisi, Nancy G., *Medieval and Early Renaissance Medicine: An Introduction to Knowledge and Practice* (Chicago: University of Chicago Press, 1990).

Smith, D. Vance, 'Body Doubles: Producing the Masculine *Corpus*', in *Becoming Male in the Middle Ages*, Jeffrey Jerome Cohen and Bonnie Wheeler (eds.), The New Middle Ages 4 (New York: Garland, 1997), pp. 3–19.

The Book of the Incipit: Beginnings in the Fourteenth Century, Medieval Cultures Series 28 (Minneapolis, MA: University of Minnesota Press, 2001).

Arts of Possession: The Medieval Household Imaginary, Medieval Cultures 33 (Minneapolis, MA: University of Minnesota Press, 2003).

Smith, R. M., 'Geographical Diversity in the Resort to Marriage in Late Medieval Europe: Work, Reputation, and Unmarried Females in the Household Formation Systems of Northern and Southern Europe', in *Woman is a Worthy Wight: Women in English Society, c. 1200–1500*, P. J. P. Goldberg (ed.) (Stroud: Alan Sutton, 1992), pp. 16–59.

Smith, Sidonie, *Subjectivity, Identity and the Body: Women's Autobiographical Practices in the Twentieth Century* (Bloomington, IA: Indiana University Press, 1993).

'Identity's Body', in *Autobiography and Postmodernism*, Kathleen Ashley, Leigh Gilmore and Gerald Peters (eds.) (Amherst: University of Massachusetts Press, 1995), pp. 266–92.

Staley, Lynn, *Margery Kempe's Dissenting Fictions* (University Park, PA: University of Pennsylvania Press, 1994).

Stanbury, Sarah, 'The Voyeur and the Private Life in *Troilus and Criseyde*', *Studies in the Age of Chaucer* 13 (1991), 141–58.

Steiner, Emily, *Documentary Culture and the Making of Medieval English Literature*, Cambridge Studies in Medieval Literature 50 (Cambridge: Cambridge University Press, 2003).

Stokes, Myra, and Burton, T. L. (eds.), *Medieval Literature and Antiquities: Studies in Honour of Basil Cottle* (Woodbridge: Brewer, 1987).

Storey, R. L., 'Gentlemen Bureaucrats', in *Profession, Vocation, and Culture in Later Medieval England: Essays Dedicated to the Memory of A. R. Myers*, Cecil H. Clough (ed.) (Liverpool: Liverpool University Press, 1982), pp. 90–129.

Strohm, Paul, 'A Note on Gower's Persona', in *Acts of Interpretation: The Text in its Contexts 700–1600. Essays on Medieval and Renaissance Literature in Honour of E. Talbot Donaldson*, Mary J. Carruthers and Elizabeth D. Kirk (eds.) (Norman, OK: Pilgrim Books, 1982), pp. 293–8.

'Politics and Poetics: Usk and Chaucer in the 1380s', in *Literary Practice and Social Change in Britain, 1380–1530*, Lee Patterson (ed.) (Berkeley: University of California Press, 1990), pp. 83–112.

Hochon's Arrow: The Social Imagination of Fourteenth-Century Texts (Princeton: Princeton University Press, 1992).

'"Lad with revel to Newegate": Chaucerian Narrative and Historical Meta-Narrative', in *Art and Context in Late Medieval English Narrative: Essays in Honor of Robert Worth Frank Jr*, Robert R. Edwards (ed.) (Cambridge: D. S. Brewer, 1994), pp. 163–76.

Summers, Joanna, 'Gower's *Vox clamantis* and Usk's *Testament of Love*', *Medium Aevum* 68 (1999), 55–62.

Sussman, Herbert, *Victorian Masculinity: Manhood and Masculine Poetics in Early Victorian Literature and Art*, Cambridge Studies in Nineteenth-Century Literature and Culture 3 (Cambridge: Cambridge University Press, 1995).

Swanson, Heather, 'The Illusion of Economic Structure: Craft Guilds in Late Medieval English Towns', *Past and Present* 121 (1988), 29–48.

Medieval British Towns (Basingstoke: Macmillan, 1999).

Tambling, Jeremy, *Confession: Sexuality, Sin, the Subject* (Manchester: Manchester University Press, 1990).

'Allegory and the Madness of the Text: Hoccleve's *Complaint*', *New Medieval Literatures* 6 (2003), 223–48.

Tavormina, M. Teresa, '"Bothe Two Ben Gode": Marriage and Virginity in *Piers Plowman* C.18.68–100', *Journal of English and Germanic Philology* 81 (1982), 320–30.

'Kindly Similitude: Langland's Matrimonial Trinity', *Modern Philology* 80 (1982), 117–28.

'"Gendre of a Generation": *Piers Plowman* B.16.222', *ELN* 27 (1989), 1–9.

Kindly Similitude: Marriage and Family in 'Piers Plowman', Piers Plowman Studies 11 (Cambridge: D. S. Brewer, 1995).

Taylor, Robert A., *et al.* (eds.), *The Centre and Its Compass: Studies in Medieval Literature in Honor of Professor Leyerle*, Studies in Medieval Culture 23 (Kalamazoo, MI: Western Michigan University Press, 1993).

Thompson, John J., 'A Poet's Contacts with the Great and the Good: Further Consideration of Thomas Hoccleve's Texts and Manuscripts', in *Prestige, Authority and Power in Late Medieval Manuscripts and Texts*, Felicity Riddy (ed.) (York: York Medieval Press, 2000), pp. 77–101.

Thomson, John A. F. (ed.), *Towns and Townspeople in the Fifteenth Century* (Gloucester: Sutton, 1988).

Thornley, Eva M., 'The Middle English Penitential Lyric and Hoccleve's Autobiographical Poetry', *Neuphilologische Mitteilungen* 68 (1967), 295–321.

Tosh, John, *A Man's Place: Masculinity and the Middle-Class Home in Victorian England* (New Haven, CT: Yale University Press, 1999).

Tracy, Charles, *English Medieval Furniture and Woodwork* (London: Victoria and Albert Museum, 1998).

Trigg, Stephanie, 'The Traffic in Medieval Women: Alice Perrers, Feminist Criticism and *Piers Plowman*', *The Yearbook of Langland Studies* 12 (1998), 5–29.

Turner, Marion, '"Certaynly his noble sayenges can I not amende": Thomas Usk and *Troilus and Criseyde*', *Chaucer Review* 37 (2002), 26–39.

Twigg, Graham, *The Black Death: A Biological Reappraisal* (London: Batsford Academic and Educational, 1984).

Tyler, Elizabeth M. (ed.), *Treasure in the Medieval West* (York: York Medieval Press, 2000).

Walker, Sue Sheridan (ed.), *Wife and Widow in Medieval England* (Ann Arbor: University of Michigan Press, 1993).

Wallace, David (ed.), *The Cambridge History of Medieval English Literature* (Cambridge: Cambridge University Press, 1999).

Wasserman, Julian N., and Blanch, Robert J. (eds.), *Chaucer in the Eighties* (Syracuse, NY: Syracuse University Press, 1986).

Waugh, Scott L., *England in the Reign of Edward III* (Cambridge: Cambridge University Press, 1992).

Weintraub, Karl Joachim, *The Value of the Individual: Self and Circumstance in Autobiography* (Chicago: The University of Chicago Press, 1978).

West, Delno C., and Zimdars-Swartz, Sandra, *Joachim of Fiore: A Study in Scriptual [sic] Perception and History* (Bloomington: Indiana University Press, 1983).

Westerdorf, K. P., 'Some Observations on the Concept of Clandestine Marriage in *Troilus and Criseyde*', *Chaucer Review* 15 (1980), 101–26.

Wetherbee, Winthrop, 'John Gower', in *The Cambridge History of Medieval English Literature*, David Wallace (ed.) (Cambridge: Cambridge University Press, 1999), pp. 589–609.

Williman, Daniel (ed.), *The Black Death: The Impact of the Fourteenth-Century Plague*, Medieval and Renaissance Texts and Studies 13 (Binghampton, NY: Centre for Medieval and Early Renaissance Studies, 1982).

Windeatt, B. A., '"Love that oughte ben secree" in Chaucer's *Troilus*', *Chaucer Review* 14 (1979), 116–31.

Wittig, Joseph S., '*Piers Plowman* B, Passus IX–X: Elements in the Design of the Inward Journey', *Traditio* 28 (1972), 211–80.

Wogan-Browne, J., *et al.* (eds.), *Medieval Women: Texts and Contexts in Late Medieval Britain. Essays for Felicity Riddy*, Medieval Women, Texts and Contexts 3 (Turnhout: Brepols, 2000).

Woolf, Rosemary, *The English Religious Lyric in the Middle Ages* (Oxford: Clarendon Press, 1968).

'The Tearing of the Pardon', in *Piers Plowman: Critical Approaches*, S. S. Hussey (ed.) (London: Methuen, 1969), pp. 50–75.

Wormald, Francis, and C. E. Wright (eds.), *The English Library before 1700* (London: Athlone, 1958).

Yeager, R. F., '*Pax poetica*: On the Pacifism of Chaucer and Gower', *Studies in the Age of Chaucer* 9 (1987), 97–121.

  Chaucer and Gower: Difference, Mutuality, Exchange, English Literary Studies 51 (Victoria, BC: University of Victoria Press, 1991).

  'The Body Politic and the Politics of Bodies in the Poetry of John Gower', in *The Body and The Soul in Medieval Literature*, Piero Boitani and Anna Torti (eds.) (Cambridge: D. S. Brewer, 1999), pp. 145–65.

  (ed.), *Fifteenth-Century Studies: Recent Essays* (Hamden, CT: Archon Books, 1984).

  (ed.), *Re-visioning Gower* (Asheville, NC: Pegasus Press, 1998).

Zeeman, Nicolette, 'Studying in the Middle Ages – and in *Piers Plowman*', *New Medieval Literatures* 3 (1999), 185–212.

Zumthor, Paul, 'Autobiography in the Middle Ages?' *Genre* 6 (1973), 29–48.

Index

Walsingham, Thomas (*c.* 1340–*c.* 1422) 43
Weber, Max 6
Weintraub, Karl 8
West, Mae 1
Wetherbee, Winthrop 84
women 143, 144, 154–7
  widows 28
  mothers and mothering 64–7
  work 13, 125

workshops 1–9, 115–16, 124, 165; *see also*
  household
Wynnere and Wastoure 13, 28
Yeager, Robert F. 16

youth 58

Zeeman, Nicolette 37, 113

For EU product safety concerns, contact us at Calle de José Abascal, 56–1°, 28003 Madrid, Spain or eugpsr@cambridge.org.

www.ingramcontent.com/pod-product-compliance
Ingram Content Group UK Ltd.
Pitfield, Milton Keynes, MK11 3LW, UK
UKHW010042140625
459647UK00012BA/1558